TELEVISION TALK SHOWS

Discourse, Performance, Spectacle

LEA's COMMUNICATION SERIES

Jennings Bryant and Dolf Zillmann, General Editors

Selected titles include:

Ellis • *Crafting Society: Ethnicity, Class, and Communication Theory*

Heath/Bryant • *Human Communication Theory and Research: Concepts, Contexts, and Challenges, Second Edition*

Leeds-Hurwitz • *Semiotics and Communication: Signs, Codes, Cultures*

Olson • *Hollywood Planet: Global Media and the Competitive Advantage of Narrative Transparency*

Penman • *Constructing Communicating: Looking to a Future*

Zillmann/Vorderer • *Media Entertainment: The Psychology of Its Appeal*

For a complete list of titles in LEA's Communication Series please contact Lawrence Erlbaum Associates, Publishers

TELEVISION TALK SHOWS

Discourse, Performance, Spectacle

Edited by

Andrew Tolson
De Montfort University

LEA LAWRENCE ERLBAUM ASSOCIATES, PUBLISHERS
2001 Mahwah, New Jersey London

Lawrence Erlbaum Associates, Inc., Publishers
10 Industrial Avenue
Mahwah, New Jersey 07430

Cover design by Kathryn Houghtaling Lacey

Library of Congress Cataloging-in-Publication Data

Television talk shows: discourse, performance, spectacle / edited by Andrew Tolson.
p. cm.
"Four of the chapters were first presented as papers at a conference on 'Identity and Performance in Broadcast Talk' held in September 1998 at the Media Research Institute of the University of Stirling"—Introd.
Includes studies of three American talk shows (Sally Jesse Raphael, Ricki Lake, and Jerry Springer), two British (Kilroy and Trisha), and one Israeli (With Meni).
Includes bibliographical references and index.
Contents: Talking about talk : the academic debates / Andrew Tolson—Performing talk / Louanne Haarman—"No YOU rioted!" : the pursuit of conflict in the management of "lay" and "expert" discourses on Kilroy / Helen Wood—The many faces of With Meni : the history and stories of one Israeli talk show / Shoshana Blum-Kulka—"Has it ever happened to you?" : talk shows as mediated performance / Joanna Thornborrow—"It makes it okay to cry" : two types of "therapy talk" in TV talk shows / Raina Brunvatne and Andrew Tolson—Confrontation as spectacle : the argumentative frame of an American talk show / Ian Hutchby—"I'm out of it; you guys argue" : making an issue of it on the Jerry Springer show / Greg Myers.
ISBN 0-8058-3746-9
1. Talk shows—United States. 2. Talk shows—Great Britain. I. Tolson, Andrew.

PN1992.8.T3 T45 2001
791.45′6—dc21 00-059322
CIP

Books published by Lawrence Erlbaum Associates are printed on acid-free paper, and their bindings are chosen for strength and durability.

Printed in the United States of America
10 9 8 7 6 5 4 3 2 1

CONTENTS

Contributors

Shoshana Blum-Kulka is Karl and Matilde Newhouse Professor of Communication at the Hebrew University of Jerusalem. Her research interests are in the fields of discourse analysis, pragmatic development, interlanguage pragmatics, ethnography of communication, language education, family discourse, and media discourse. She is co-author and co-editor of *Cross Cultural Pragmatics: Requests and Apologies* (Ablex, 1989) and *Interlanguage Pragmatics* (Oxford University Press, 1993). Her most recent books are *Dinner Talk: Cultural Patterns of Sociability and Socialization* (Lawrence Erlbaum Associates, 1997) and *Talking With Adults: The Contribution of Multiparty Talk to Language Development* (co-authored with Catherine Snow, Lawrence Erlbaum Associates, in press).

Raina Brunvatne is a graduate of Communication Studies at Queen Margaret University College, Edinburgh, UK, and a postgraduate student in Cultural Studies at Goldsmiths College, University of London.

Louann Haarman teaches English at the University of Bologna, Italy. Her main research interests are in research methodology in applied linguistics and television studies. Recent publications include *Talk About Shows: la parola e lo spettacolo* (CLUEB: Bologna, 1999) and "Television Talk" in *Massed Medias: Linguistic Tools for Interpreting Media Discourse* (LED: Milan, 1999). She is currently engaged in a large-scale research project on linguistic characteristics of political reporting and commentary in English print, broadcasting, and electronic media.

Ian Hutchby is Senior Lecturer in Sociology and Communication at Brunel University, West London. He has research interests in broadcast talk, the technological mediation of interaction, and children's communicative competencies. He is the author of *Confrontation Talk: Arguments, Asymmetries, and Power on Talk Radio* (Lawrence Erlbaum Associates, 1996), *Conversation Analysis* (Polity Press, 1998) and *Conversation and Technology: From the Telephone to the Internet* (Polity Press, 2000). His articles have appeared in *Sociology, Discourse and Society, The Journal of Sociolinguistics, Discourse Processes, Text*, and *Research on Language and Social Interaction.*

Greg Myers teaches in Linguistics and in Culture and Communication at Lancaster University, UK. Among his publications are *Words in Ads* (Arnold, 1994), *Ad Worlds* (Arnold, 1999), and recent articles in *Media, Culture and Society, Text*, and *Applied Linguistics.* He is currently working on a study of the expression of opinion in conversation.

Joanna Thornborrow is Lecturer in Language and Communication at Cardiff University, Wales, UK. Her research interests are in three main areas: media discourse analysis, social and insititutional interaction, and discourse stylistics. Publications include articles in *Text, Discourse and Society, Language in Society*, and *Discourse Studies*; and *Power Talk*, a book on language and social interaction, is currently in press (Longman). She is co-editor of a special issue of *Discourse Studies*, on authenticity in media discourse (forthcoming).

Andrew Tolson is Principal Lecturer in Media Studies at De Montfort University, Leicester, UK. He has research interests in broadcast talk, political communication, and the culture of celebrity. Previous publications include *Mediations: Text and Discourse in Media Studies* (Arnold, 1996) and contributions to P. Scannell (Ed.), *Broadcast Talk* (Sage Publications, 1991). An article "Publicness: The Construction of Authenticity in News Interviews" is to appear in *Communication Review* in 2001.

Helen Wood teaches media and cultural studies at the University of Wolverhampton, UK. She has research interests in media discourse, gender and media consumption, and has recently completed her PhD thesis on women's interaction with British daytime television.

Introduction: The Talk Show Phenomenon

Andrew Tolson

Two British news stories from 1999: In February it was reported that two producers and a researcher working on the BBC talk show *Vanessa* had been suspended following a revelation that some guests on the program were fakes (*Guardian*, 1999a). What was particularly scandalous was that two strippers, purporting to be "feuding sisters" had been knowingly recruited from an entertainment agency. This was too much for the BBC hierarchy, who produced a statement concluding that "audiences must be able to believe in the integrity of our programs." The *Guardian* article drew comparisons with *Vanessa's* ITV rival *Trisha*, where producers claimed they had been duped into featuring fakes. Later in 1999, *Vanessa* was axed by the BBC, having lost its ratings battle with *Trisha*.

Then in April, news reports reached Britain of another development in the infamous *Jenny Jones* murder case. Now the family of the man murdered in 1995 by the object of his homosexual desires, after appearing on the program, was initiating a lawsuit against the production company (Telepictures Productions) and the distributors (Time Warner). Here the *Guardian's* report (1999b) set the case in the wider context of U.S. legal rulings on media responsibility for criminal acts. Clearly an "effects" agenda had entered the U.S. courts to the extent that not only were the media being cited as a possible influence, but also they were now potentially, legally culpable as a direct cause of crime.

From such reports, it would seem that the TV talk show is in something of a double bind. They are damned if they do feature fakes (at least in the high-minded ideology of British public service broadcasting), and damned if they don't (the *Jenny Jones* case being an extreme example of the alleged exploitation of participants). Either way, in continuous press coverage of this sort, talk shows have now become the most controversial TV genre since the American quiz show scandal of the 1950s. They have also, in America, become the target for concerted public campaigns. In 1998, *The Jerry Springer Show* was forced to review its editorial policy following representations to its production company from the Dump Springer Coalition (*Guardian*, 1998). As Shattuc (1997) has described, Springer is only one of a group of talk shows criticized by the right-wing Empower America campaign, and the institute Contract with America.

On the other hand, Shattuc also claims that in the 1990s, talk shows became the most popular genre on American TV, citing in particular the popularity of Oprah Winfrey. If this is the case in America, it is certainly not true elsewhere: In Britain, soap operas and drama series still command the highest ratings. What is incontrovertible, however, is that the talk show has become ubiquitous, and a major focus for critical discussion by academic commentators as well as journalists. And what is most interesting about the *Vanessa* fiasco is that the BBC felt it had to dabble in this sort of programming at all. The talk show has become emblematic of a series of developments in the modern media economy: cheap to produce, daytime programming, stripped across the schedules, heading (according to its critics) increasingly downmarket towards the murky depths of "trash" TV. Here then, by way of illustration, is the list of talk shows available on U.K. television on a typical weekday, Monday, March 6, 2000:

Time	Program	Channel
9 a.m.	*The Roseanne Show*	Ch 5
9 a.m.	*Kilroy*	BBC 1
9:25 a.m.	*Trisha*	ITV
10 a.m.	*Jerry Springer*	Living
11 a.m.	*Jenny Jones*	Sky 1
11:40 a.m.	*Maury Povich*	Living
12 p.m.	*Sally Jesse Raphael*	Sky 1
1 p.m.	*The Oprah Winfrey Show*	Ch 5
3 p.m.	*Jenny Jones*	Sky 1
3:30 p.m.	*Esther*	BBC 2
4 p.m.	*Montel Williams*	Granada
4:40 p.m.	*Maury Povich*	Living
4:55 p.m.	*Montel Williams*	Ch 4*
6:10 p.m.	*Jerry Springer*	Living

*alternates through the week with *Ricki Lake*

In other words, with one break in the early afternoon, it is possible for the British viewer to watch talk shows every weekday, all day long. There are a couple of further points to make about this list. First, it ranges across channels; in fact, it ranges across all significant channels that offer mixed programming. It is of course also possible to watch quiz shows, comedy shows, and sports events continuously, on the channels that are dedicated to those genres, but the ubiquity of the talk show is such that it is multichannel. Second, it is also apparent that in the United Kingdom, only the major terrestrial (public service) channels produce their own talk shows; all the rest (8 from this list of 11) are imported from the United States.

One reason for producing this book on talk shows then, is because they matter. They matter because they are a focus for considerable public debate and because they are crucial to the landscape of popular television. But also, as demonstrated in this volume, their significance has crucially to do with the fact that talk shows revolve around the *performance of talk*. That is to say, the controversy and the popularity of talk shows is fundamentally rooted in the pleasures of watching and listening to people talking in particular ways—and for the most part these are ordinary people who are engaged in colloquial forms of talk. This itself is a remarkable phenomenon in an age fascinated by glamor and by spectacle. Whether or not the guests are "real," and however they may or may not be exploited, there is a discursive dynamic to this performance of talk which engages contemporary audiences. That at least is the premise of this book and is the focus for its investigations.

In this connection, it should be also clear that if the term *talk show* has a wide and varying provenance (and in America it can also include *chat* or celebrity interview), there is one specific type of talk show that is the main concern. This is illustrated by the list previously supplied which, with some variations, are all shows with certain key elements in common. Crucially, they all feature groups of guests, not individual interviewees, and they all involve audience participation. That is to say, the studio audience is not only visible (it is invisible on many chat shows) but also it is given the opportunity to comment and intervene, not simply to respond. The host then typically acts as a mediator between the guests and the studio audience, often moving around studio spaces with a mobile microphone. It is this kind of talk show whose discursive dynamics we seek to explore in this volume, for of course, it is this kind of talk show that constitutes the talk show *phenomenon*.

By investigating the *talk* of talk shows, we are making a new contribution to their academic analysis. As noted, the talk show has been the focus for some previous academic commentary, but with two exceptions this work has largely ignored the actual talk produced on these shows. This work is reviewed in the first chapter, which suggests that much academic debate about talk shows has been very generalized and often highly speculative. There are some academic references to some shows (particularly to *Oprah Winfrey*) but very little in the way of sustained empirical analysis. Even the two exceptions to this rule, namely Carbaugh (1988) and Livingstone and Lunt (1994) are, in their different ways, problematic. They contain interesting insights, but from the point of view of this volume, they lack a coherent methodology for analyzing broadcast talk.

A distinctive feature of this book is that it offers a systematic empirical study of the broadcast talk in talk shows. Thereby, we hope to illuminate how talk shows work as media experiences. This systematic approach has been developed since the mid-1980s, by importing methods of verbal discourse analysis into media studies. These methods are derived, broadly speaking, from sociolinguistics, conversation analysis (CA), and pragmatics. I introduce this approach at the end of chapter 1, which explains how these disciplinary perspectives have cohered into a set of protocols for analyzing broadcast talk. Following this, subsequent chapters build on what has now become a distinctive body of work in media studies, ranging from early studies of news interviews (Heritage, 1985; Heritage & Greatbatch, 1991) and "DJ talk" (Montgomery, 1986) to more recent work on radio phone-ins (Hutchby, 1996a) and sports commentary (Marriott, 1996). In this field, there has been some work on chat shows (Montgomery, 1999; Tolson, 1991) but apart from some previous work by contributors to this volume (Haarman, 1999; Thornborrow, 1997) very little attention has been given to the kinds of talk shows considered here.

One feature of the methodology employed in this book, which will be immediately apparent to the reader, is that it takes a particular approach to the presentation of data. Data takes the form of transcripts of broadcast talk, but these are clearly not reproductions of original recordings, nor are they "quotations" of the dialogue that took place. Rather, the transcripts presented here should be regarded as strategic interventions into the recorded material, designed to highlight salient features of talk as verbal interaction. Transcripts thus incorporate a set of conventions developed in CA for representing such features as overlapping turn-taking, patterns of stress and intonation, paralinguistic punctuations (such as pauses and intakes of breath), and audience response. There are some variations of presentation in the contributions to this book (in particular, two chapters make systematic reference to the visual as well as the verbal channels of communication), but generally all chapters with original data make use of the transcription conventions that are set out in the appendix to chapter 2 and discussed in further detail by Hutchby and Woffitt (1998).

Thus, the book is in two parts. In part one, we offer a critical review of previous academic work on talk shows, outline the parameters of our own approach, and begin to map out the range of talk show formats, or subgenres, included in our definition. Basically these formats range from issue-oriented debates, through explorations of personal experiences, to the kinds of staging and performance sometimes dismissed as "trash" TV. In part two, we then present six empirical case studies. With one exception (Thornborrow, chapter 5) which looks at narrative strategies in various programs, these chapters focus on particular shows, across the range of subgenres previously identified. Three of the shows are American (*Sally Jesse Raphael*, *Ricki Lake*, and *Jerry Springer*), two are British (*Kilroy*, *Trisha*) and one is Israeli (*With Meni*). Apart from one previous article (Krause & Goering, 1995), this is also the first study to offer an international perspective.

The contributors to this book are members of an international network of researchers interested in the study of broadcast talk. All, with one exception, have participated in the Ross Priory broadcast talk seminar, held annually at Strathclyde University in Scotland. Four of the chapters were first presented as papers at a conference on "Identity and Performance in Broadcast Talk" held in September 1998 at the Media Research Institute of the University of Stirling. The authors would therefore particularly like to acknowledge the efforts of the conference organizer, Stephanie Marriott, and the contributions of all co-participants and members of the Ross Priory group. This is in every sense a collective piece of work, where the contributions of named authors have been informed by discussions across the network, for a number of years. We hope this volume stimulates the further development of research into broadcast talk.

ACKNOWLEDGMENTS

I would like to thank Emily Wilkinson of Lawrence Erlbaum Associates for her faith in this project and Eileen Bosher for her hospitality during its preparation.

—*Andrew Tolson*

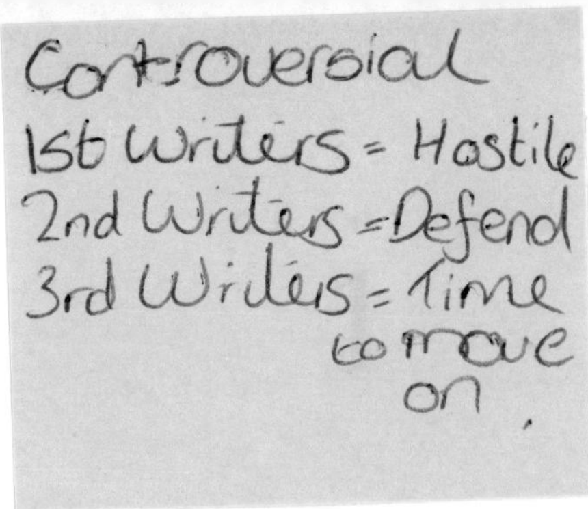

Controversial
1st Writers = Hostile
2nd Writers = Defend
3rd Writers = Time
to move
on

Talking About Talk: The Academic Debates

Andrew Tolson

In the wake of its notoriety, the talk show phenomenon has attracted a range of academic commentary and discussion. This chapter reviews that work, partly to introduce the range of theoretical perspectives, but also to develop a case for the kinds of empirical analysis that follow. Some of this academic work touches on what we see as interesting issues, and of course we acknowledge that. Equally, however, much discussion seems to be overwhelmed by the phenomenon with which it is engaged. If the talk show is the most controversial TV genre, then much academic commentary seems impelled to line up either for or against the terms of the controversy. In the first camp there are some writers who express profound moral ambivalence or even hostility toward the talk show. These writers are then contradicted by others who seek to defend the genre, sometimes in political or, more precisely, sexual-political terms. Finally, there is a third twist in some writings which are critical of the terms of this defense and which suggest, we think, that it is time to move on.

FROM "MORAL PANIC" TO POSTMODERNISM

First, then, we can point to a number of contributions whose agenda seems directly to reflect the public controversy about talk shows. In sociological terms (Cohen, 1972; Thompson, 1998), it is possible to see the more extreme contributions as part of a "moral panic" where religious leaders and journalists are now joined by some academics in their condemnation of these shows. In fact, some elements in this academic commentary bear an uncanny resemblance to the kinds of journalistic reports previously considered. Discussions therefore range from the apparent fraudulence of some talk show productions to broader pronouncements on their victimization of guests and their generally negative effects on American culture. It is interesting, then, to note that the generality of these pronouncements has some affinity with other familiar kinds of cultural criticism.

The management of the BBC should not have been surprised by the fake guests recruited to *Vanessa*. This is a practice widely recognized in America and indeed there is some evidence that it is part of the attraction of these shows for dedicated fans.[1] The practice of faking is also discussed in an academic paper by Nelson and Robinson (1994). In an entertaining piece of ethnography, the article recounts how principal author Nelson (a sociologist with research interests in deviance and gender) was invited to appear on a talk show on the topic of male escorts. She reports that initially her expert role was prescripted, in that she was provided with a "blueprint" for the show; subsequently it became clear that the role of every other participant was also scripted, with several being performed by members of an escort agency. In particular, the "women who pay men for sex" were revealed to be an escort and a dancer posing as a lawyer and a public relations executive. For Nelson, this undermined the show's claim to be engaged in serious investigative journalism; and there is a very interesting account of the host's performance of feigned spontaneity, even surprise, in what was clearly a collusive set-up.

So faking in this sense is a routine practice—the question is what do we make of it? In fact, Nelson and Robinson (1994) draw two sorts of conclusions, the first of which is far more interesting than the second. At first, Nelson compares the show's presentation of this form of gender "deviance" with her own research-based understanding of its complexity. She is struck by a conservative agenda which amounts to denigrating and punishing women's assertion of sexual autonomy. The show thus presented a simplified and manageable "morality tale" in which "normative gender roles were unthinkingly taken for granted . . ." (p. 73). Further evidence is offered in this book to suggest that "morality tales" are indeed a central feature of some kinds of talk show, and as narratives, their claim to reality may be interestingly ambiguous. Whether real or fake, the primary function of participants is to act as characters in the stories being told.

---

[1]On the Internet site, TVTalkShows.com, which announces itself as "the world's largest TV talk show fan website!" contributions are invited on "fake guests," or rather guests who have been seen making multiple appearances on various shows. Apparently guest-spotting of this sort is one of the activities of dedicated fandom.

On the other hand, the very fraudulence of the show's production, together with its oversimplification of the topic, might be enough to condemn it. Nelson and Robinson (1994) conclude their article by speculating on the "effects" of such shows, and I return to this question shortly. For other commentators, however, there is no debate over what the effects of such talk shows might be. With a "moral panic" agenda firmly in place, Abt and Seesholtz (1994) regard talk shows as an attack on the American way of life:

> To experience the virtual realities of television talk shows is to confront a crisis in the social construction of reality. Television talk shows create audiences by breaking cultural rules, by managed shocks, by shifting our conceptions of what is acceptable, by transforming our ideas about what is possible, by undermining the bases for cultural judgement, by redefining deviance and appropriate reactions to it, by eroding social barriers, inhibitions and cultural distinctions. (p. 171)

Indeed there may be interesting questions to ask about the "social construction of reality" in talk shows and it may be useful to investigate the "management of shocks" and the "breaking of cultural rules." For Abt and Seesholtz, however, such ambiguities or transgressions can only amount to an undermining of cultural values. From fake guests to tragic victims, talk shows are an embodiment of the worst excesses of the commercialization of popular culture.

There seem to be two main aspects to the argument. The first relates to what Abt and Seesholtz (1994) define as ersatz community and the second concerns "psychobabble." First then, the problem with talk shows is that they encourage a "blurring of boundaries," of categories that were fundamental to traditional forms of social order: distinctions between normal and deviant, public and private, real and fictional. In deconstructing these categories, "television talk shows create an ersatz community without any of the social and personal responsibilities that are attached to real life" (p. 175). It is interesting (and we see why shortly) that what is projected in this criticism is a notion of real community characterized by a "functional ecology" and a sense of "neighborliness."

The second part of the argument concerns the kinds of talk which are encouraged on these shows. Abt and Seesholtz (1994) do not actually analyze any talk, but they do make claims ranging from the suggestion that "psychobabble" is full of cliches, to speculation that public confessions on television might be damaging to participants. Here "therapy as entertainment" meets "managed outrage and other cynical distortions" (pp. 178–179). Participants might thus be victimized by their instant quasi-therapeutic encounters with unlicensed gurus and unqualified hosts. Again, we see later that Abt and Seesholtz might have something of a point here, but this point is hardly clarified by their appeal to commonsense wisdom about not "washing dirty linen in public." For in essence this condemnation of the talk show is a rhetorical exercise designed to promote the moral panic. It is a ritualistic appeal to traditional values that the talk show allegedly (for no evidence is provided) undermines.

From this line of argument, it is then just a small step to speculation about the effects of talk shows on viewers. What are the effects of continual exposure to a diet of deviant behaviors, or as Abt and Seesholtz put it, the erosion of boundaries and distinctions? There is, of course, a long established tradition of effects research in the study of mass communication (McQuail, 1994), and there is a critique that questions its efficacy (Barker & Petley, 1997). My point in this context is simply to confirm that such questions can only be asked, because they only make sense, from a conservative perspective on mass media. For if media (in this case talk shows) are inherently problematic, morally dubious, and viewed with suspicion, then from this perspective it seems inevitable to enquire into their negative effects on audiences.

Which is precisely the starting point for Davis and Mares' (1998) study of the "effects of talk show viewing on adolescents." Why adolescents? As Davis and Mares state, it is not because young people have now become a major target audience for talk shows (cf. Shattuc, 1997), or even because students provide a convenient population for academic surveys—rather it is because adolescents have been thought, in some journalistic commentaries, to be particularly vulnerable to talk shows. Hypothetically, four types of effect have been supposed. First, it has been imagined that in their "blurring of boundaries," talk shows might distort viewers' sense of reality. Second, it might be thought that viewers might become "desensitized" to "depictions of human conflict and suffering." Third, viewers might be encouraged to make simplistic judgments about complex social issues. Fourth, Davis and Mares pick up an argument about "perceived realism" to hypothesize that viewers who perceive talk shows to be unrealistic are more likely to be negatively affected because they are less likely to make critical judgments.

With these hypotheses, and duly citing Abt and Seesholtz as a key source, Davis and Mares proceeded to sample 282 high school students using quantitative questionnaires. The results, interestingly enough, showed that only the first hypothesis had any measure of credibility, insofar as teenagers were inclined to overestimate the real occurrence of teen-related (but not adult-related) problems. Otherwise, high levels of talk show viewing did not correlate with any measures of desensitization; on the contrary, Davis and Mares (1998) argue that viewers are encouraged to take issues seriously because (echoing Nelson and Robinson) "talk shows serve as cautionary tales" (p. 83). Far from undermining the basis for moral judg-

ment, therefore, talk shows actually seem to encourage it, forcing Davis and Mares to conclude:

> "that the primary value of this study lies in taking a piece of conventional wisdom (ie. talk shows are harmful) that has been bandied about by people with considerable power, and testing it. As usual, it appears that conventional wisdom is overly pessimistic and much too simplistic."

But of course disproving the hypothesis about negative effects is not in itself an answer to the moral panic, nor is it quite the end of the line for speculative arguments about the cultural impact of talk shows. A further interesting twist, producing an unlikely alliance of critics, is provided by another sort of rhetoric that makes reference to "postmodernism." Funnily enough, the description of the genre provided in the major example of postmodernist argumentation (Munson, 1993) is virtually identical to that provided by its conservative critics. Here, the talk show is a "postmodern" construct because it undermines the certainties of modernism, in particular the possibility of a unified subjectivity. It has a "productive instability" which:

> has become a paradigm for a commodified medium–spectator relationship that responds to postmodern conditions in which meaning constantly fluctuates. It reproduces the consumer culture's shifting array of goods and the lifestyle connotations necessary to their appeal. Its ever-changing "throw-away" form appealingly and effectively (re)produces information in bite-sized packages for the information-overloaded subject. (p. 45)

We should acknowledge that this quotation is taken from a section of *All Talk* where Munson is discussing call-in radio programs. Indeed, the real strength of his book is its detailed history of the development of radio talk in America and the influence of this on subsequent televisual forms. However, as a form of rhetoric, the slogan "productive instability" is made to apply to all modern forms of talk show, and it is here, once again, that we encounter arguments about the blurring of boundaries. Scattered throughout the book are references to the blurring of the pre-modern (oral culture) and modernity (mediated spectacle); to modernist postures of subjectivity and "postmodern" emotional investments; to the mixing of genres in new hybrid forms and the manifestly blurred category of *infotainment*. As a consequence of this, the talk show is regarded as particularly heterogenous and discontinuous: It creates an effect of "fluid spectatorship": "Confronting boredom and channel clutter with constant, intensified novelty and 'reality' talkshows offer a variety of Others to the fluid spectatorial self" (Munson, 1993, p. 15).

In Munson's argument, it would seem that the postmodern heterogeneity of the talk show can be located on a variety of dimensions. As the previous quotation suggests, it is present in the diversity of voices included both in phone-in programs and in TV talk shows. It is further evident in the new conditions (in the 1990s) of TV production and consumption, with stripped, throwaway programming on multiple channels visited instantaneously by the "zapping" viewer. It is also manifest in the intertextuality of talk shows which, as hybrid genres, refer outwards (and to each other) as a network of lifestyles and consumer cultures. In the end Munson (1993), and he is not the only example, seems to regard the talk show as emblematic of contemporary televisuality; here he is driven to further speculation about new forms of mediated experience:

> It is my view that a medium like the talk show creates not "placelessness" but a hyperlocal or cyberspatial "place". Old lines are being erased, but new ones are being drawn—new social and political connections, new "neighborhoods". The talkshow is not so much the *last* neighborhood in America—however apocalyptic some of the talk about it—as the newest and least understood. (p. 18)

An "ersatz community" perhaps? From a British perspective, one is tempted to ask, "What is it about Americans and 'neighborhoods,' or more precisely, the figure of the 'neighborhood' in a type of cultural rhetoric?" The point is that Munson is now on the same terrain as Abt and Seesholtz, and despite his disclaimer, he is equally as apocalyptic. The talk show is symptomatic of American TV culture, and that culture is in the business of deconstructing old and reconstructing new forms of community (or sense of "place" in the terms of Meyrowitz [1985] to whom Munson is here referring). Now, one might lament this transformation or one may attempt to engage with it, as Munson does. Either way, it is characterized as a whirl of diverse, ambiguous, and confusing tendencies that radically disorientate the (post) modern spectator. All in all, it takes an effort of will to remind ourselves that we are only watching television.

FROM POSTMODERNISM TO THE PUBLIC SPHERE

In the context of his historical survey of the roots of the contemporary talk show, Munson (1993) refers to a 1960s American TV program, *Art Linkletter's House Party*. As the title suggests, and from Munson's description, this program was the type of homey audience participation, consisting of humorous performances by ordinary people and with the direct involvement of a studio audience, which Scannell (1996) has identified as the

aspect of *sociability* in broadcasting. However, as an antecedent of the talk show (and Munson argues that *House Party* specifically "presaged Donahue"), what is most significant is the development of new formats for participatory television that construct new forms of "spectatorship," as Munson (1993) puts it:

> *House Party* offered the simulated sociality of a "party" by bringing the housewife into the studio—and the advertised products into her home. The borders between home, stage and marketplace—between spectacle and dialogue—seemed to have collapsed. The co-presence of the spectator's and the host's body and vocality, the performance space, and the media apparatus were all redefining "spectatorship" by inscribing aspects of folk culture and interpersonal rituals, "people are funny" storytelling and anecdotal personal experience. (pp. 53–54)

Again there is a blurring of boundaries, but here Munson is not referring to general cultural categories (reality–fiction, information–entertainment) so much as describing the development of a specific televisual genre. It is the organization of the set, the camerawork, and the movement from the stage to the studio audience, that technically construct the "copresence" of this experience. Two further significant points are made: first, that this is a genre that prefers particular ways of speaking, defined as anecdotal storytelling; and second, that the composition of the studio audience and indeed the target market for the show is overwhelmingly female.

In *Art Linkletter's House Party*, Munson finds an example that brings into focus a number of key issues for the subsequent debate about TV talk shows. The point about gender is reserved for the next section of this chapter; initially I focus on the question of *spectatorship*, because this clearly links to another very influential assessment of the significance of talk shows, first developed by Paulo Carpignano and his associates at the CUNY Graduate School (Carpignano, Anderson, Aronowitz, & Defazio, 1990). In this account, a transformation of spectatorship is at the center of a major realignment of contemporary media culture. It is apparent in changing news formats, as well as in audience participation programs. It hinges around "new social relationships of communication embodied in the television medium which have progressively undermined the structural dichotomy between performance and audience" (p. 35). A further crucial development is then made when Carpignano et al. claim that this dichotomy is essential to representative politics and thus to the category of the "public":

> For representative politics is built on the same separation of performance and audience that characterises the structure of theatrical communication . . . Most importantly, it is on the structural separation between performance and audience that the ideological category of the public is constructed. (p. 34)

There may be a questionable ingenuity in an argument that conflates representational politics with traditional forms of theatre. Leaving that aside, however, it becomes clear that the argument has interesting consequences; if contemporary theatrical spaces are changing, as they clearly are in shows like *House Party* with their deconstruction of the space between stage and audience, then this might begin to transform the "ideological category of the public." Here Carpignano et al. are invoking Habermas' concept of the "public sphere" (Habermas, 1984); and the argument goes on to suggest that new televisual spaces of performance, with their changing forms of audience participation, are involved in the construction of new types of public sphere.

Recall that for Habermas (1984), the classic (bourgeois) public sphere is a forum outside the control of particular interests where, through reasoned debate and discussion "something approaching public opinion can be formed" (p. 198). Habermas' account was closely tied to the development of traditional forms of journalism within an informed and democratic community of citizens. Carpignano et al. (1990) argue that this is now changing in at least two ways. First, because of the impact of electronic news gathering, news is no longer reported so much as monitored. We no longer rely on journalists for reports of news because we see news happening on our screens, in real time. The status of the reporter diminishes to that of a commentator; and here we are offered a new spectatorial role: "The 'mediating' narrative of reporting establishes a relationship between a recipient of information and an event. The watching of a live space establishes a relationship between an act of monitoring and a happening" (p. 42). This has consequence[illegible] Carpignano et al., for the way TV news increasingly presents itself [illegible]

The second example of [illegible] ng forms of spectatorship and categor[illegible] e the argument consists of three m[illegible] n's description of *House Party*. Fir[illegible] of performance diverge from tradit[illegible] tween host, participants, and studio [illegible] fixed, more mobile, and not averse t[illegible] tography. As a consequence, the TV [illegible] io audience, which is itself involved [illegible] show is the most eloquent example of the [illegible] ignano et al., 1990, p. 49).

What is then articulated in talk shows? If we recall the point about anecdotal storytelling, Carpignano et al. go on to argue that this is essentially about the production of commonsense, "not as a balance of viewpoints," but spoken "in a serial association of testimonials" (p. 51). These testimonials, we can assume, frequently take a narrative form (this is a focus for several chapters in this volume). More generally, it is suggested that they amount to a repetition of statements with the emphasis more on diversity than reaching conclusive resolutions. In this way:

> Common sense in this perspective would not be limited to a set of assumptions derived from life experiences . . . Common sense could also be conceived as a product of an electronically defined common place which, by virtue of being electronically reproduced, can be considered a public place. In its most elementary form, going public today means going on air. (p. 50)

In short, talk shows deliver a new kind of public forum that allows a diversity of voices to be heard. Carpignano et al. again point out that some of these are voices previously marginalized in the classic public sphere, particularly the voices of women. More generally, these are the voices of ordinary people who are permitted, in this genre, to present a challenge to the status of expertise. The range of topics discussed extends beyond those previously thought to be relevant to formal political agendas, and so the authors conclude, somewhat elliptically, that "a common place that formulates and propagates common senses and metaphors that govern our lives might be at the crossroad of a reconceptualization of collective practices" (p. 54).

It is, of course not clear what this means. Is this a new public sphere? It seems that Carpignano et al. (1990) would like to think so, but cannot quite bring themselves to say it. Nevertheless it is apparent that a major reevaluation of talk shows is underway in this argument, for they now appear not so much symptomatic of the "postmodern condition," as both aesthetically interesting and culturally progressive. With hindsight it is amazing how influential this reevaluation has been. We turn to the feminist argument shortly, but there are at least two other reasons why the "public sphere" argument might have proved to be popular in some academic contexts. First, it certainly provides a counter to the negative perspective with its moral panic and cultural pessimism. More particularly, however, this is an argument that speaks to a widespread concern about the demise of conventional politics and a "crisis of public communication" (Blumler & Gurevitch, 1995). It has become common to read accounts of contemporary political communication that refer to talk shows as an interesting prospect or as a suggestive pointer to the future of public discourse (Dahlgren, 1995; Garnham, 1995; van Zoonen, 1998).

However, the fullest development of this perspective is still to be found in the work of Livingstone and Lunt (1994). This work takes the discussion of talk shows into new areas of genre analysis and audience research, but it is the link to Carpignano et al., to whom Livingstone and Lunt directly refer, that I want to examine here. There are two main issues that explored at length, and they are worth further consideration not least because they provide the context for some contributions to this book (cf. Haarman, chapter 2, and Wood, chapter 3). So first I examine Livingstone and Lunt's detailed discussion of commonsense discourse, and second, I return to their arguments about the public sphere.

As we have seen, an important feature of the talk show for Carpignano et al. is the way it allows for the articulation of common sense. Here common sense is regarded not simply as an ideology, but as a product of the discursive exchanges that talk shows stage as an electronic "public place." In their account, Livingstone and Lunt show how this production operates, and they do this with reference to the work of Erving Goffman. Specifically, what is at stake here is Goffman's discussion of *participation frameworks* and *footings*.

In his later work, Goffman (1974, 1981) develops a critique of dyadic models of communication (sometimes referred to as transmission models) that pre-suppose singular categories of *speaker* and *hearer*. His argument is that, for many types of speech communication, these categories are too simplistic. For instance, the category "hearer" can be broken down into "ratified listeners" and those who might be overhearers or "eavesdroppers." Similarly, the category "speaker" elides not just different ways of speaking (in particular forms of speech, such as storytelling) but also the different relationships it is possible to have to the words one speaks. Speakers might be the "authors" of their own words, or they might "animate" the words of others (when speaking from a script, etc.) or they can speak as "principals" on behalf of some institution or authority. These different possibilities are defined by Goffman as "footings" (p. 124) in the act of speaking; and particularly in public places, speakers often shift footings, now speaking institutionally, now speaking on their own behalf, etc. (cf. Livingstone & Lunt, 1994, pp. 54–55).

Now the question becomes: What is the participation framework of the talk show? As in all forms of broadcast talk, it is crucial that we recognize that the talk is always produced for an "overhearing audience" (Heritage, 1985); that is to say, all broadcast talk is performed, and the modalities of such performance are a major concern for several contributors to this volume. Livingstone and Lunt (1994), however, do not particularly focus on this aspect of the participation framework. Rather, they consider the footings characteristically adopted by speakers on talk shows, and they argue that talk shows routinely stage confrontations between lay persons (who speak in their own words) and experts (who speak institutional discourse). Again, "common sense" can be understood to be the outcome of this confrontation. Thus:

> The subject position of "ordinary person" is created when the studio audience "tell their own story." They construct the folk category of speaker in

> which animator, author and principal are the same, and so gain communicative power through the construction of authenticity. As the experts frequently speak for other experts, they are thus reduced to a mouthpiece, the animator, who speaks for another expert . . . or, more nebulously still, speaks in defence of "expertise" or "the profession" . . .
>
> In sum, experts speak for others while the audience speaks for themselves. Thus it is difficult for experts to construct an authentic and credible persona on the screen, and yet authenticity and credibility rather than, say, intellectual argument or verified evidence are, simultaneously, being constructed as the rules of the discourse. As experts are trained to develop arguments carefully, at length, citing supporting evidence, rebutting refutations and noting qualifications, they are doomed to failure in discussion programmes. They appear fragmented rather than whole, cold rather than warm and alienated rather than authentic. (pp. 129–130)

Actually, "doomed to failure" might be a little too strong, for Livingstone and Lunt do go on to discuss the particular challenge afforded to the expert, to translate the language of expertise into the language of lay experience, and so establish a new sort of legitimacy for expert knowledge. However, leaving that aside for the moment, let us pause to consider the significance of this argument in the context of the discussion so far. I suggest that it makes two significant contributions. First, it shows that some claims made about talk shows, such as the challenge to expertise by common sense, can be illuminated (and, we see later, also tested) by close analytical attention to forms of discourse. That, to repeat, is the rationale for this book. Secondly, however, Livingstone and Lunt's theoretically informed argument at this point decisively contradicts the rhetorical speculation we have previously encountered in arguments about the deconstruction of social categories in forms of "fluid spectatorship." There may be interesting aesthetic features of talk shows that place domestic viewers in the position of the studio audience (mobile camerawork, etc.), but what is then activated are highly determinate social categories of expert and lay person (or "system" and "lifeworld") embedded in the distinct footings through which these categories are articulated.

These points are taken further in the course of this book. Now, however, let us return briefly to the major question posed by Carpignano et al., that is, the question of the public sphere. What is Livingstone and Lunt's answer to this question? Logically, this now becomes a matter of whether the challenge to expertise by common sense, in the terms already outlined, can qualify as a public sphere. It may be a "public place" (Carpignano et al.) but is it a public sphere—a place where public opinion can be formed? Livingstone and Lunt's (1994) answer seems to be almost, but not quite:

> In the audience discussion programme we observe the media appropriation of conversation, public opinion, protest and political accountability, all tai-

> lored to a daily programme slot and thereby intertwined with the rest of popular culture. To the extent that social and political opinion acts as a constraint on political, economic and social decision makers, this process is increasingly managed within popular culture . . .
>
> . . . Even if the audience discussion programme is in some ways a parody of the serious public sphere advocated by Habermas, it still offers an opportunity not present under post-war political and social civic culture for minority groups, protest groups and ordinary people to gain access to mediated communication. (p. 176)

The problem is that gaining access to the media is not the same thing as influencing civic public opinion. Certainly, in the last decade, there have been instances of this, the most publicized being the impact of Oprah Winfrey's pronouncements on beef and BSE. It may be also that public opinion of some public services, for instance the police force in its treatment of ethnic minorities, might have been affected by talk show discussions, and in this book Wood (chapter 3) provides an example of the kind of program that might function in this way. But she also points to a contradiction: that insofar as talk shows wish to retain a focus on such issues, then close analysis of the debate demonstrates that it is carefully managed and controlled by the host to the detriment of some expressions of lay discourse. In this type of show, people are not free to speak their experiences or tell their stories, unless these closely conform to the dominant agenda.

In the end, Livingstone and Lunt fall back on what looks like a compromise position: the concept of the "oppositional public sphere." Derived from Negt and Kluge (1990) rather than Habermas, this stops short of the formation of public opinion, to refer instead to a forum where different discourses are in circulation, where opposing voices are juxtaposed, but where closure in the form of decisions or demands is less likely to be reached. The most that can be said for such a forum is that it "may not generate a clear and consensual position but rather offers a range of diverse positions, providing an active role for the viewer in debate . . . To debate without conclusion is to celebrate the wisdom of the populace but to fight shy of promoting the insight of popular decisions beyond the bounds of the programme" (p. 301).

This, it seems to me, makes a final important point: that however we assess their significance, the contribution of talk shows to the public sphere cannot be determined by considering particular programs, or even the genre as a whole. For the public sphere is not located in a particular place, and it is by no means restricted to television. Rather it is a circulation of public discourses through a range of sites, institutions, and other forms of publication in which talk shows might, just might, play a very marginal role.

FROM FEMINISM TO MELODRAMA

In any case, much of the "public sphere" argument ignores the point that most talk shows, particularly the ones complained about by the critics, do not feature debates or discussions at all. This point is mentioned by Livingstone and Lunt (1994), who recognize that for some talk shows, the emphasis is more towards a *therapy genre* involving "the creation of intimacy and . . . emotional self-disclosure" (p. 67); and this might be picking up on the observation by Carpignano et al. (1990) about a "serial association of testimonials," particularly where topics are seen as "women's issues" which redefine "the relationship between the public and the private" (p. 51). In fact, by far the greatest number of contributions to the academic debate about talk shows has been made by writers concerned with their feminist potential, as a genre that traditionally has had women as its target audience. Here the focus of debate has been on the display of intimacy in public contexts, rather than the formation of public opinion in classic forms of debate.

This is, then, quite a large literature, in which we can distinguish between three broad perspectives. First, there exists what we might call a positive, or even utopian, feminist perspective that is concerned to promote the talk show's feminist credentials. This then becomes precisely the point of contention for several contributions that might be defined as coming from a second, "critical feminist" perspective. Finally, in the third category is a group of writers who argue that the forms of discourse under discussion here, particularly "therapy talk," can be seen as culturally specific. The argument is that these forms of talk have their roots in American popular culture, exported around the globe, but by no means universal.

First then, let us consider the positive feminist argument, which includes the contributions of Gray (1989), Haag (1993), Squire (1994), and Masciarotte (1991). In this argument, daytime talk shows operate as a "women's network" (Gray, 1989), which foregrounds the "construction of intimacy" (Haag, 1993) and with some qualifications is working towards "the empowerment of women" (Squire, 1994). Singled out for particular attention here is Oprah Winfrey (Haag, 1993; Masciarotte, 1991; Squire, 1994) though Phil Donahue also receives positive (Gray, 1989) and more qualified commentary (Masciarotte, 1991). Note that the reference here is to these personalities as individuals as much as to the shows in which they appear. In particular, Winfrey's qualifications for this type of feminist endorsement have to do with the fact that she is a Black women who has publicly disclosed aspects of her own troubled personal history (from her struggles with weight to her abuse as a child) and that she now appears as something of an icon, or "legend" (Haag, 1993) for feminist self-help.

Some commentaries focus on Oprah's communicative style. She displays a tactile intimacy with her studio audience and has several "voices" ranging from the formal and serious to the playful Black vernacular (Haag, 1993). Her willingness, on occasion, to talk "black American," "gives a public voice to marginalized phenomena" (Squire, 1994, p. 70). This argument goes on to suggest that the sheer diversity of voices on *The Oprah Winfrey Show* creates an effect of "super-realism," that is, an impact that cannot be contained within the show's ostensible narrative structure. As Squire (1994) put it:

> Daytime talk shows like *Oprah* try to reach a realist truth by interleaving information and entertainment, and deploying narratives of personal growth to pull this "infotainment" together. Sometimes, they do not manage the integration and super-realism, a realism torn out of shape by excess of emotion or empiricism, disrupts the explanatory framework. (p. 75)

For Squire, such forms of disruption are found, for instance, in the repetition of narratives of sexual abuse or in moments when the intensity of emotion challenges conventional psychological explanation. There is a familiar rhetoric here, namely that a certain authenticity is produced by the transcendence of structure, where structure establishes a framework that is disturbed, broken, or even "scandalized" by an excessive act of communication. Bursting into tears is such an excessive act, where raw emotion signified at the level of the voice and the body takes over from coherent speech. For Squire, this is Oprah's "super-realism," but for Masciarotte (1991), in what is the most theoreticist example of this argument, *The Oprah Winfrey Show* stages nothing less than a challenge to the patriarchal symbolic order, where we can discover a voice that is resistant to the systems that claim to know it:

> The talk show's speaking subject is constituted in the speaking of its subjection to a system(s), of its struggle with the necessary determinants of subjectivity. The talk show subject is known only in the instance of speaking its struggle with the system(s) that represents it. It is the resistance of the voice silenced . . . as a critique of the very systems that claim to know it. It is not coincidental that this displacement comes as therapeutic discourse moves into the mass culture subjectivity. The move from individual to mass exposes the necessary bourgeois illusion of the distinction between public and private . . . Given the scandal position of the feminine in representation, it is also no coincidence that this move occurs alongside the articulation of a feminine subject, a public feminine authority. The coordination and reconfiguration of that move say that the healthy, the nonvictim speak from a position of denial. (p. 98)

It is one thing to argue that talk shows stage confrontations between common sense and expertise where the latter (because of the footing it occupies) is constructed as inauthentic. However, Masciarotte is arguing that expertise is in unconscious denial (of its own violence, of the arbitrary categories it imposes) even as the talk show subject voices its protest. Conversely, the talk show subject is afforded an essential rather than a constructed authenticity which is ultimately guaranteed by the fact that it is "feminine" and therefore a priori "scandalous." It is the public visibility and hearability of the body and voice of the oppressed that is enough to make this rhetorical gesture.

To bring matters down to earth, it is very interesting to consider what actually was happening on *The Oprah Winfrey Show* as Masciarotte (1991) arrived at her interpretation:

> One of the best examples of [Oprah's] promotion of narrative, operatic excess is a program on sex addiction in which the guest was recalling her history in the language of ego psychology, the language of cured addict, the language of case study, not story. Oprah was unsatisfied with this recounting and prodded the women into telling the graphic details of her addictive behavior . . . Oprah extracted from the cured voice stories of compulsive, hourly sex, sex with a mentally handicapped boy, stories of sexual betrayal of a husband on a honeymoon, making a spectacle of the individual caught in a narcissistic blackout and dramatizing a systematic lack of self-esteem. In soliciting a painful story of the abject feminine . . . after the rehearsal of these details Oprah made this woman cry and the audience squirm. Then the audience began to confess their addictions too: one man told the story of his shoplifting addiction after invoking the line "I understand. My experience is just like yours . . ." (p. 97)

In the critical feminist perspective (Landeman, 1995; Lupton, 1994; McLaughlin, 1993; Peck, 1995; Probyn, 1993), it is not enough that talk shows provide a public forum in which oppressed voices can speak. What needs further consideration are the practices of speaking, the kinds of things that are said, and the use that is made of this speech in the wider context of the show. The starting point for this might be to question Oprah's power to "make a spectacle" of this woman, and to make her cry, but not simply at the level of claiming that some guests are victimized by these shows. Rather, what Masciarotte is describing seems to be a species of *confession* as a "ritual of discourse" famously described by Foucault (1978):

> The confession is a ritual of discourse in which the speaking subject is also the subject of the statement; it is also a ritual that unfolds within a power relationship, for one does not confess without the presence (or virtual pres-

> ence) of a partner who is not simply the interlocutor but the authority who requires the confession, prescribes and appreciates it, and intervenes in order to judge, punish, forgive, console and reconcile; a ritual in which the truth is corroborated by the obstacles and resistances it has to surmount in order to be formulated; and finally, a ritual in which the expression alone, independently of its external consequences, produces intrinsic modifications in the person who articulates it: it exonerates, redeems and purifies him (sic); it unburdens him of his wrongs, liberates him and promises him salvation. For centuries the truth of sex was, at least for the most part, caught up in this discursive form. (pp. 61–62)

In this perspective then, the "abject feminine" on *Oprah Winfrey* is not at all the transcendence of structure (excess or scandal), but rather the routine product of an established social practice. For Foucault, it is a carefully modulated technique, often professionally deployed, for producing confessional statements. These, in the manner of their articulation, seem to insist on a subjective truth. On this basis, as is equally well known, Foucault (1982) proceeded to discuss the social consequences of this form of subjectivity, as the production of subjects with a conscience who are thereby amenable to the exercise of disciplinary power. Discipline, in modern forms of *governmentality*, requires the constant policing of boundaries between normality and deviance, and subjects who have internalized these distinctions. In this account, the confession only provides an apparent liberation; it actually serves to bind the subject ever more tightly into the social order.

Several feminist discussions of talk shows demonstrate a familiarity with Foucault's theory, without, however, in all cases remaining strictly within its protocols. The most orthodox account is provided in Lupton's (1994) discussion of a *Donahue* program that featured heterosexual couples where one of the partners is bisexual. Lupton demonstrates that the program operated with a double standard, where the imperative to confess as a positive form of self-expression was then framed by a discourse of moral indignation, cultivated between Phil Donahue and his audience. Normalizing judgments were formed where Donahue constantly reinforced the "otherness" of the guests' relationships and reinforced the position of the audience as "normal" (p. 56), so much so that:

> such shows can be regarded as the modern equivalent of the stocks as well as a secularized version of the confessional, in which offenders are held up to public ridicule and chastised for their sins, accepting their punishment in return for experiencing a cathartic release of guilt. (pp. 61–62)

Of course, as Lupton emphasizes, it is significant that the confessions produced in talk shows are enacted in public. In this respect, as "testimonials," they differ from the classic form of the ritual described by Foucault, or perhaps we could say that a further level of "ritualization" has been added. (We return to this point in chapter 6.) At the same time, however, such "therapeutic" talk shows do seem to be operating broadly in the Foucaultian territory, as is also evident in McLaughlin's (1993) discussion of talk shows on the topic of prostitution. Her main point here is that prostitution is inevitably cast as deviant, against the self-definition of sex workers who claim to be professionals, and this is constructed in a consensus where the views of experts and lay persons coincide. In other words, there is no necessary confrontation in talk shows between discourse of expertise and common sense, and with this evidence, McLaughlin offers a counterargument to Carpignano et al. (1990), attacking the notion of an oppositional public sphere.

From a feminist perspective, the key point about such arguments does not concern the making of moral judgements per se, as that the judgments made in these talk shows are resolutely (hetero)sexist and patriarchal. The incitement to confession in *Oprah Winfrey* therefore needs to be assessed in a wider political context where women's claims to sexual autonomy are stigmatized (cf. Nelson & Robinson, 1994) and where the normality of the heterosexual couple and the sanctity of the family are routinely reaffirmed. The same point is confirmed by White's (1992) analysis of dating game shows, in the context of a broader exploration of therapeutic discourse on American television. A further dimension is added in discussions which point out that the domestic housewife is the primary target for these shows, and where "women demographics" (Shattuc, 1997) determine that talk show confessions intersect with the promotion of domestic/women-oriented consumer goods to create an "uncanny" effect of disturbance and yet reinforcement of "normal" domesticity (Probyn, 1993).

There is also a broader political engagement in some feminist discussions. For Landeman (1995) and Peck (1995), the issue is that confessional discourse works as a form of management by displacement of structural social problems. This becomes (in Peck's terms) a familiar argument about "ideological labor," whereby the definition of issues in personal terms mystifies and masks their wider social construction—"containment through personalization," as she puts it. For example, an *Oprah Winfrey Show* entitled "Secrets from the Past" presents a narrative of child abuse as "toxic shame" to be overcome through confession, rather than set in a social context of child poverty and deprivation. Within the confines of talk shows, Peck (1995) argues, "all problems seem to be amenable to therapeutic intervention" (p. 75) and she neatly draws the distinction between this and political speech:

> Therapeutic discourse translates the political into the psychological—problems are personal (or familial) and have no origin or target outside one's

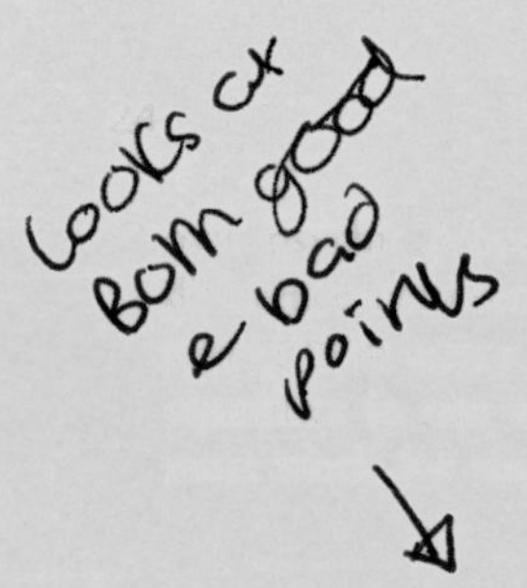

. Compare this to the language of politics: there is a ying 'I'm ill, I've been abused, I need recovery", and oppressed, my exploitation is based on structural in- ty, I share this experience with others with whom I change." (pp. 75–76)

passing that there is a difference between Peck's ar- ultian view that confessions do not so much mask social inequalities as construct them. This is the basic difference between theories of ideology and discourse in media and cultural studies. However, in this context, both theories are united in offering a counter-argument against the views of the utopian feminists, Masciarotte, Squire et al. For instance there seems to be a direct contradiction between Peck's (1995) argument and Squire's (1994) claim that the productivity of *Oprah Winfrey* lies in its "display [of] the contradictions which traverse our subjectivities rather than to opt for social determinist explanations of problems . . ." (p. 74). In one argument, *Oprah* is progressive because it transcends social structures; in the other, it is regressive because it fails critically to engage with them.

So where does this leave the feminist perspective? There would seem to be an impasse, but in the rest of this chapter I explore the possibility of moving things on by changing the terms of the debate. In all the accounts summarized so far, though some interesting suggestions are made, the dominant agenda is *evaluative*: the discussion engages with talk shows in terms of their generally negative or positive cultural implications. As we have seen, there are moral condemnations and feminist critiques, just as there are positive claims for an "oppositional" public sphere and/or the "empowerment of women." Given the seemingly irreconcilable differences here, however, perhaps it would be more productive to start from a different place, working toward a critical analysis of talk show culture rather than a general judgment of it. A useful place to begin, I think, is another strand to the discussion of "therapeutic discourse" in talk shows, which has recognized that what is promoted and performed in this context has quite specific cultural roots.

The starting point for a more analytical approach to the talk show has to be Carbaugh's (1988) wonderfully idiosyncratic study of *Donahue*. In this, the first book-length study of the genre, *Donahue* is considered from an ethnographic, or more precisely, ethnolinguistic perspective. That is to say, Carbaugh is concerned with cultural categories of speech, and what these categories suggest about the cultures in which they are located. The cultural categories of speech are identified by members' definitions, and on *Donahue* these are made through a metalanguage that uses terms like "being honest," "sharing," and (good) "communication." The use of these terms is then related to the cultural framework (we might say, ideology) that supports them. This framework defines participants as individuals with "rights" (to speak, to choose) who tread a fine line between personal freedom and constraint or obligation to others, and who possess a concept of "self" as an inner, essential core.

Typically then, shows like *Donahue* are dedicated to the exploration and display of "self" as a precondition for effective individuality. The *optimal self* is defined as "independent, aware and communicative" (Carbaugh, 1988, p. 69), so self-aware individuals will express themselves by "being honest" and "sharing." Carbaugh's account thus provides an understanding of (good) communication as a way of "working through" the problems it presupposes, such as forms of repression and denial. More to the point, however, is Carbaugh's insistence that this whole approach to speaking in these categories is culturally specific. Other cultures do not have such concepts of individuality and self, nor do they share these communicative values. Participants on *Donahue* are therefore engaged in a particular, and perhaps peculiar, form of cultural activity which Carbaugh characterizes as "talking American."

In a context where the favored strategy is to engage in a cultural evaluation of talk shows, this has to be a major insight. Carbaugh does not so much evaluate the speech forms he identifies as attempt to dissect the cultural context in which they operate. Following Carbaugh, other commentators have sought, in passing, to define the cultural provenance of ways of speaking on talk shows: a common argument notes their similarity to the Protestant activity of testifying to one's sins before a group as a ritual of membership (Lupton, 1994; Masciarotte, 1991). If there are religious antecedents here, however, it needs to be stressed again that these might be distinctively American. In a useful cross-cultural comparison, Krause and Goering (1995) point to a series of differences between American and German talk shows. The German shows are more concerned with a national public sphere, whereas "American talk shows often have the feel of mini-therapy sessions" (p. 202).

A further observation made by Krause and Goering is that the American talk shows tend to be more "dramatic." This point needs to be made carefully, for they also note that the German shows retain a conventional theatrical form of presentation. The argument is that not only are the performance spaces more fluid on American shows, allowing for audience participation (cf. Carpignano et al., 1990); the performance of the talk itself is different. The display of the self in the activity of testifying has a dramatic performative potential beyond that found in more conventional discussions: "As each guest shares his/her personal story, he/she becomes the 'star' for the moment . . . the talk show becomes more like a series of vignettes or one-act plays on a central theme" (pp. 198–199). Furthermore:

> Interestingly, whereas inarticulateness (sic) on German talk shows is seen as a sign of incompetence, on American talk shows, it is often equated with individual authenticity. Halting, groping speech and the inability to put feelings into words somehow lend credibility and magnitude to a guest's story. (p. 202)

From these observations, it is possible to begin to form a sense of what would be required in an analytical approach to talk shows. Both Carbaugh and Krause and Goering draw our attention to cultural preferences for particular forms of talk. Here, previous observations about the articulation of common sense on talk shows, or their use of confessional discourse, can now be related to specific popular cultural identities and pleasures. Most significantly, in our understanding of these pleasures we need to explore the ways in which talk is *performed*. Clearly the act of "testifying" is not just a personal narrative, it is also its dramatic enactment for an audience. This warrants our attention to the practices or—as Carbaugh would say—the rituals of talk, rather than the ideological "what is talked about." There is one last contribution to the literature that also begins to define this ground, and interestingly relates it back to previous feminist concerns.

In some ways Shattuc's (1997) important book on talk shows can be seen as a contribution to the feminist debate that, at the same time, begins to break new ground. It achieves this by taking on board the point about cultural specificity first introduced by Carbaugh. It is not always clear that Shattuc herself is fully aware of its significance, particularly when she returns to the question of the feminist credentials of Oprah Winfrey; but her key contribution is to show that the cultural significance of American talk shows can be related to a long history of American tabloid journalism, in the melodramatic "sob sisters" genre. Her argument suggests that the talk show represents a commercial repackaging of that tradition for television, particularly oriented to "women demographics" which largely define the target audience for daytime television. *The Oprah Winfrey Show* has been the most successful of these products, reaching its zenith in terms of ratings in 1994. Subsequently, Shattuc traces a shift in the market toward a more youthful audience which accounts for the rise of the "trash" type of talk show, represented by *Ricki Lake* and *Jerry Springer*.

The important point here is that an evaluation of the contents of particular shows is not the main issue. Rather, our attention is drawn to the industrial context of talk show production, and in her suggestion that the shows are a contemporary form of melodrama, Shattuc achieves two things. First, she relocates Carbaugh's argument about "talking American," with its possible religious links, in a genre of popular culture, a genre which, furthermore, has long been associated with a particular appeal to women (Gledhill, 1987). Feminist or not, and one suspects this will be endlessly debated, this is the cultural sphere of talk show production.

Second, however, this now allows us to turn to the *talk* of talk shows with the emphasis on its *performance*, precisely in a context where this might be seen as melodramatic. Here we have a popular form of drama where the scenarios are not (we are led to believe) performed by actors, but by ordinary people who have learned how to speak melodramatically:

> Unlike medicine shows and vaudeville, everyone performs on talk shows. They are closer to public performances of personal narratives of emotional pain, frustration and recovery. The guests and audience members do not come as naïve to the TV arena. Audience members primp in the restroom upon arrival to look 'good' if the camera catches them. Before taping they play musical chairs as they shift seats in order to get as close as they can to the host and the microphone. They vie to ask questions. They have watched the programs and have absorbed many of the conventions. They call the hosts by first names. Generally, they know what are permissable questions and behavior (many are savvy enough to ask their questions straight to the camera). They have thought out their narratives beforehand. They speak the language of talk shows and therapy. (Shattuc, 1997, p. 127)

"They speak the language of talk shows . . ." but what kind of language is this and how is it spoken? Shattuc brings us finally to the question we explore further in this book; but first let us briefly review what we have learned so far. It has been suggested that this is the language of *common sense*, which can be identified in the *footings* of lay discourse as opposed to expertise. There might also be some use of confessional discourse, suitably performed for public consumption. More generally there is the kind of "therapy talk" that can be related to the practice of "testifying" before an audience. Carbaugh defined this as "talking American" in rituals that Shattuc suggested are a form of melodrama. In short, the phenomenal success of the TV talk show seems to be related to the popularity of the melodramatic performance of talk. How do we begin to analyze this phenomenon?

THE TALK SHOW AS BROADCAST TALK

As outlined in the introduction, the remaining chapters of this book take a particular approach to the analysis of talk show talk. Though its validity is tested in the case studies that form these chapters, it will be helpful to the reader who is unfamiliar with this methodology if a short introduction is provided here. Essentially, as we have said, we consider talk shows as a species of broadcast talk, and this means that the talk has three defining features. First, this talk has some affinities with the patterns of verbal interaction normally found in everyday conversation. Second, however, unlike ordinary conversation, this talk must be understood as "institutional;"

that is, talk produced in an institutional setting. Third, unlike any other kind of institutional talk, this talk is produced for, and oriented toward, an "overhearing audience"—that is, whatever else might be happening in the studio, there is always a wider audience which is not co-present, invisible and (usually) unheard.

Institutional talk has previously been studied in a variety of contexts such as classrooms, courtrooms, and clinical interviews (cf. Drew & Heritage, 1992). A basic approach here is to recognize that while such talk can be compared to ordinary conversation, in some respects its features are different. In many studies, ordinary conversation is taken as prototypical talk, and institutional talk is then examined in terms of how it differs from the prototype. Ordinary conversation has been studied through the methods of Conversation Analysis, which pays particular attention to the ways in which interactive talk is locally managed and organized, for instance in regular patterns of turn-taking. The turn-taking patterns of institutional talk are then investigated for their differences from ordinary conversation, particularly where who takes what turns at speaking is institutionally predetermined (cf. Hutchby & Wooffitt, 1998).

As far as broadcast talk is concerned, it is clear that several institutional factors impinge on the talk that occurs. If we consider, for instance, the widely studied news interview (Greatbatch, 1986, 1992; Heritage, 1985; Heritage & Greatbatch, 1991), it is clear that, at the most basic level, patterns of turn-taking are heavily influenced by the pre-allocation of roles of interviewer and interviewee. So it is expected that one party will ask questions, and a second party (which may, of course, be more than one person) will answer them. That is the most basic point, but now consider that in many news interviews, interviewers are not expected to ask questions on their own behalf, but rather on behalf of the audience, sometimes defined as the "public." This means that the organization of interviewer turns is also predetermined: not only must interviewers produce questions, but these must also be hearably impartial, or "public-spirited," and this can involve the interviewer recycling public statements using an "animator" footing (Clayman, 1992).

Furthermore, if the role of interviewer demands a particular alignment to the questions produced, it also requires a more general alignment to the audience. This is where the third defining feature of broadcast talk becomes relevant: that the talk is directed toward an unseen, distant audience. Not only must the participants talk generally in ways that are acceptable to that audience (or else they will switch off), but also the talk has several specific features which are designed for that audience to relate to. Heritage's (1985) pioneering analysis of the news interview shows how interviewers often follow interviewees statements by "formulating" them for the audience: that is, by summing up, "furnishing the gist," or probing what has just been said. A further key dimension to the analysis of broadcast talk is then introduced by Heritage's further observation that these formulations can be more, or less, "cooperative," in that the interviewee may find them an acceptable summary, or not. I return to this shortly.

First, however, let us consider a further implication of our third defining feature of broadcast talk. If, in broadcasting, the talk is always oriented to an "overhearing audience" whether or not a studio audience is present, then that talk is always, in a general sense, performed. Furthermore, if that talk is to be performed in ways that are acceptable to the audience, then all sorts of generic considerations come into play. "Speech genres" are a feature of ordinary conversation, in the sense that we are able to distinguish between stories, jokes, sales talk, etc. (Bakhtin, 1986). In broadcasting the production of speech genres must be judged both in terms of their appropriateness for the immediate context and for the intended audience. There is a "double articulation," or a piece of doublethink, in any form of broadcast talk (Scannell, 1991b). For instance, it might be thought that a story will be out of place in a news interview, but much more appropriate for a sociable occasion such as a chat show, but the participant in a news interview might take the risk with a story if it is calculated that a favorable impression may be gained (Tolson, 1991).

Which brings us back to "cooperativeness." A further defining feature of ordinary conversation is its *cooperative principle*. This is specified in the well-known conversational maxims of Grice (1975), namely that contributions to conversation should be appropriate in terms of quantity (length of turns), quality (truthfulness), relevance, and manner. That is to say, it becomes noticeable if these maxims are flouted in any way: for example, if speakers talk for too long, are ambiguous or obscure or (in a phrase used by British politicians) "economical with the truth." Speakers can be deemed to be less than fully cooperative and can be held normatively accountable for their behavior. More generally still, *manner* covers the expectation that ordinary conversation will normally be conducted politely and with reference to the "face wants" (i.e., respect) of others (Brown & Levinson, 1987). From this perspective, ordinary conversation is a fundamentally cooperative activity, in which, as co-conversationalists, we constantly reaffirm each other's identities.

In the performance of talk for overhearing audiences, however, the cooperative principle can become very complicated. We can distinguish between three kinds of situation which, in broadcast talk, regularly occur. In the first place, there are some genres of broadcasting where talk that might normally be judged to be contrary to the conversational maxims or principles of politeness is routinely produced. For instance, in Britain at least, we have become accustomed to forms of chat show where hosts routinely insult guests (Montgomery, 1999); but of course, this is still, in a sense, cooperative when it occurs within a genre where all participants are aware of the rules of the game being played. At the other extreme from this are those occasions where the participants, knowing the rules, refuse to abide by them. Such instances of rank uncooperativeness are extremely rare, but they are very memorable, such as the moment when the Bee Gees walked off the Clive Anderson talk show or when defense minister John Knott refused to answer any further questions in a news interview with Robin Day.

More interesting still, and a major characteristic of contemporary broadcasting, are those situations where we do not know for sure. That is, because of the double articulation in broadcasting, it is possible for the talk to appear to be normatively problematic and yet be acceptable to the more general requirement for "good television." Further levels of entertainment are provided by shows that seem to test how far you can go: the activities of shock jocks fall into this category. Then there are shows that transgress boundaries of taste, decency, and even functional human behavior, but where the situation may or may not be a set-up, or where the performers may or may not be real. This is, of course, where we came in: it is a key issue for the talk show phenomenon. Suffice it to say that, where others have seen this as the talk show's "postmodernism," in this volume we prefer to analyze it as a form of play with the pragmatic expectations of conversational practice.

Therefore, we now turn to the discourse analysis of talk shows. We start in chapter 2 with an overview, and then we move to the analysis of particular programs as case studies. We take with us a set of protocols that define broadcast talk as a conversational practice, institutionally located and always "doubly articulated" both to the immediate situation and to the overhearing audience. As such, this talk is institutionally produced for target audiences and is designed to appeal to them. It may reproduce established conventions, or it may play with them, in explicit or covert ways. It may look like ordinary conversation or it may not; either way, the basic expectations of conversational practice are mobilized in audience responses. However, if this talk is melodramatic, perhaps it is also performed in such a way that it can be perceived to be a form of acting; except, of course, that we are also led to believe that the actors are, in some sense, real.

CHAPTER

2

Performing Talk

Louann Haarman

This chapter provides an overview of the daytime talk show, possibly the most familiar and popular manifestation of a vast and fluid genre that embraces an impressive variety of television formats. These include conversation between elite peers, round table or group discussions, interviews, debates, mock courtroom proceedings, and topical discussions between experts and ordinary people. The characterizing feature of all such formats is the performance of talk before an audience, but there is immense variety in the performers, the content and style of the talk, the procedures followed, and the characteristics and interventions of the participating and/or overhearing audiences. Indeed, even within discernible subgenres such as the daytime talk show, significant variations in content, style, and procedure combine to determine recognizably different products.

Specifically, this chapter explores the structural and discursive features of the three principal types of daytime talk shows: the audience discussion show, the issue-oriented talk show centering on social problems in a personal perspective, and the trash talk show, where social and personal problems are presented as spectacle.[1] Although these different products share the same ultimate goal, that of entertainment through talk, particular aspects of format and procedure give rise to three very different types

[1]An earlier version of this paper appears in Haarman (1999) where I also discuss the evening celebrity show (*Jay Leno*) and the current affairs talk show (*Jonathan Dimbleby*).

of performance, each of which involves recurring and characteristic patterns of linguistic behavior that are not only substantially different from everyday conversation, but that at times vary in important respects even among the different talk show types.

The analytical approach adopted corresponds essentially to what Fairclough (1995, p. 31) has called a cultural–generic approach. This pays particular attention to the role of context in the interactive construction of meaning and to the particular characteristics of a form of broadcast talk where coparticipants engage in a prearranged discursive event that is deliberately intended to be overheard by others. By virtue of its public, asymmetrical, goal-oriented character, talk show talk is taken as institutional talk that can be examined from a conversation analytic perspective in order to highlight recurrent patterns in interaction. I begin by setting out the essential components of the talk show as genre; then, with reference to specific programs, I describe how these components are deployed in daytime talk show types.

COMPONENTS OF TALK SHOW FORMATS

The daytime talk show (with its three main subvariants) is defined here as a particular talk show format, which can be distinguished from other principal types such as the current affairs debate or panel interview (Greatbatch, 1992) or the evening chat show (Montgomery, 1999; Tolson, 1991). One basis for making such typological distinctions is the different deployment, in the various formats, of these key elements, taken as necessary components of a talk show: a host, a special guest or guests, a studio audience, and a focus for talk.

Hosts are responsible for the flow of the performance. They are the point of contact between the television studio and the audience at home, and—within the studio—between the special guests, eventual experts, and the studio audience. As program manager, they introduce the object of discussion, present the guests and experts, and direct the proceedings, handling also technical aspects such as interruptions for commercial announcements. Their power and control are visually conveyed by their mobility: They are, in fact, the only persons other than the technical crew who are entitled to rise and walk in the studio, selecting speakers, proffering the microphone to members of the studio audience, withdrawing it at their discretion. Control is also exerted through linguistic patterns typically utilized by all hosts, who open, frame, and close the talk, selecting the topic, allocating turns, soliciting and guiding interventions through, for example, questions, interruptions, and formulations. Although linguistic mechanisms for the maintenance of control are common to all hosts, the style of the host's performance varies according to the kind of guests invited and topics discussed, the social composition of the studio audience, eventual constraints on the possibility of intervention arising from the physical layout of the studio, and ultimately the preplanned format of the show.

There tends to emerge in all talk show types a feeling of intimacy and familiarity between host and members of the studio audience and, indirectly, spectators at home. Horton and Wohl (1956) describe this curiously close and trusting relationship between viewers and media personalities as *para-social*, whereby viewers relate to the media personalities as if they actually know them, "in somewhat the same way they know their chosen friends: through direct observation and interpretation of appearance, gestures and voice, conversation and conduct in a variety of situations" (p. 213, cited in Peck, 1995).[2] The creation of this confidential para-social relationship, potentially common to any television genre centering on a personality, is particularly encouraged by talk show formats and procedures. First, the presence of an actively invoked and participating studio audience increases the feeling of involvement of the viewing audience. Peck (1995) notes, for example, that the studio audience acts as "an identificatory bridge between viewers and hosts/guests" (p. 63). Furthermore, the persona of the talk show host is constructed in the media in such a way as to underline his or her normality, accessibility, and similarity to ordinary viewers. One of the spin-off effects of this is what Fairclough (1989) has termed *synthetic personalization*, leading to "the simulation of private face-to-face discourse in public mass-audience discourse," a tendency that, along with a "democratization" of talk, is "linked to a spread of conversational discourse from the private domain of the lifeworld into institutional domains" (p. 98). We shall see the particular asymmetrical character of conversational discourse produced in an institutional setting and how this is favored by talk show procedures.

According to the specific type of talk show, the guests are persons who are in some way newsworthy, authoritative, representative, or simply

---

[2]Horton and Wohl's essay, originally published in *Psychiatry* in 1956, analyzed the American evening talk shows of the 1950s (e.g., Steve Allen's *Tonight*). Although their intuitions and description of the para-social relationship remain substantially valid, many of their conclusions, as Munson (1993, pp. 115–117) suggests in his discussion of their work, were conditioned by prevailing contemporary approaches to television criticism, which tended to conceive of the television viewer as unreflecting and highly impressionable. Thus, their view that talk shows were "deceptive and hazardous" because the "spectator may be hoodwinked by the talk show into the 'twilight zone' of para-social relations and a greater belief in the 'reality' of that interaction—'experienced as of the same order as, and related to, the network of actual social relations'[. . .]".

deemed by host or show producers to be intrinsically interesting.[3] Frequently talk shows include among the special guests one or more experts, such as psychologists, social workers, sociologists, academics, members of government, or others with presumably specialized knowledge in the topic under consideration, whose comments and counsel are meant to "make sense" of the problem at hand. By lending authority and credibility to the proceedings, the figure of the expert functions as the representative of the public, institutional sphere in these programs. The role of the studio audience varies according to the particular type of talk show, from that of nominated addressee, occasionally responding to questions put by the host, to continuously active player, where interventions may range from considered and articulate questions and statements to outbursts of approval or disapproval, laughter, applause, or derision.

According to the type of talk show, the focus for talk may be simply chat (agreeable talk ostensibly for its own sake) typical of the evening celebrity talk show, or an issue or theme ranging from political and social matters and current events to topics pertaining more strictly to the private domain, like jealousy or infidelity. The guests engage in talk for as long as the host and programming constraints permit.

As we shall see, there is a convergence between topic, kind of participants, communicative styles, and scheduling time that creates a characteristic context of situation[4] in talk shows. Current affairs or politically oriented talk shows featuring politicians, members of government, journalists, etc., often scheduled for prime time or Sunday, tend to be more sedate than talk shows featuring celebrities (scheduled for late evening, including music and transgressive humor) or the daytime shows, where ordinary people are gathered to discuss in serious, often tragic and intimate tones, "social" issues related to the personal sphere. Each of these different contexts of situation functions according to specific interactive rules and linguistic behavior that shape the proceedings. As mentioned earlier, in all contexts talk is highly controlled by the host in opening and closing moves and in the allocation of turns and selection of topic, but the end products may be quite dissimilar. For example, lexical field and register may vary considerably, with talk pertaining to the private sphere tending more closely to resemble stretches of ordinary talk in length of utterance, overlaps, pauses, false starts, and repairs, whereas talk on programs referring to the

---

[3]Heaton and Wilson (1995, pp. 69–93) discuss daytime talk show guests at some length, including methods of recruitment, preshow preparation and briefing, motivation, and aspects of their "performance." In this regard see also Priest (1995), who discusses in a social psychological perspective the propensity of guests to disclose such private matters to literal (but not virtual) strangers, and Masciarotte (1991), who treats the phenomenon from a psychoanalytic perspective.

[4]See Firth, 1950; Halliday and Hasan, 1985; Hymes, 1967, 1974.

public sphere is predictably more formal. These differences in the kind of talk produced are compatible and consistent with the different social and linguistic constructions of the players themselves. Hosts, guests, experts, and studio audience in each of the principal talk show types constitute a sort of social microcosm embodying a discernible, particular configuration of personal and institutional expectations within which certain kinds of discourses and interactive patterns are considered appropriate and accessible.[5]

In what follows I address the performance of talk in three types of shows that comprise the daytime subgenre, beginning with the British audience discussion format, then moving on to the two quite different American varieties, the issue-oriented format (associated with *Oprah Winfrey*), and the trash talk show (exemplified by *Jerry Springer*).

THE AUDIENCE DISCUSSION FORMAT

In this format, members of the studio audience, normally composed of 50 to 70 ordinary people and others who are presented as having expertise in the topic considered (politicians, doctors, academics) engage in discussion. Thus, all talk is produced entirely by the studio audience, not simply expanded by it as in the other two daytime models considered here. In its purest form, the audience discussion show is represented by BBC's long-running *Kilroy*, and I focus here on this program.

The format opens with the host's entrance in the studio, which presents an almost intimate, semicircular and tiered seating arrangement. An educated, elegant ex-Labour Member of Parliament, Robert Kilroy-Silk walks through the audience under the theme music toward the camera, where he stops, his back to the studio audience, and introduces the topic of discussion to the viewing audience. (This is the only time the viewing audience is directly addressed until the end of the program, when he signs off.) He then opens the discussion as he turns to the studio audience, where experts are normally seated in the first row, their titles or positions appearing in subscript on screen the first few times they speak. There is no visible editing, and, unlike the other talk shows considered here, no interruption for commercial announcements in the 45-minute program.

Topics for discussion range from the public domain, such as poverty and the elderly or job discrimination, to intimate and private matters like

[5]The nonarbitrary nature of this state of affairs is underlined by the fact that very few talk shows are broadcast live, or are broadcast without some degree of editing, a fact that allows talk show producers a further opportunity to polish, refine, and adjust the construction of the product. Those rare talk shows that are broadcast live are generally political or current affairs shows on breaking news produced by networks. Elsewhere, editing is done with varying degrees of transparency or invasiveness. American daytime shows, for example, produced and distributed by specialised production houses that tape up to two programs at a time, are quite obviously constructed on the editing table, as we shall see.

domestic violence and casual sex, spanning topics broached in the current affairs format (not discussed here) as well as those more typical of the daytime subgenre, where social issues are cast in a personal perspective. As the topics vary in public or private focus, the program assumes the discursive patterns of the debate, the therapy session, and/or what Livingstone and Lunt (1994) have called the romantic narrative, to which we later return.

The discussants themselves represent an assortment of different discursive styles and competence that require different modes of guiding talk and of actually managing the proceedings. During the interventions, Kilroy moves among the public, sitting beside speakers (making room for himself, edging between two audience members in a familiar, informal way) as he listens to their contributions. Indeed, the importance of studio geography and especially seating arrangements for the conduct of such group discussion cannot be underestimated. Generally, the larger the audience and the more "isolating" the seating arrangements (with a great distance between potential interactants, or all seats facing forward so as to make eye contact between audience members difficult), the less the interaction and the more talk tends to be monologic, or performed predominantly by experts, host, and a few host-selected lay persons.[6] The *Kilroy* set is such that he may move with some agility through the public, eliciting or accepting interventions from all quarters, "binding" the studio audience by virtue of this movement and implicitly legitimating all members as potential speakers.

Indeed, the very fact that Kilroy's attention during the entire discussion is directed solely to the studio audience (to whom he thus commits allegiance, ignoring the viewing audience) is also, I suggest, significant for the creation of a social context conducive to interventions from them. His skill in the management of discussion is considerable. In selecting speakers, he often calls them by name and is apparently aware of the probable content of their interventions;[7] he initiates, or ratifies audience-initiated, topic changes; he provokes disagreement; he maintains discipline, chiefly through interruptions and reprimands; he passes judgment, praises, comforts, and consoles, as appropriate to the social and discursive contexts determined by the topic of discussion, the characteristics of the discussants, and the framing of talk (i.e., whether in a debate or therapy mode).

Kilroy's program on high salaries to ex-Ministers who accept directorships in companies they privatized while in office, falls neatly in the discur-

---

[6]Seating arrangements for *The Time, the Place*, for example, which is no longer broadcast, did not encourage interaction and did not permit the host easy access to individual audience members. Not surprisingly, most talk took place between the host and a nominated speaker.

[7]The program is preceded by a warm-up session in which Kilroy speaks with the audience members. The lay members of the audience are recruited through announcements of upcoming programs that appear on screen under the closing credits. Experts are invited by program producers.

sive category of debate. Clearly a social and political issue, the topic is presented and pursued in such a way as to encourage conflict and disagreement, which is actively sought by the host in soliciting interventions, as may be seen in Extract 1. Invited experts on this program include one Conservative and one Labour MP, a representative of the General Municipal and Boilermakers Union, an Independent Pay Advisor, a Pay and Benefits Consultant, and the Director of the Institute for Health Service Management. Interventions from the lay audience come from some middle-aged or older women, some apparently small businessmen, and others who identify themselves during their talk as a worker, a chartered accountant, an old age pensioner, a bank clerk, and shareholders. The extract, taken from the beginning of this program, shows Kilroy's introduction of the topic and his usual selection of a lay member of the audience, here an elderly woman, to make the first contribution. The passage illustrates the asymmetrical nature of the talk, which tends to repress the kind of negotiation of topic and turns typical of everyday conversation, and highlights some common devices through which the host controls audience interventions. (Transcription conventions are given in the Appendix.)

Extract 1

Kilroy		[. . .] and this of course ca:me very hot on the
		heels of utility company chiefs being fo:rced (.)
		to justify pay rises of 75 per cent
		in some case taking their salaries (.)
		to over a million pounds a year.
		(0.6)
	1→	first, what do you feel Lilly
		about those (.) former Tory ministers
		who have gone and joined the board of companies
		(.)when they were (0.5) ministers [in government?
Lilly		[well really I
		feel sorry for the poor souls (.)
		talk about the med- the government ( )
		they're taking a cut in sa:lary
		all they're doin' really is jumping on the
		bandwagon Robert.
Kilroy	2→	what's the bandwagon.
Lilly		what do you think the bandwagon is.
		they're in for all they can get out of it.
Kilroy	3→	you feel that. you feel [that they actually-
Lilly		[I I feel that strongly.
		[that's all they're in for it
Kilroy	4→	[that it's the gravy train
		it's a gravy train
Lilly		you call it gravy train

		I call it bandwagon,
		you call it the gravy train.
		it's just the same thing Robert,
		no matter what they're doing,
		(0.75)
		pretending (.) it's in our interest,
		it's not in our interest at all.
Kilroy	5→	they're on a gravy train, Michael,
		your former colleagues

Note at arrows 1 to 4 how Kilroy probes the *feelings* of a lay member of the public, presumably representative of the opinion of the larger viewing audience, and clarifies the inappropriate metaphor of the bandwagon, through two questions (arrows 1 and 2) and two declaratives functioning as cues (arrows 3 and 4). He then abruptly abandons Lilly in a move that would have been extremely face-threatening in everyday conversation, and turns at arrow 5 to Sir Michael Grylles, a Conservative MP, to challenge the other side by formulating the gist of Lilly's turns in a provocative statement implicitly inviting Michael's intervention.

As host, Kilroy rarely remains neutral on social and political issues. At his arrowed turns in the following exchanges he consistently takes the side of the ordinary people, constructing the experts as evasive, challenging their arguments, even silencing them with accusations of unfairness, at times quite aggressively.

Extract 2

Michael		[. . .] **to Man 2**
		you asked me a question
		let me just answer.
		I mean he's a man of great experience
		he he he obviously knows a lot about accountancy
		I agree he may need to buff it up
Man 2		possibly in the past he knew a lot about
		accountancy
Michael		right right but a lot of the basics of
		accountancy don't change, [a lot of details change-
Man 2		[would you take a
		mechanic to do your car
		that hadn't touched a car for 15 or 20 years?
Audience		hhhhh[hhhhh (2.5 sec.)
Michael		[I think- we- I think ( )
Kilroy	→	he's asking you a question now Michael
Man 2		I'm asking you a question.
		would you take someone

who had previous experience doing
who hadn't done that job for 15 o
had done something diametrically
to do that job on your car. (0.5)
would you do that?
[answer the question please.
Michael [I have not felt- I'm trying to answer it,
can't seem to get a word in
Kilroy → yes or no, Michael (.) yes or no,
[yes or no, yes or no
Michael [( )
[. . .]
Kilroy → [the answer's no but he doesn't want to say it.

This extract illustrates aspects of what Livingstone and Lunt (1994) have called the *romantic narrative influence* on audience discussion shows, mentioned previously and evident here in Kilroy's overt support of the lay members of the audience vis-à-vis the experts. This feature accommodates a reading of the proceedings as quest for social order, which is quite consonant with Kilroy's fast-moving, intense conduct of the discussion, especially, but not only, on programs framed as debates. Livingstone and Lunt (1994) describe it thus:

> In the audience discussion program, as in the romance, we start with a social problem which directly affects the studio audience, who represent the inhabitants of the "kingdom". [. . .] the host plays a central role as the hero who undertakes to solve the problem affecting the kingdom (the public) and restore social order (through advice, understanding or validation of experiences). Consequently, he or she strides through the mythical kingdom (studio), setting out on a journey of discovery, brandishing his or her sword (microphone). On the way, the hero encounters those who can offer information and advice, and those who hinder by posing problems and undermining information [. . .]. Having attained the goal—an understanding, a decision, a body of evidence—the hero returns triumphant to the community in need, for whom social order is restored and celebrated (pp. 59–60).

Evident, however, in such debate is not only Kilroy's support of the lay public, but the lay members' own aggressive and outspoken stance toward the experts. The demeanor and accent of Man 2 in Extract 2 is clearly working class, and he is only one among the lay public who openly express their anger at experts attempting to justify the very high salaries under discussion. Such unreserved aggression toward experts is, in fact, so recurrent that I suggest it may be considered a generic trait of the audience discussion show, much as exuberant audience participation—as we shall see—is a generic trait of the trash talk show.

This tension, which is sometimes artfully constructed between expert and lay participants, has been addressed by many previous commentators.[8] As widely observed, it is reflected most obviously in particular and sometimes radically different uses of language. Experts tend to formulate their contributions using technical terminology or jargon (bureaucratic, medical, etc.), facts or statistics, longer turns, and more frequent metadiscursive markers. They address the issues and the conduct of the discussion, whereas lay participants focus on the concrete and everyday: Man 2 in Extract 2 offers a clear and down-to-earth analogy in order to challenge the appropriateness of ex-Ministers picking up jobs after the passage of years ("would you take a mechanic to do your car that hadn't touched a car for 15 or 20 years?"). Similarly, lay participants invoke their personal experience. Concordance software applied to a *Kilroy* episode on children and poverty analyzed in Haarman (1997) shows that lay participants uttered 31 of the 34 occurrences of "I have" or "I've" (a pattern typical of the personal grounding of experience), and 13 of the 14 occurrences of "I was." Experts in that episode and in the episode on high salaries do not offer any significant personal information or anecdotes, but these are recurrent in lay discourse, because it is their experience that gives lay members expertise.

The privileged mode of lay discourse is thus the personal story. Stories occur in a remarkable 36% of the turns in the episode on children and poverty, where they actually underlie and give form to lay argumentation.[9] Not surprisingly, such stories comprise a very large part of those episodes dealing specifically with the private domain (e.g., jealousy, broken families), which tend to pivot on self-disclosure and group solidarity and eventually counseling on the part of the host or experts. They also occur, however, in programs in which political issues are debated. Thornborrow (1997) has noted that they often serve as a means of "establishing the speaker's position in the debate, and particularly [. . .] in opposition to one other participant" (p. 255). In the program on high salaries, for example, Man 1 intervenes after Michael speaks in support of ex-Ministers who take jobs in privatized industry, to state:

Extract 3

1	Man 1	But Robert does this mean that they're good
2		managers and they're good <u>com</u>pany people?

[8]See, for example, Fairclough (1995), Haag (1993), Livingstone and Lunt (1992, 1994), Peck (1995).

[9]In Haarman (1997) I give several examples of argumentative discourse in conflictual exchanges between lay members of the studio audience and experts, where working class housewives prove equal or superior to a Conservative MP, a doctor, and a university professor. See especially pages 76–83.

		because I worked for Ford Motor Company,
		I recalls [sic] a young man Albert Caspars
		who grew and grew,
		and now he's chairman of Ford of Europe
		and chairman of his own company in Germany.
		now that lad worked hard,
		worked his way all the way up and (.) I don't
		mind if he's being (.) paid (.) value for money
		but=
Kilroy	1→	=but what we're talking about here
		is not somebody who's worked their way up,
		we're talking about [former ministers=
Man 1	2→	[but these-
Kilroy		=who have been in a position of power and
		responsibility who have made decisions that
		affect (.) the companies that were privatized,
		be they the water company, or Cable and Wireless
		or British Telecom and then subsequently
		being appointed to the boards of those companies
Man 1	3→	but the point I'm trying to make is,
		if you want a good company
		it's got to be managed well.
		now what guarantee are these people
		that they are good managers . . .

In his arrowed turn Kilroy, responsible for the orderly development of discussion, interrupts Man 1's story, not immediately relevant to the context, to bring the talk back on track in a metadiscursive formulation of the topic of discussion, and continues to hold the floor over Man 1's attempted interruption at arrow 2. In the following turn (arrow 3), Man 1 explicates his story (after a metadiscursive introduction, "but the point I'm trying to make is") and reveals its relevance for the present discussion. This excerpt is also a good illustration of Kilroy's sensitivity to the potential danger of losing the rhythm and thread of discourse through "random" story-telling, a situation that he is careful to avoid, especially in the case of programs with several experts (as this program—untypically—was) centering on complex issues.

Kilroy is also sensitive to the role of stories in forwarding the talk, especially when through them lay participants construct their social identities. The following excerpt from a program on children in broken families represents a familiar sequence in audience discussion shows, particularly on topics pertinent to the private domain, where one participant's story triggers a joint clarification and elaboration of the topic of discussion. The excerpt begins with a young woman's answer to Kilroy's question about how she learned that her parents had broken up:

Extract 4

1	Woman 9		well I had just started my final year at school,
2			and um Mum was upset
3			and she was upset all the time
4			and I didn't have any idea why
5			and then then she started crying
6			which she used to do a lot,
7			and then there ( ) I said what's wrong
8			and she sat me down and she said
9			I've had to ask Dad to leave
10			and from that point I was crying all the time
11			because I'd had such a good relationship
12			with my Mum and my Dad
13			and they were like my idols,
14			I loved them together
15			and we had such good times
16			and and it just destroyed me.
17	Kilroy	1→	what do you mean by destroyed you?
18	Woman 9		well because I've always seen them together
19			and they from my point of view
20			they've always looked happy
21	Kilroy	2→	what did you do?
22			was there anything that could have helped?
23			I see you two **mother and daughter** holding
24			hands here like this heh heh do you (.)
25			is there anything could have helped you?
26			could it have been handled in a way
27			either advice or counseling or an outside
28			person?
29	Woman 9		well I'd started going out with my boyfriend
30			just after they'd split up
32			and he was a big help for me and (.)
33			but I did have my Mum to speak to
34			[I couldn't
35	Kilroy		[you needed somebody else
36			[to lean on, to talk to
37	Woman 9	3→	[I did need somebody else from the
38			fam- outside the family
39			and I had my friends and I had my boyfriend
40			and they really did help me
41	Kilroy	4→	**to Woman 6** does counseling help?
42	Woman 6		I think it should help but it costs money
43	Expert		not if you use, well we operate in Basingstoke,
44			Relateen, which is a counseling service for
45			young people and it's completely free [. . .]
46			so there are beginning to be-

47	Woman 6	isn't it a shame we need that?
48	Woman 7	terrible
49	Karen	I had counseling on the National Health [. . .]

Note here Woman 9's long and very detailed account of how she discovered her parents' breakup, delivered in calm, serious tones, and her devastating evaluation of the account ("and and it just destroyed me"), which Kilroy immediately follows up at arrow 1 ("What do you mean by destroyed you?"). Kilroy clearly means "in what sense, how" it destroyed her; she responds with "why" ("they've always looked happy"). He then pursues (at arrow 2) the central theme of the program, which is focused on how to help children through the ordeal of separation, by asking her if there was anything that "could have helped," like counseling or an outside person, and guides her through two turns to her statement at arrow 3 that she had her friends and her boyfriend and "they really did help me." At this point he can effectively operate a transition from the story to address, at least for the moment, the central issue of the program. Extending the microphone to another woman sitting next to the expert, he asks at arrow 4 "does counseling help," ready then to take in the subsequent turn the expert who self-selects to describe the services offered by her counseling service. The introduction of the topic of counseling by the expert and Woman 6's comment on the cost of counseling prompt the initiation of another story, again through self-selection, by Karen (a woman who has already spoken at length of her parents' troubled life together and eventual separation), who begins to tell of her own counseling obtained through the National Health Service.

Kilroy's discussion, then, unwinds in a complex, "spiraling" interactive discourse with a social message that is jointly constructed by the stories offered and developed in talk between host and audience members. Kilroy keeps close control on the talk produced, but the format itself offers a context in which self-selection and some local negotiation of turn and topic are possible. As we shall see, this is much less the case in the issue-oriented daytime model, where talk is performed predominantly by guests, experts, and host.

THE ISSUE-ORIENTED TALK SHOW: SOCIAL ISSUES IN A PERSONAL PERSPECTIVE

The highly functional and efficient format of this subgenre, introduced by Donahue in 1967 and consolidated by Oprah Winfrey from 1984, is also used in the trash talk shows (discussed below). Both types of program present different degrees of linguistic and structural formality in combination with different types of content and the host's style of interaction. The format differs markedly from the audience discussion model in procedure, sequencing, and studio geography. As the show opens, the host introduces the guest or guests to the studio audience and/or directly to the spectators at home, then begins the discussion by engaging the guests in talk that in form and rhythm is very similar to a standard media interview. The special guests—occasionally celebrities or "protagonists," but predominantly ordinary people—are seated at center: on a slightly raised platform before sections of tiered seats (*Oprah, Jerry Springer*); at the center of a semicircular amphitheater (*Donahue*); or on center stage (*Geraldo, Ricki Lake*). Interventions from the studio audience are, at the host's discretion, permitted and solicited. Before each commercial break, the host may provide a summary of what has been said and usually offers a preview of what is to come in the next segment.

As noted earlier, seating arrangements and the physical characteristics of the studio may condition the kind of interaction typical of the program. On some shows (e.g., *Oprah*), the host may move between the guests and the studio audience, managing interventions from both sides and underlining by his or her own movement the interactive character of the talk, which often centers on the expression of solidarity or therapeutic advice. Where the studio layout does not permit such easy access to both guests and audience (as in *Ricki Lake* and *Geraldo*, both taped in a large auditorium), the host may simply remain standing and move among the studio audience, thus suggesting the sense of difference between audience and guests, and the often confrontational nature of talk (though solidarity and therapeutic advice are not uncommon here as well). I return to these aspects in some detail later.

Daytime programs centering on social issues in a personal perspective are represented by what Shattuc (1997) calls the first generation of American daytime talk shows (*Donahue, Oprah, Sally*, and *Geraldo*), which have focused consistently on topics closely related to the private sphere. Issues relating specifically and solely to the public sphere, common on *Kilroy*, are virtually never treated. As Shattuc (1997) notes, "most often, the problem is introduced as a personal problem (for example, obesity, HIV+, a bisexual spouse) but then generalized to a large social issue" (p. 95), so that the issues emerge from and are anchored in a domestic, personalized context. Topics range from subjects that are personal but not necessarily intimate, like "Best friends" (*Vanessa*), "Saving money" (*Oprah*), "Smoking and children" (*Oprah*), to much more private, titillating topics like "Adultery" (*Oprah*), "Transsexuals" (*Vanessa*), and "Gay today, straight tomorrow" (*Geraldo*).

The following excerpts from *The Oprah Winfrey Show*[10] illustrate typical features of talk and procedure. In the first exchange, from a program on smoking and children, Oprah is acknowledging requests to intervene from the audience. Note the difference between the rather formal language of the doctor, speaking from the audience as expert, and the interventions of Woman 1 and Woman 2.

Extract 5

Doctor [. . .] when we talk about children and
environmental tobacco smoke
in fact we haven't known what we know
about lung cancer and direct smoking (.)
it's only been studied about(.)15 or 20 years,
and now we really s- are understanding,
as physicians (0.5)
we are teaching our medical students,
we are teaching other doctors in (0.5) courses
we are talking to patients, talking to parents
it is a harmful thing
there is no safe lower level of exposure
to environmental tobacco smoke for children
Oprah **walking close to the audience** okay, okay.
somebody over here wanted to say something.
moving up the tiered seats you wanted to say what?
yes?, ma'am. (0.5) and it is?
extending the microphone
Woman 1 I am a daughter of a smoker for over 25 years.
I (.) think that the ploy is smoking (.)
if (0.5) say your wife has an unsafe car,
she's- (.) the daughter is in that car every day
is that unsafe? is that a child abuse case,
also because the car might be unsafe?
and they could get an accident?
Oprah **indicating another woman, extending the microphone**
you say yes it is.

[10]In very recent years Oprah's guests have been almost exclusively celebrities or others in the news, rather than ordinary people, although the topics have remained substantially unchanged. Programs in February 2000 include "Dr. Phil McGraw discusses sexless marriages"; "Saved by a stranger" (a couple who rescued a young mother from the trunk of a car when she was attacked and abducted by her ex-boyfriend); "Newly divorced women"; "Should you be doing that?" (family who tells how their daughter was killed when she accepted a ride from a friend whose car had other teens in it). The programs cited in this chapter were recorded in 1995.

28 Woman 2 yes Oprah I do: say yes (.) it's very important-
29 Oprah =if you're driving a car that's unsafe,
30 and you know that car's unsafe-

The doctor's speech is formal and fluent as he constructs himself as a member of the scientific community ("now *we* really are understanding *as physicians*, *we* are teaching *our medical students* [. . .] it is a harmful thing") and speaks confidently with the authority this membership confers on him. Oprah's and the women's interventions show instead typical features of spontaneous spoken language, namely:

- *Informal, ambiguous, and unusual formulations*: Oprah's "You wanted to say what" (= What did you want to say?); Woman 1's "I am a daughter of a smoker for over 25 years" (Is she 25 years old? Has her mother or father smoked for over 25 years?) and "I think the ploy is smoking" (given the previous context, the expected formulation of this phrase would have been "I think the smoking is a ploy" referring to one ex-husband's motivations for gaining custody of his daughter);
- *False starts*: "if- (.) say your wife has an unsafe car, she's- the daughter is in that car every day"
- *Mistakes*: "they could get an accident"
- *Interruptions:* Oprah's interruption of Woman 2.

Yet, despite the naturalness of talk at a microlinguistic level (syntactic, lexical, phonological, and prosodic features), evident in this passage are differences at a higher level (e.g., topic selection, openings and closings, turn-taking). Just as we observed in Extract 1 as Kilroy opens the program on high salaries for ex-ministers, these differences derive from the asymmetry of power and the institutional nature of talk. Thus, when the doctor concludes his intervention, Oprah simply walks away, without a word, to call on audience members who have asked for the floor, offering the microphone to Woman 1, then withdrawing it suddenly to extend it to Woman 2, and finally removing it from Woman 2 to offer her own comment. Her behavior, linguistic and interactive, is dictated by the necessity to move the show forward, and this precludes the possibility for lengthy and complex negotiation of turn and topic that characterizes ordinary conversation.

In addition to the host's control, the example also illustrates Oprah's concern to involve the studio audience in the proceedings and to solicit their opinions, and it captures the feeling of intimacy between host and members of the studio and viewing audiences. The establishment of this para-social relationship, as mentioned earlier, is dependent in large part on the construction of the host as "normal" and accessible, one of us. This is a status that Oprah achieves, for example, by revealing information about her personal life both during the program itself and in special targeted media coverage in secondary texts such as radio, newspapers, and magazines. This lends credibility to the host's broadcasting role as concerned and intimate friend who has herself suffered personal problems and now offers solidarity and (therapeutic) advice, the latter chiefly in the form of specialized assistance by experts.

The strong sense of familiarity thus encoded in program semantics and semiotics is, of course, consistent with the production of talk in the private, often intensely personal domain. Haag (1993) has noted in this regard that interactive behavior on talk shows is similar to interactive norms in same-sex female relationships, where the disclosure of personal information is encouraged through supportive listening behavior and discursive strategies that facilitate talk. The following example illustrates some of these strategies. It is taken from a program dealing with adultery, in which Oprah interviews a family composed of husband and wife (Bob and Mary), a daughter and son in their teens, and a younger boy (Corey) about 11 or 12 years old. The extract begins with Oprah's framing of the interview, the second of the program.

Extract 6

1	Oprah	[. . .] This family is also trying to figure out (0.5)
2		how to keep going after not one but two affairs
3		(.) shook their marriage, first? (.)
4		Mary had an affair twelve years ago (.)
5		Bob found out about it, they separated
6		they got back together, then Bob had an affair
7		that just ended a year and a half ago (.)
8		things were so bad (.) they held a family meeting
9		with their three children (.)
10		Chris and Corey and Elisabeth (.)
11		they all say that they're still trying to make
12		things right (.) again (.)
13		I found it interesting because (0.75)
14		as I understand it Chris you blamed yourself?
15		(1.0)
16	Chris	No I didn't blame myself, I just blamed
17		(1.0)
18		the lady that (0.5) my dad had the affair with
19		because (.) I'd seen her before and I just didn't
20		know that (0.5) [that
21	Oprah	[But you didn't think it was your
22		fault
		[3 turns]
23	Oprah	How did you find out about it?

	(2.0)
Chris	[Well
Corey	[I was
Oprah	**looking at Corey pointing** you we::re
Corey	I was in my room at night and (.)
	I'm right by the driveway so (0.5)
	I heard it through the window
	(1.2)
Oprah	you heard your dad?
Corey	and mom
Oprah	hm hmm
	(2.2)
Corey	I didn't like it **crying softly**
Oprah	**softly** of course you didn't like it
	(1.1)
	and you were very hurt by it becau:se- (0.5)
	it's okay
Corey	**crying** they didn't tell me? and I had to find out
	the hard way?
	[4 turns]
Oprah	so then Corey after you heard it that that first
	ti:me did you go to your mom or your dad?
	and in America this is why affairs are so bad (.)
	because it destroys? (0.6) it destr- (.)
	not only your relationship, but just (1.5)
	i- in ways that we will never understand damages the
	children (.) for life.

A number of typical linguistic and interactional features emerge from this extract, particularly the host's control over the flow of talk, a control achieved principally through the deployment of discursive strategies such as framing, speaker nomination, cueing,[11] reiteration and formulation, and, of course, questions, which indicate prior knowledge of key information pertaining to the guests.[12] In Oprah's first turn, for example, the exchange

---

[11]Cueing is accomplished through utterances implicitly inviting the addressee to speak to a specific topic. Declaratives are a common type of cue. Cues are often signalled by tag questions (generally uttered without rising intonation), by which the host, possibly accessing his or her prior knowledge, guides the speaker's discourse in such a way that eventual gaps in the audience's information are filled and/or selected topics are introduced into the talk. Holmes (1995, p. 85) cites studies showing that tag questions "occur more frequently in the speech of those who have some kind of responsibility for the success of an interaction."

[12]This information is gathered by the show's producers, who—with or without the host (depending on the show)—select the topics and the guests, brief guests and hosts, and block out the various phases of the interview before taping. See Shattuc (1997, pp. 47–84) for a description of the entire talk show production process, and Nelson and Robinson (1994) for a personal account of a "pre-scripted" talk show.

with the family is framed in her introduction to the collective interview, and she significantly chooses to begin talk with one of the children, not the parents, for the children, and the devastating effects on them of the parents' adultery, will be the principal focus of the interview. Thus Oprah's nomination of Chris as first speaker and cue for him to address his own emotional response: "as I understand it Chris you blamed yourself" (and, unusually, evidence of wrong information: "no I didn't blame myself"); and later the selection of Corey to speak by pointing at him and repeating the words he uttered in overlap with his brother Chris ("you were . . ."). Corey's audible sobbing and tearful replies to Oprah's questions and solicitations to speak ("and you were very hurt by it becau:se . . .") are picked up by the camera, which provides extreme close-ups of the weeping child, justifying Oprah's urgently expressed comment, "in America this is why affairs are so bad because it destroys not only your relationship, but just in ways that we will never understand damages the children for life."

This rather maudlin introduction is followed by a series of probing questions to the father and mother that illustrate well Oprah's interviewing style: outspoken, often abrupt questions, frequent feedback through back channeling, repetitions, token responses and expressions of solidarity, formulations, and interim summing up with an eye to the maintenance of ongoing comprehension both in the studio and for the viewing audience. The arrowed turns mark some of Oprah's techniques in conducting the talk and involving studio and viewing audiences in the proceedings:

Extract 7

1	Oprah		Bob how long had you been having the affair?
2			(1.5)
3	Bob		about 11 months
4	Oprah		11 months
5			(1.4)
6			and <u>why</u> did you have the affair Bob?
7			(1.6)
8	Bob		well, ha (.) I [guess
9	Oprah	1→	[for all the reasons that we've
10			been talking about?
11	Bob		well some reasons that's been said before
12			(1.2)
13			we didn't communicate,
14			there's some things that
15			(1.0)
16			we just - (.)
17			we'd been married for like 17 years at that time
18			and uh
19			(1.3)

20			we just kinda (.) growing apart for
21			one reason or another
22	Oprah		hm hmm (.)
23	Bob		and uh (0.5) we didn't talk (.)
24			and didn't (.) communicate our feelings
25	Oprah		hm hmm
26	Bob		and that.
27	Oprah	2→	**turning toward studio audience, louder**
28			and as I said earlier what I've learned
29			over the years is that
30			(1.8)
31			people don't lea:ve
32			because the other person is pre:ttier,
33			because a lot of times the women'll say
34			why I can't believe,
35			she didn't look as good as I did (.)
36			but (.) they don't leave because of that,
37		3→	**to Bob** they leave because of the way the other
38			person makes them feel.
39	Bob		exactly
40	Oprah	4→	=is that correct?
41	Bob		yeah
42	Oprah	5→	for you too
43	Bob		yes
44	Oprah	6→	so you had lost those feelings with your wife,
45			did not know how to regain those feelings
46			[. . .]

Evident in this exchange is Oprah's skill in drawing out talk. Her potentially face-threatening comments and questions are counterbalanced with positive feedback in the form of "continuers" or "acknowledgement tokens" (like "hm hmm," "uh huh," "yeah") and by showing generally affiliative listening behavior (e.g., leaning forward, encouraging the guest to continue speaking). She is also sensitive to the studio audience, picking up (at arrow 1) what had been said in the interview of the previous adulterous couple and the woman's husband: "all the reasons that we've been talking about." By using "we" she includes not only the previous trio but also the studio audience, thus drawing it and the audience at home into this conversation with Bob. Note also her comment at arrow 2 ("and as I said earlier what I've learned over the years . . ."), addressed in a louder voice to the studio audience as she turns slightly toward them, whereas the last line of this turn at arrow 3 is spoken more softly directly to Bob ("they leave because of the way the other person makes them feel"). At arrow 4 ("is that correct?") and arrow 5 ("for you too") she then twice confirms Bob's agreement, marking this as an important point in the discussion, also broached in the first interview of the program, and subsequently in the final segment.

As mentioned earlier, the role of the expert on daytime talk shows, giving authoritative advice based on special knowledge, lends an institutional voice and point of reference to the proceedings. In the program on smoking and children, the doctor offers statistics and other information on the danger of environmental tobacco smoke, and, although he gently corrects Oprah's own statements on smoking twice, she treats him cordially and with respect. However, the figure of the expert with his or her specialized knowledge and confident, precise speech may sometimes be taken as suspect. It is not uncommon, in fact, for the expert's authority to be questioned by members of the audience and/or by the host (as we have seen in Kilroy's exchanges with Michael, the Conservative MP), who in turn constructs himself or herself as champion of the ordinary people in the audience, checking and verifying the expert's interventions. In the talk show on adultery, we have a good example of such a challenge when Oprah confronts the expert, Dr. Bonnie Eaker Weil, on the reliability of her statistics:

Extract 8

Oprah		joining us now is Dr. Bonnie Eaker Weil
		who now has the task of trying to offer some
		clarity to this (.) confusing situation.
		Bonnie is the author of a book on this very
		subject,
		it's called adultery the forgivable (.) sin,
		and I was asking the au:dience after hearing
		this story briefly for the first (.)
		y'know ten minutes of this show
		whether or not Bonnie they now belie:ve (.)
		[. . .] is adultery now the forgivable sin?
Bonnie		[. . .] I think it's forgivable,
		[. . .] and I think we have to stop judging adultery
		I think we have to do something about-
		there's an epidemic out there (0.5)
		one person in 80 per cent of marriages (0.6)
		commits adultery.
		(0.7)
		that's 70 per cent of men and 50 per cent of women
		that's very high.
		(1.5)
Oprah		that's high.
		codeswitching into nonstandard English
	→	where we get that statistic from Bonnie?
Bonnie		well it's in my book
		and I got it from all the different theorists
		[( )
Oprah	→	[yeah I hear I hear tha- i- i-
		in standard English is it like one out of seven-?

		is it one out of seven men?
		or (0.6) seventy percent of men.
Bonnie		70 per cent of men and 50 per cent of women
		and it's going higher for women as- as we sit here
		today
		(0.75)
		okay?
		and there's an emotional [( )
Oprah		[70 per cent of married
		men are- [have an affair=
Bonnie		[yes.
Oprah		=[at some time!?
Bonnie		[yes. (0.5) and 50 per cent of women and that's
		pretty high.
Oprah	→	**codeswitching into nonstandard English**
		so they mus' be repeatin' some uh the same women
		then.
Audience		[hhhhhhhhhhhhhhhhhhhhhhhhhhhh (3.5 secs.)
Bonnie		[hhhhhhhhhhhhhhhhhhhhh (3 secs.) right on.
Oprah	→	right. some of the same women are goin' with the
		70 per cent,
		it's not enough women to go around but anyway.
Bonnie		but Oprah the (.) biggest part of this whole thing
		is that in second marriages, adultery and divorce
		are even higher [than in the first marriages
Oprah		**in standard English** [in the second marriage?
	→	that's hard to believe.
Bonnie		absolutely true
Oprah	→	yeah. **looking at audience**
		we we find that hard to believe don't we audience?
		that's hard to believe.
Audience		yea::h

Bonnie substantiates her claims by citing statistics in her first turn, but Oprah immediately challenges these, often marking her challenge by codeswitching into a nonstandard accent and intonation, synonymous with down-to-earth common sense and concrete knowledge (see her arrowed turns). She not only questions the statistics (in truth, Bonnie's sources are hardly convincing), she also questions the credibility of Bonnie's statement regarding divorces in second marriages, even involving the studio audience in her disbelief ("we find that hard to believe don't we audience?"). This example is a good illustration of how the role of the expert is in large part *constructed* by the host, who may at his or her discretion either exploit and legitimate the expert's authority as a purveyor of (good, credible) institutional knowledge, as in the case of the doctor speaking of environmental tobacco smoke, or challenge the expert's information and preparation, presenting him or her as unreliable, biased, or possibly incompetent, as in Extract 8.

As the excerpts confirm, one of the principal features of these daytime talk shows is the constant recourse to therapeutic discourse through the solicitation of free-flowing talk around deeply personal matters, but also in the general focus on psychological and sociopsychological issues. Exchanges like those with the distraught family—the pathos, the crying child, the crying parents, the pained admission of wrongdoing and guilt—are highly recurrent on daytime shows. In the program on adultery, Bob and Mary deliver their remarks with sadness and remorse, their words and demeanor express a profound conviction that what they have done is morally and socially wrong, and the camera follows and focuses meaningfully and insistently on their tears and clasped hands in close-up and extreme close-up. As discussed in the previous chapter, several academic commentators have seen similarities between these practices and Foucault's (1978) account of the confession, though because of its public nature, this is in fact more similar to the Protestant practice of "testifying to one's sins." It is a form of bearing witness where authenticity is guaranteed by the physical confirmation of remorse.

The talk show confession may also be read, however, in a broader social perspective as a personal performance that implicitly confirms the existence of a shared moral–ethical code and a common understanding of what is to be taken as deviance and transgression. Acland (1995) in this regard speaks of a "drama of social inclusion, always with the implication of the stability of the social order" (p. 104), whereby the individual who has committed some deviant act that has determined his or her social exclusion offers a confession in order to be allowed to reenter a stable social order. The performance of the confession on national television underlines the existence of that social order, and the host—a foot squarely placed in both public and private domains—often articulates and reiterates it even as he or she solicits and receives the deeply personal disclosure. In the following extract, for instance, Oprah moves from an emotional exchange with Mary to a more formal and didactic tone in which she first turns to the studio audience and then addresses the viewing audience (at line 4) to deliver a general moral lesson: "so affairs are dangerous":

Extract 9

Oprah Now we're not just talkin' about sex here either
Mary no!
Oprah no (.) **turning toward studio audience**
so (.) affairs are dangerous in so many ways uh
those of you who are having them
especially if you have children (.)
because it serves as a model (.)

when you don't recognize that it's serving as a
model, so Elisabeth and Corey and Chris
who grew up in this family (0.5)
no matter what is said to them,
if you grow up in a family where it's ha:ppened?
it happened twice,
chances are, when you (.) marry,
you end up imitating that
in ways that you you swear you're not gonna do it
[. . .]

This feature of the daytime show is also very much present in the model discussed in the following section, although the primary emphasis in these latter programs, as we shall see, is clearly less on the "talk" and more on the "show" constructed in and by the talk.

PERSONAL AND SOCIAL ISSUES AS SPECTACLE: THE TRASH TALK SHOWS

The trash show dating from the early 1990s represents what Shattuc (1997) calls the second generation of the American daytime shows.[13] This model exaggerates the focus on the private domain, which is carried to grotesque extremes in an effort to incite confrontation and conflict both between the special guests themselves, and between the guests and the studio audience. The ostensible social framing that characterizes the first generation model has been reduced, although guests are often rather crudely displayed as emblematic of "deviant" classes or categories of society (e.g., gays, juvenile delinquents, single parents). Some programs in this category have entirely eliminated the presence of experts that in other daytime shows give authority and institutional credibility to the proceedings. Here, in fact, nearly all the voices are lacking social or professional accreditation: both special guests and the studio audience belong in large part to the culturally underprivileged. Their interventions are unpredictable, provocative, and playful, a carnivalesque parody of the generally serious, somewhat self-important, therapeutic pretensions of *Donahue* and *Oprah*.

Although the trash talk show unfolds within the same structural framework as the previous two subgenres (introduction by host; presentation of special guests; interview and talk; interventions from the audience; and summing up by host, time permitting), there are major differences in the

[13]Shattuc counts *Donahue, Oprah, Sally*, and *Geraldo* as first generation talk shows; *Ricki Lake, Jerry Springer, Jenny Jones, Gordon Elliot, Mark Wahlberg, Maury, Rolonda* as second generation shows, falling under her category of "trash" programs. In my own data, however, both *Sally* and *Geraldo*, though dating from the 1980s, consistently present special guests and topics that are more characteristic of the trash shows.

way the product looks, in the construction of the guests and the studio audience, and in the language used. The different "look" of the product is traceable to the rather invasive editing, which in other talk show types, in order to maintain the semblance of "liveness," is barely perceptible. During the editing process, not only are labels identifying the special guests superimposed on the tape, but some programs are assembled very much as if they were a product of fiction (a sitcom or series), with video clips of what is to come running under the opening credits and before each commercial break, and trailers for the next program before the current episode ends. Thus, Jerry Springer begins a program entitled "My wife's sleeping with my aunt" speaking to the viewing audience from what appears to be his office, leafing through an album with snapshots of the special guests to come:

> Hi and welcome. Today's show we're gonna meet a family whose story has more twists and turns than a soap opera. Let's begin with Beckey. You see she's married to Dale, but having an affair with Chris. But what Dale and Chris don't know is that she's also sleeping with Sharon, Dale's aunt. Meanwhile Aunt Sharon's fifteen year old daughter Jessica is dating Richard, but claims she is bisexual and is longing to be with Kathleen, the woman she babysits for. Well this seems like one happy wild family. Okay let's see what happens. Come on.

This operation positions the viewing audience, now aware of the principal characters and revelations of the show, on a different footing from the studio audience, which experiences during the taping the surprise and delight of discovering the intricate relationships in the "wild family" as they unfold before the cameras. (Indeed, from the very title of the show the viewing audience knows the key and most surprising development even before the program begins.) Unlike other models, then, where the viewing audience and the studio audience are both positioned as naive and unknowing, here the studio audience is constructed as one of the active players on the show, and its reactions are as integral a part of the proceedings as the stories of the guests. This is a major difference from the first generation shows where the audience's role is that of participant–observer representing or standing in for the viewers at home.

The language of guests and most audience members is in large part nonstandard and often heavily accented by ethnic group (Black and Hispanic) and class (working, noneducated). Because of the frequent conflictual and confrontational nature of the topics and of guests' interventions, there are many overlaps and loud, excited speech, including taboo words—sometimes obscured during editing by an overlapping sound (beep)—and frequent appeals by hosts to "Watch your language! You're on national television." Further, interventions by single audience members are generally qualitatively different from those in the audience discussion show or the first generation daytime shows, which tend to orient toward the issue at hand, as in Extract 5 from *Oprah*. Here, instead, interventions are usually rapid one-liners in keeping with the fast rhythm and production priorities of the programs, which favor confrontation or simple expressions of solidarity over discussion. Thus single audience members may offer advice, sometimes supported by aphorisms, or simple insults, as in the arrowed turns in the following extracts.

Extract 10

Ricki		do you want him back?
		(0.6)
Joani		I would take him back.
Audience		NOOOOOOOOO (5 secs.)
Ricki		**walking to woman in audience, extending microphone**
		stand up, ma'am, you're saying no.
		(0.8)
Woman	→	I wouldn't take him back
		(0.75)
		no way, after he left you when you have two kids
		(0.75)
Joani		I love him
		(0.6)
Woman	→	love is only a word
		(1.2)
	→	and love is blind.
		[(2 turns)]
Ricki		**walking toward man in audience, extending**
		microphone yes (.) sir.
		(2.0)
Man		yeah.
Ricki		stand up please.
Man		**to Joani** I would say you get the stuff
		and just move on,
	→	better men in the sea,
	→	[and a dog is always a dog
Audience		[xxxxxxxxxxxxxxxxxxxxxxxxxxxxx (8 secs.)

Extract 11

Jerry		is there anything about this that strikes you as
		wrong?
Beckey		all but it's his aunt, other than that, no.
Audience		NOOOOOOOOOOOO (3 secs.)
Woman 1	→	you're sick!
		[. . .]
Woman 2	→	this is for Beckey.
		I don' wanna put you down like everybody else
		but you nasty !

Moreover, as may be seen in these extracts, the audience participates collectively in the proceedings to a much greater extent than in other talk shows, showing solidarity and approval through applause, and calling out agreement or approval (YEEESSS or YEEAAHH), disagreement or disapproval (NOOO or BOOO), or by commenting or protesting with various other noises often combined with laughter and possibly applause.[14] Some guests intrinsically provoke audience response by their behavior or appearance, but it is also actively sought by the host in two principal ways: by eliciting from the guests comments likely to be taken as provocative or outrageous, and by direct questions to the audience (prior to the introduction of another guest, for example), which automatically elicit audience response. Some of these characteristics can be seen in Extract 12. (Notice also Ricki's rather simple introduction to this new segment of the program compared to Oprah's more elaborate framing operation in Extract 6.)

Extract 12

Ricki		what happens when the man you love is loving
		somebody else
		and you didn't even know it
		until he left you for that other woman.
		that is exactly what happened to my next guest
		Angel (.)
		Angel, did you ever think that your boyfriend Pete
		would leave you?
		(0.8)
Angel		no (.) heh (0.5) uh
		(1.2)
		we when we was together,
		I mean we had our ups and downs
		but I loved him.
		I loved him more than the world
		(1.2)
		uh (.) the first time he left me
		(1.2)
	1→	he left me for a prostitute
Audience		NOISE (3.5 secs.)
		[(1 turn)]
Angel		he (2.3)
		when we hooked up the second time uh,
		he was (.) paying me (0.6) for damage
	2→	he did to my car when he beat me up

[14]Anderson (1999) and Montgomery (1999) both offer a close treatment of laughter and applause, the first in *Jonathan Dimbleby* and *Question Time* (British current affairs talk shows), the second in the British chat show *Mrs Merton*.

		and beat my car up
Audience		NOISE (2.5 secs.)
Angel		heh
Ricki		so this man was abusive to you?
Angel		uhm the doctor said that if-
	3→	'cuz he body slammed me twice when he beat me up
		heh
Audience		NOISE (2.5)
Angel		they said that (.) I woulda been paralyzed for life
		(.) if (.) it'd been a hairline (.) either way.
		(2.0)
		so yeah [. . .]
		I used to be 300 pounds
		(1.3)
	4 →	I lost- (.) I got down to 120 pounds
Audience		NOISExxxxxxxxxxxxxxxxxxxxxxxxx (9 secs.)
		[. . .]
Ricki		so you lost this weight for this man
Angel		uhm
Ricki		to keep him?
Angel		no I lost this weight (.) before I met him,
		and I kept, I lost even more weight after he got
		me 'cuz I quit eatin'
		I quit wantin' to live,
	5 →	honestly (.) just wanted to die
Audience		nooo
Ricki	6→	do you wanna meet this guy Pete?
Audience		YEEE[ESSSSSSS (3.2 secs.)
Ricki	7→	[me too, Pete come on out.
Audience		NOISE (15 secs.)
Ricki		hi Pete, gotta lotta friends in the audience today
Pete		yeah, really!

Evident in this segment is the variety of functions of collective audience response. It is elicited here first by the guest's comment that her boyfriend left her for a prostitute (at arrow 1); by her affirmation that he physically abused her (at arrows 2 and 3); once (with applause) by her announcement of her massive weight loss (arrow 4); again in response to her account of the pain he had caused her (arrow 5); in answer to Ricki's direct question asking whether they wanted to meet him (arrow 6); and finally in response to his arrival on stage. In some cases the collective intervention seems clearly to mark solidarity, as in response to Angel's weight loss and her account of the hurt Pete caused her. Elsewhere solidarity appears to be mixed with indignation and disapproval of the reported event or situation, as in the reaction to Angel's physical abuse and Pete's abandonment of her for a prostitute. In general, audience intervention marks all important moments in the rhythm of the trash talk show, effectively acting as a foil to the guests' stories, confessions, and revelations.

But not only is the role of the studio audience different in this model; also significantly different from the first generation shows is the linguistic and emotional context in which the personal and intimate disclosures of the talk show guests are offered. Jerry Springer's opening exchange with Beckey in Extract 13 is not untypical. Note at the arrows Springer's appeal for collaboration, revealing his prior knowledge of her story, and Beckey's immediate compliance by completing Springer's utterance.

Extract 13

Jerry		welcome to the show.
		today we are talking to a family in crisis.
		first I want you to meet Beckey.
		she's a married woman, but a month and a half ago
		Beckey began having an affair with another man
Audience		BOOOOOO (7 secs.)
Jerry		Beckey, all right, hold on, hold on,
		Beckey why did you cheat on your husband?
Beckey		why did I cheat on my husband?
		because I was tired of the same wee wee.
Jerry		you what?
Beckey		I was tired of the same wee wee all the time.
Audience		NOISE (15 secs.)
Jerry		when uh when you married him
		did you think he was gonna get a new one?
Audience		NOISE hhhhhhhhhhhh (8 secs.)
Jerry	→	tell me I mean you know you said=
Beckey	→	=not only that he's overly jealous
		when I go somewhere
		I gotta call when I get there
		whenever I leave I gotta call
		whenever I'm ready to leave
		he's very abusive, he hits on me.

This is a considerably different approach to the topic of adultery from that of Bob and Mary on *Oprah*. If we take confession or the Protestant act of testifying to be grounded in an implicit acknowledgment of wrongful behavior according to some common standards of right and wrong, then this definitely appears to be something else. Far from remorseful, the most colorful trash show guest seems quite unaware that she or he has behaved in a way not consonant with appropriate standards of behavior. In this sense the trash shows are examples of *carnival* in the medieval sense of popular, bodily pleasure, offensiveness, bad taste, and degradation, as opposed to a display of morality, discipline, and social control (Bakhtin 1968). They also offer "excessive gestures, exploited to the limit of their meanings," as Barthes writes about wrestling (1972, p. 17). The physicality of the guests erupts on screen: they strut and saunter in, they shake their fists, they stand off, nose to nose. They try to hit one another and are pulled apart by the host and security guards, or they play the victim who has suffered at the hands of lovers or family members or been abused by life in general. They shout and weep, they curse and insult and offend each other, and they tell stories of betrayal, sexual promiscuity and abuse, abandoned children, drunkenness, drugs, and every other kind and combination of deviancy that can be imagined.

Similarly, the audience expresses joy and pleasure in witnessing the breaking of the rules of social control. Like Barthes' (1972) wrestling fans, the studio audience, itself "not in easy accommodation with the dominant ideology," revels in the "evasion, or at least negotiation, of dominant ideological practice" (p. 234). The camera, which in first generation talk shows pans the audience, lingering on tears and sympathetic faces, here zooms in on expressions of unbelieving and amused wonder or horror at such stories. The audience collectively shouts approval, disapproval, or outrage, but as we have seen, the cheers and jeers and boos are part of the performance, and they are at times as excessive as the stories they accompany, as in this exchange from *Jerry Springer*:

Extract 14

Dale		before we get started,
		she's saying I'm abusive to her?
		(0.7)
		no no no no.
Jerry		okay.
Dale		I've hit her twice.
Audience		NO[ISE (5 secs.)
Dale		[we've been married- the first time I hit her-
Jerry		okay let's hear
	→	let's [hear, I'm not excusing it let's hear it.
Dale		[she was drunk,
		sitting on my chest, slapping me re[peatedly.
Beckey		[he's hit me
		six times.
Dale		I have not, I've hit her twice.
Jerry		do you hit him ?
Beckey		he socked me he put a knife in my face.
		if that's the case ( ) I mean be for real.
Jerry		okay. do you hit him?
Beckey		yeah I hit him. ( )

21	Audience		NOI[SExxxxxxxxxxxxxxxxxx (7 secs.)
22	Jerry	→	[wait a second, okay wait wait a second.
23			now I don't understand the audience
24			I'm not suggesting that there's any justification
25			for hitting her
26			but why are you cheering because she hits him?
27	Audience		NOISE

The amused concern that Springer voices at the arrowed lines is consistent with the host's framing of the talk on these shows against the backdrop of middle class morality and standards for social conduct. Not only in *Jerry Springer*, but in every trash talk show in my own corpus, the host and/or eventual psychologists and counselors remind the errant and the deviant of social values and responsibilities, and/or (as in the first generation daytime shows) offer therapeutic counseling in order to resolve problems in relationships, as may be seen in the following extracts:

Extract 15

1	Jerry	**to Beckey** do you think your behavior in this
2		marriage has been appropriate?
3		you're the mother of three children,
4		you said you you'd love him till death do you part

Extract 16

1	Jerry	**to Chris, Beckey's lover** okay, so long as Beckey
2		is still in this marriage with uh Dale
3		isn't it appropriate for you to say (.)
4		you have to put your own considerations aside,
5		they've got to give their marriage a chance,
6		they've got three kids,
7		they gotta give those kids
8		a chance to grow up in a solid household,
9		so shouldn't you just say, hey I may really like
10		you but I gotta back off you're married.
11	Audience	xxxxxxxxxxxxxxxxxxxxxxxxxxxxxx (8 secs.)

Extract 17

1	Sonny	**a relationship expert on Ricki** yeah,
2		and what Angel and Pete really need to do
3		I'd like to see them walk not run [sic?]
4		to take a look at a book called getting the love
5		you want, because what each of you are doing,
6		is you're replicating what you experienced
7		earlier.

uh what you're replicating Angel
is a household in which the man gets his way (.)
whatever his way is, he just gets it.
and you really need to take a look at,
you're gonna keep doing that?
and you can get rid of Pete,
but you're gonna replace him
with someone that looks just like Pete
[. . .]
and Pete what you're doing with your life
is you're picking women that you can abuse
Audience YEAHHHHHHxxxxxxxxxxxxxxxxxxxxx (5 secs.)
Sonny and it may be that early in your life
what you learned about relationships (.)
is that abusive love is still love,
and that's the best kind of love that you can get.
because if that's all you could get as a kid
that's what you think love is

So, although the trash talk show manipulates and flaunts in carnivalesque fashion "the weird, twisted, and depraved" for the delight and pleasure of a disinherited audience, it manages at the same time to "contain" such deviance in a flexible bourgeois frame: a highly complex ideological operation that belies the simplistic crudeness of the players and their stories.

CONCLUSIONS

This overview of the three principal models of the daytime talk show aimed to illuminate similarities and differences in the realization of the genre by examining procedural, linguistic, and interactional frameworks operating in the various formats. I have suggested that the different profiles and deployment of basic components of the talk show (hosts, guests, studio audience, and a focus for talk) determine different contexts of situation that in turn give rise to particular institutional expectations regarding the construction of the players and the type of verbal interaction produced. In other words, the host's personality and demeanor, the topic chosen (public or private domain), the studio layout, the personal and social background of the guests and studio audience, and their assigned role in the show's format (to provide expert advice; to provoke pity, anger, or praise; to share experiences; to offer solidarity, etc.) all contribute to the context of situation which constrains the production of talk within predictable boundaries.

Thus, while the performance of talk before an audience is common to all formats, the particular manifestation of talk depends on the specific series of factors that characterize each communicative event (Hymes, 1967). Furthermore, as discussed in the previous chapter, all broadcast talk is institutional talk and characterized by asymmetrical relations of power in interaction. Thus, as we have repeatedly seen, unlike conversational procedures in ordinary conversation, here it is the host who opens and closes sequences, selects and frames the topic, allocates turns and guides the production of talk in the interests of institutional priorities like time and topic constraints. The examples show that whereas talk at a microlinguistic level generally presents lexical, syntactic, phonological, and prosodic features of ordinary conversation, at macrolinguistic levels such as framing and turn allocation, the host is in control; and even where this control is temporarily relinquished in the interests of spectacle and heated argument, this nevertheless remains within the bounds of generic norms and expectations.

Among these factors is the ultimate goal of such an event, namely broadcast media entertainment. This is a common goal, but it is differently realized in the three formats considered here. The entertainment value of the audience discussion show seems to be linked to the orchestration of multiple, contrasting voices in a joint construction of public meanings (as we saw in Extract 4 from the program on children in broken families). The American first generation daytime shows, instead, focusing on social issues in a personal perspective, appear to attach entertainment value to episodes of "testifying" and self-disclosure, favoring a performance that tends to display persons and issues in a moralistic frame. Oprah's adulterous couple, with their poignant confessions and weeping children, are shown as victims and bearers of a social message posed in strongly didactic terms.

Finally, the entertainment value of the trash programs, as the examples show, lies in parody and exaggeration, taken to the limits of the absurd and grotesque, and in the active role of the studio audience as a player in the performance. Jerry Springer's "My wife's sleeping with my aunt" is representative of the cumulative effect of increasingly outlandish characters and situations and the incredulous hilarity (or disgust) they provoke. The trash show, more than any other daytime format, is thus purposefully constructed as spectacle through extensive editing and strategies for retaining the audience through commercial breaks, which have some similarities with forms of TV drama. It is not, then, surprising that the "reality" of these shows has been questioned, for whatever the circumstances of their production, they bear the closest resemblance to scenarios from popular fiction.

APPENDIX: TRANSCRIPTION CONVENTIONS

( )	If empty, indicates unclear portions of text; otherwise, a guess at what was said: (word).
bold	Description of nonverbal behavior or other information.
(1.5)	Length of pause in seconds.
(.)	Pause of less than .5 seconds.
=	Indicates that utterance follows immediately on previous utterance, or is latched to separate parts of a continuous utterance by the same speaker.
[	Indicates the point at which overlap with another speaker begins.
word-	Hyphen indicates word has been cut off sharply.
<u>word</u>	Underlining indicates stress given to word or syllable.
WORD	Uppercase letters indicate increased volume.
sho::w	Colons indicate lengthening of vowel sound.
.	Terminal falling intonation.
,	Brief pause ("list" intonation).
?	Rising intonation.
!	Excited intonation.
[. . .(n turns)]	Omitted turns.
[. . .]	Omitted utterances.
.hh	Audible intake of breath.
hh	Audible exhalation.
heh	Laugh token.
hhhhh	Extended laughter. Where appropriate for the analysis, the length of the laughter response in seconds is indicated in parentheses.
xxxxx	Applause. Where appropriate for the analysis, the length of the applause in seconds is indicated in parentheses.
xx x xxx	Sporadic applause.

Note also:

- As indicated above, conventional punctuation marks such as full stops and commas are to be taken as markers of intonation and not of syntax. In order to facilitate reading, lines usually represent relatively complete syntactic units.
- Where a pause of 0.6 seconds or more occurs at the end of a syntactically complete unit, I have placed the pause on a separate line, interpreting it as a point of possible turn transition or difficulty of some sort.
- Transcriptions are given in a form consonant with the level of delicacy appropriate to the analysis at hand (i.e., sometimes very little more than the verbal text is provided).

CHAPTER

3

"No, YOU Rioted!": The Pursuit of Conflict in the Management of "Lay" and "Expert" Discourses on *Kilroy*

Helen Wood

As previously discussed, the phenomenon of the television talk show has often been afforded a rather privileged position within current debates about the nature of a mediated public sphere. Offering a discursive space where ordinary people meet and interact with institutional representatives in a public forum, the talk show format has been lauded for its democratic potential. One of the key critical expositions of this point of view can be found in Carpignano et al. (1990), where the authors claim that the talk show attempts to present "an exercise in electronic democracy." In this view, the talk show is distinctive in its promise of participation and apparent challenging of traditional hierarchies. It involves real people, talking about real life experiences in real time, which gives them a claim to authenticity that assists in the talk show's championing of the ordinary citizen.

The construction of the talk show's format, such as the cues that serve to blur the distinctions between the studio and the home audience, facilitate a feeling of "live" commonsense debate that is, in Habermasian terms, more akin to the "life-world" than to the "system." According to Livingstone and Lunt (1994), the commonsense stories of lay participants are often even privileged over the institutional discourses of the expert, disrupting normative power dynamics. In such a forum, therefore, the traditional polarization of the public and private is often eroded. This, it is claimed, accounts for an oppositional public sphere that encompasses the lived experiences of the citizen (the *lifeworld*) alongside the critique of bureaucracy (the *system*). For some, therefore, the talk show presents a phenomenon whereby "Communication between representatives of the system world and the life-world establishes links between those realms and so potentially generates critical knowledge which could overcome the separation of these realms" (Livingstone & Lunt, 1994, p. 180).

However, what is being neglected here is a discussion of exactly what the spectacle of the television medium means in terms of the structure of conversational debate. One cannot ignore what Dahlgren (1995) referred to as television's "entertainment bias." In this view, the construction of the talk show is located at the intersection of audience participation and spectacle because the discourse follows a particular institutional agenda of the *televisual*. What was missing from earlier discussions about the democratic potential of talk was detailed analyses of how these forms of talk are produced and thus to some extent stage-managed. Haarman, in chapter 2, this volume, emphasizes from the outset an understanding of talk show discourse as *performed* and highlights the extent to which discursive frameworks are embedded within the institutional context.

In fact, Livingstone and Lunt (1994) themselves recognized that there are checks to be made on assumptions of spontaneity in talk shows: "While on the one level, all interactions are spontaneous and unique, conversations are highly rule-governed, frequently repetitive, and commonly used to repeat handed-down or unoriginal ideas (i.e., common sense)" (p. 163). It is this *rule-governed* nature of the talk that I discuss here. Talk shows are, after all, television programs that are carefully researched, produced, and to some extent pre-scripted. Ultimately the talk in question is produced with an overhearing audience in mind, and it is in this context that *televisuality* works as the production constraint that most characterizes the talk show as a specialized form of interaction. In this chapter, I argue that the pursuit of televisual drama is the main goal that affects the management and construction of talk show debate, where it translates into the pursuit and maintenance of conflict between expert and lay discourses as a form of dramatic entertainment.

THE DATA

In this chapter, I offer an analysis of the construction of the interaction in one specific program of *Kilroy*.[1] This is a British program that models itself on the American tradition represented by *Donahue*. It conforms to the genre of talk show that Haarman, in chapter 2, refers to as the audience discussion format. It is hosted by Robert Kilroy-Silk, a former Member of

[1]Broadcast January 1997.

Parliament who styles himself as champion of the people. This particular edition of *Kilroy* is selected because it presents a typical version of the conflict of expert versus lay discourses—in this particular case, citizens versus the police force—that translates into "us versus them" confrontation.

The key themes that arise throughout the program are: Do the public trust the police? Do the police do enough to fight crime? Are the police overzealous? Are the police racist?

Key "lay" speakers are people who have specific stories to tell about mistreatment by the police and key "experts" consist of representatives of the police force, an ex-policeman who is now an academic, and a Member of Parliament. The experts' primary role is to contest the descriptions of police actions put forward by members of the studio audience.

In this analysis of the program, I intend to investigate how the discourse develops throughout its 45-minute scheduled duration. What is the host's role in the production of the talk? How are the "commonsense" discourses of the audience elicited and managed? How are the expert's discourses produced, and at what points do the key points of dramatic televisual tension and conflict emerge?

ESTABLISHING THE ROLE OF THE HOST—KILROY AS "ONE OF US"

Audience discussion talk shows are, almost without exception, identified by the persona of the host—*Oprah*, *Donahue*, *Ricky Lake*, and in this case *Kilroy*. The centrality of the host is therefore established from the outset and (as Haarman notes in chapter 2) Livingstone and Lunt (1994) described the host's role as that of romantic "hero" defending the right to speak of the populace. Central to understanding the construction of the interaction in talk shows is the knowledge that the host is ultimately responsible for deciding who can take the floor in the debate. Mostly this is explicit in the power to select participants to speak, but occasionally speakers gain the floor through self-selection. Either way, ultimately the host is responsible for allowing speakers to retain the floor.

Livingstone and Lunt's (1994) description of the host as romantic hero suggests that the host situates himself against established power. My main argument here is that Kilroy's production of his own "authenticity" and the positioning of himself (although a former Labour MP) as hero on the side of "ordinary" people can be explained in terms of his management of the production of talk in the studio. Kilroy's positioning as "one of the people," rather than the impartial journalistic figure that is encouraged in other kinds of television interview, is apparent from the program's opening:

Extract 1:

Kilroy: **(direct address to camera)**
Hello and good morning. Do you trust the police? Do they do enough: to fight crime. (.) Are they over zealous (.) heavy handed (.) racist? We:ll the courts seem to think they are sometimes (.) Last week one man was awarded one hundred and eight thousand pounds after the police used false evidence against him. Another was awarded three hundred and two thousand pounds after he was brutally treated by the police (.)
(moves up the stage to a member of the audience)
And yet often the police don't seem to do what we want them to do do they Michelle, do they do enough to deal with the problem that you've got in your area?

There are some relatively obvious points to be made about this setting of the scene. First, in his direct address opening, Kilroy assumes a relationship with the general wider public—"Do *you* trust the police." Second, he moves to cite real cases of true stories that establish the primacy of the real event before moving to Michelle, given authenticity by reference to her first name, to invite her to relate her story about her area. On the other hand, "the police" in this introduction remain a faceless, homogenous entity. Clearly the distinction here between "us" and "them" has already been drawn, and this particular edition is chosen for its exemplary illustration of such a division.[2] In this show, the emphasis on the authority of the "authentic" over the "professional" is particularly marked and is evidenced in one MP's frustrated outburst that the show is one-sided and unfair. This, I show, has little to do with time allocated to participants from either side, but rather with the way in which these competing discourses are managed by the host.

THE PROCESS OF MANAGING THE DEBATE

Livingstone and Lunt (1994) did, to some extent, discuss how the host manages the debate to support lay voices over those of those of the expert. However, their analysis was mostly descriptive and did not pay close attention to the way in which turns are taken. I intend to look more closely at the kind of turn-type pre-allocation system that applies here.

In the data, there is clearly a pattern that emerges in the flow of the discourse throughout the show. Firstly, we see from the outset that Kilroy se-

[2] Not all versions of audience discussion programs have such clear emphasis. More recently with the popularity of these shows there has been a shift away from more public issue oriented programs.

lects a lay person whom he invites and helps to tell their story through question and answer sequences and supportive feedback. Secondly, he reformulates or summarizes the story, and thirdly, he presents the problem to an expert of his choice. After this point there may finally be some competition for turns from the audience, and occasionally the floor may open up to allow any speaker access. It is here that there is the greatest opportunity for conflict to escalate beyond the control of the host. This pattern is regular and is consistently repeated through the thematic shifts in the program. I suggest, therefore, that the process of managing the audience talk show debate might look like this:

1. selection of a lay speaker and elicitation of their narrative
2. reformulation or summary of the narrative
3. passing of the point of injustice/ tension to the selected expert
4. possibility of the floor to open up, it is here points of conflict usually emerge.

The regularity of this pattern demonstrates the control the host has over the debate. Despite the appearance that it may have of being open and random, the discussion is actually rather neatly executed and artfully managed in favor of lay speakers.

Selecting Speakers and Eliciting Narratives

The pre-scripted nature of the show is evident in Kilroy's sense of the spatial orientation of the speakers and the roles they will play in the discussion. In most instances the host selects both lay and expert speakers by reference to their first names. At the beginning of the management cycle just outlined, Kilroy selects a narrator by choosing a member of the audience to relate his or her personal story. The manner in which key lay speakers are introduced to the floor is interesting because if Kilroy addresses them by their first names, his prior knowledge of their experience also allows him to assign the narrative context from which they are to speak. If we take the opening question from extract 1, Kilroy has prior knowledge that Michelle has a problem in the area where she lives. Here he selects Jonathon, a Black man, to tell a story about police racism:

Extract 2: [K = Kilroy, J = Jonathon]

1 K: Jonathon are the police racist? Jonathon?
2 J: I think in some cases the police are very racist . . .
(. . .)
3 K: Do they treat you in a discriminatory way?

After Kilroy's prompting question, Jonathon proceeds to tell a story about having been stopped by the police on several occasions. It is clearly not a lucky guess that this man has an experience to tell about racist treatment, as Kilroy accurately seeks Jonathon out among the audience at a pertinent moment of the discussion.

Furthermore, some of Kilroy's responses to key speakers betray the fact that he is already familiar with the events within their narrative:

Extract 3: [M = Michelle]

1 M: Well first of all prior to this they've got my
2 second son Dean hah hung him from the balcony on
3 the second floor by his ankles erm (.) he::'s got
learning disabilities so he's backward so=
4 K: =n: this group of youths you say that they have
5 been terrorizing the neighborhood as well as your
6 own son's to the extent that you've had to move to
→ what a safe house=
7 M: = a safe house

In this extract, Kilroy introduces a piece of detail, referring to Michelle having to move to a safe house, which she had not volunteered previously. It is clear in Kilroy's selection of speakers, and the interaction that ensues, that the pre-production phases of the programming provide Kilroy with considerable knowledge of the details of contributors and their experiences. How the host then uses this knowledge of the "life-world" of the audience becomes interesting in the strategies used to control the discourse.

Question and Answer Sequences

Having selected a lay speaker, Kilroy and the chosen interlocutor embark on a question and answer sequence. In everyday conversation, Searle (1969) suggested that there are two types of question: the "real," whereby the questioner asks about something he or she does not know, or the "exam," whereby the questioner tests the other speaker about something he or she already knows. As described before, one of the features of this talk show is that Kilroy has prior knowledge of lay participants stories and therefore the type of questioning might reflect an exam style question under Searle's criteria. However, in this institutional context, the questioning is not so much a test but rather a device involved in mediating communication. The question and answer sequence here does not, therefore, approximate those found in everyday conversation, but rather takes the form of an interview where the questions are being asked to elicit information (in these cases personal stories) for the overhearing audience. In this capacity, Kilroy's questions tend to be confined to asking for more detail or clarifying and expanding on certain parts of the relevant story as in the following two extracts.

Extract 4

1	M:		erm I've gone to em on several occasions with er
2			threats that 'ave been made to my son and er no one's taken me seriously
3	K:	→	What kind of threats?
4	M:		um threat that they were gonna kill my eldest son
5	K:	→	Who's this?
6	M:		A gang of youths where I live (.) they call
7			themselves the Bronx posse er they've terrorized people on my estate for quite a quite a number of [years
8	K:	→	[How did they terrorize you what kind of things do
9			they do?
10	M:		um it all started back in October of la::st year
11			(.) one of the youths asked my son for a cigarette
12			which e didn't have er the same evening, knocked on the door and punched my boy in the face=
13	K:	→	=nnd what happened since then what kind of things have they done to you?
14	M:		erm well, we've had to be moved out to a safe home
15			er me and the children and er its still ongoing

Extract 5: [W = falsely accused woman]

1	W:		I: was arrested (.) me 'us- cut a long story short
2			me 'usband got shot (.) I got arrested (0.2) got
3			sent to prison (.) stood tri:al (.) cost three quarters of a million (.) n [they got the wrong person
4	K:	→	['n what were you
5			arrested for?
6	W:		Conspiracy te murder
7	K:		Who?
8	W:		Me 'usband
9	K:	→	Who'd murdered your husband?
10	W:		Don't know

These are two examples of typical question and answer sequences that serve the function of assisting the exposition of the lay narrative and clarifying the salient points of the story for the overhearing audience in the studio and at home. These exchanges seem neutrally to be about the uncovering of "true" life-world experiences.

Framing Agendas in Question and Answer Sequences

Lay participants' stories, however, do not necessarily emerge spontaneously and develop freely. Thornborrow (1997) suggested that they are mutually produced by participant and host, and often what becomes of key concern is not so much the story itself as the subsequent evaluation of it (p. 252). I suggest that the centrality of the evaluation is a result of the narrative's subjection to the host's own framing, which conforms to an agenda agreed on before production. For instance, the prior knowledge of speakers and their stories not only allows Kilroy to elicit certain material at pertinent points in the programming, but it also allows him a kind of editorial control. In Michelle's case, when Kilroy presents her problem in this way, he has already made a subjective judgment about the police having not done enough in this case: "And yet often the police don't seem to do what we want them to do do they Michelle, do they do enough to deal with the problem in your area?" Similarly, in the case of a woman who was falsely tried for murdering her husband, Kilroy has already framed the point of issue within which the woman is allowed to contribute her narrative:

Extract 6

K: . . . we don't want them to be overzealous we don't
→ want them to exceed their powers (.) is there a
feeling also that perhaps sometimes they make an
arrest because they need to make an arrest just to
get somebody?
(Kilroy takes the microphone to woman who he knows will answer positively)
W: Definitely

These questions therefore accomplish more than to reveal information for the overhearing audience (as in the news interview); they also work to reproduce an agenda within which information is to be interpreted.

Pursuing Agendas

Where talk shows have pre-scripted agendas, narratives are not produced at liberty, but rather points of issue are pursued by the host in accordance with the particular framing. Therefore, although the question and answer sequences appear to be about the telling of a narrative, that narrative does not stand as testimony alone, but must be related to the agenda, which is established at the outset of the exchange. It is the frame, not the narrative, that takes precedence. For instance, in the case of Michelle's contribution, she is repeatedly asked versions of the same question about what the police did (Kilroy's frame being "Do the police do enough?"):

Extract 7

K: n they moved you out so you can't be bothered what
were you feeling when all this was happening?
M: Sacred to death (.) [terrified
K: → [what did j- n what did the
police do?
M: Nothing
K: Why?
M: I suppose they just didn't take it seriously
K: Did you keep ca:lling the police?
M: Yeh
K: → What did they say?
M: erm well they started burgling my home 'cos
everything was left in there all my contents=
K: =the boys not the police
M: No [its was he boys n:d er the-I've had four=
K: [heh, heh,
M: =[burglaries
K: [you mean after you left you left all your stuff
there?
M: yeh, it was a case of having to get out there and
then a firework was put through the letterbox
which subsequently (.) caught the dra:ught
excluder alight (.) singed all the door erm we
have been told that these youths have petrol
bombed places before and I just couldn't risk my
children's lives
K: → What did the police say?
M: Nothing
K: n what do you feel about the police?
M: I hate them
K: hate them?
M: I: hate them
K: Why?
M: Because I just don't feel that I've had (.) the
support from the police that I feel I should've

Kilroy persistently asks versions of a similar question (lines 4, 5, 11, and 27) until finally Michelle's story about victimization by a gang of youths is evaluated in terms of the inactivity of the police. The exchange culminates in the aggressive declaration "I hate them," which is repeated and thus reformulated by Kilroy. Ultimately Michelle declares that she has not had enough support from the police and the story is thus evaluated in accordance with the agenda.

In the next extract, Kilroy is shifting the floor from one speaker to another, and at the same time shifting the topic (this can occur as a result of issues being clearly pre-allocated to individual informants). As he does so, he is also framing the forthcoming speaker's narrative within the issue of "racism in the police force," before the woman even begins her story:

Extract 8: [M = man, C = Cora]

M: ... the chap was clean shaven with unruly hair why
pull a man with a beard are they blind.
K: → Cora (.) they may not be blind Cora are they
racist?
C: Very (0.2) in my opinion they're very racist
because I've er::m about six weeks ago (.) about
Friday morning early ho- sorry early hours of
Saturday morning .hh a cousin of mine they we- the
police were called to his house for a domestic
affair and they came to the house and erm (.)
basically he came out peacefully (0.3) he went
into the van peacefully without handcuffs=

At line 3, Kilroy shifts the topic by linking together the last speaker and the next with a topic shift to racism. Cora then embarks on the narrative of her cousin's brutal treatment by the police. Considering the content of the subsequent narrative, Cora's contribution could have been framed within a discussion about police brutality, as she does not refer to race at any point in the telling of her story. However, because her story has already been assigned to the agenda of racism, Kilroy's questioning, after initially supporting and clarifying the details of her story, must pursue this line, which is arguably more contentious. Thus, as is evidenced in the interaction that follows, Kilroy must introduce the issue of racism himself:

Extract 9

C: ... about two minutes after (.) he was dead (o.3) t and
[basically the CS-
K: [Withou- without in any way wishing I'm trying to be
careful of the words I use here but I [do
C: [yes
K: and they are diff:cult to u- b-
but nobody is suggesting em that that should
have happened or was in any way excusable .h but
→ wasn't because he was black was it?
(.)
C: We:ll lets see becaus:e obviously now we've been told
that CS gas was used whi:le he's was handcuffed this

has been confirmed he was already handcuff [ed and
then
K: [but white
→ men die but white men die in custody
C: ↑NOT MANY FIVE five (.) in the last year five [Seegee
Lepito they crushed=
K: → [five
what five white men?
C: =His voice box (.) Black
K: → Five black men
C: Seegee Lepito they crushed his voice box they crushed
it (.) and they've=
M: ( )
=just got a verdict of unlawful killin (.) wh::y why
did they need to t- use so much force on hhh voice
box.
K: They're racist

In this example, Cora tells her narrative by explaining the violence used by the police, which Kilroy interrupts at line 8–9 with an agenda-seeking question about whether it was because her cousin was Black. Cora, however, continues with her original narrative thread, which primarily focuses on violence. Kilroy again interrupts at line 16, "but white men die in custody." This is a curious turn as it suggests a contradiction to an answer that Cora never gave to his previous question.

However, this does have some of the desired consequence in that Cora gets louder as she proclaims that five men have died and yet she still has not specifically addressed the issue of their race. At line 19, Kilroy responds by asking a question to which he knows the subsequent answer, until Cora finally asserts "black," which he repeats. Ultimately, it is Kilroy who produces the declaration "They're racist," clearly pursuing his version of the course the interaction should take.

The issue here is not whether Cora's experiences were actually a result of racism. (It is clear from latter parts of the program that Cora had attended the debate to argue that they were.) Rather, it is the way in which the narrative is allowed to evolve that is interesting to this discussion of the management of interaction. Cora's telling of her life-world experience does not evolve freely but is continually pressed into the confines of Kilroy's predefined agenda.

Pursuing Closures to Question and Answer Sequences

The host often looks for closure, in accordance with his own framing, before shifting the topic of discussion. In the case just described, he eventually produces the required assertion himself, but in the next example he finds the desired closure in an alternative speaker to the owner of the narrative:

Extract 10: [W = falsely accused woman]

K: . . . we want the police to arrest people we want the
thugs the vandals, the murderers, the robbers all
the rest of it .hh we don't want them to be
overzealous we don't want them to exceed their
→ powers (.) is there a feeling that also that
sometimes they make an arrest because they need to
make an arrest because they need to make an arrest
just to get somebody?
W: yes

Here Kilroy has shifted the topic from overzealous policing to police making arrests "just to get somebody" by asking the question of a woman he can, from his prior knowledge about her, assume will agree. As we see in the next extract, he then encourages her to embark on her own narrative and asks her two questions (lines 1 and 4) about why she thinks she was arrested, clearly in pursuit of his agenda:

Extract 11: [W = falsely accused woman, S = woman's son, C = Chris Waterton Chairman of the Committee of Local Police Authorities, M = man]

K: Why did they get it wrong?
W: hh I don't know (.) they even convinces me
'usband I did it while 'e wah pumped full of
morphine in the hospital
K: → Why would they do that to you why would they just
get somebody
W: I don't know and they've done nothing to find out
who actually did it
K: Chris?
(. . .)
W: Bu- but why have they done nothing since to find
out who actually did shoot him
C: → I [assume-
S: → [Th- the: not bothered what they do anyway
they're not bothered who they convict about
anything (.) [they're just after more stripes
K: [it was your father that was shot
W: Yeh
S: Yeh
K: This is your mum
S: Yeh

22	W:	→	yeh m=
23	K:		=go on what were you gonna say ha=
			(takes microphone to the son)
24	S:	→	=all they're doin is after more stripes they're
25			after heh(.) they're after bein 'igher all the
26		→	ti:me they're not bothered who they arrest
27			whatever
28	C:		Ye must y' must un[derstand
29	K:	→	[No wait a minute they're there
30			to find out who did the crime they don't want to
31			stitch up an innocent man do they they wa nna
32			[fi-
33	W:		[the police know who did it
34	S:		they do :::
35	K:		Why, [why do you feel that? **(to son)**
36	M:		[Robert-
37	S:		They're just- I: feel they're just after it fu
38			the stripes

Kilroy's questions about why the police would "get it wrong" do not produce an answer that accords with his frame. The woman simply replies that she does not know. Kilroy's response to this is intriguing. In his second question, he suggests himself that they were "just trying to get somebody." However, again the woman refuses to take up this evaluation of the issue as it is presented by Kilroy, and thus resists the agenda by reasserting that she does not know. What eventually emerges however, is that the woman's son interrupts the expert's attempts to address his mother's case. This contribution is much more useful to Kilroy because it is the son who will more accurately echo the agenda—why the police "just want to get somebody." Hearing the son's interruption about the police not being "bothered" and being "after more stripes" (lines 15 and 16), Kilroy takes the microphone to him, cutting off the expert's invited response to the problem. The son's interjection takes precedence over both the expert's attempts to address the issue (lines 13 and 28) and the woman's attempts (lines 22 and 33) to return to what is, in the first instance, her narrative.

Thus, what is interesting about Kilroy's management of these personal narratives, through questions and answer sequences and his control of the floor, is that while he assists in the telling of stories and stresses the primacy of the narrative form, these personal narratives are still under pressure to be interpreted in a particular way. Evaluations have already been decided in the management and organization of the program prior to the seemingly spontaneous discussion that takes place. However, despite Kilroy's insight into his participants, they do not always produce the desired response immediately and therefore he must pursue the agenda in whatever manner is open to him to create the desired closure.

FORMULATING "LAY" STORIES

In the management process outlined earlier, I suggested that after eliciting the story through the question and answer sequence, Kilroy then must formulate the narrative as it has been related, before presenting the issue to the expert. Heritage (1985) described formulating as "summarizing, glossing or developing the gist of an informant's earlier statements" (p. 100) for the benefit of the overhearing audience. It is thus more common in institutional contexts such as courtrooms and news interviews than in ordinary conversation.

Cooperative Formulations—Assisting the Narrative

Sometimes formulations operate in a neutral or even a co-operative way to assist the communication of the lay story. Heritage referred to these as either *prompts* or *cooperative recycles*. An example of a cooperative recycle in this talk show would be:

Extract 12: [P = Photographer arrested at demonstration]

K: What happened to you?
P: I was hit in the face by a policeman, [I was
dragged off
K: [wh- where
where
P: Demonstration I'm a professional photographer I
was photographing a demonstration (.) I had a
press card I had my cameras around me the
policeman ran u p and he [smacked-
K: [wh- what were you taking
pictures of?
The demonstration (.) arrests arrests
K: It was a
→ demonstration arrests so it was arrests. There was
a bit of a kerffufle (.) a bit of argy-bargy

At lines 14 and 15 Kilroy formulates the gist of the photographer's narrative to clarify the information for the overhearer. I include this exchange to emphasize the difference between this kind of formulation and the type that I discuss in the next section. In this instance, Kilroy's formulation can be said to be a fairly supportive summary of the details of the speaker's "life-world" event.

"MIS"FORMULATIONS—ASSISTING THE AGENDA

Although many formulations perform the function of cooperatively assisting the lay person to construct his or her narrative for the audience, others also perform another function. This is to "re"formulate the narrative in terms of the program's agenda:

Extract 13 [PW = petrol station worker, B = Bertram, neighborhood watch co-ordinator]

PW: Well really I was robbed at gunpoint three
consecutive times .hh and when I asked one of the
police er why it took thirty five minutes for them
to travel (. . ? . .) about half a mile from the
police station to the petrol station where I was
working I was told well this is in Salford sticks
if there's a chap that can come here nine times
out of ten he's gonna have a gun if we turn up
very quickly =
K: = Salford near Manchester=
PW: =Yes, that's right erm, they're gonna shoot at us
so we're gonna hang back n take the evidence of
the vide[o camera and
B: [heh, heh, [heh
K: [that's not funny Bertram heh
heh eh
B: no, I'm horrified to think that that was the case
I thought they'd get there very quickly
PW: → Well, you've gotta take their point of view as
well I -I=
K: → = You mean the police don't get there quickly
enough
PW: That's true
K → They don't take it seriously enough or they don't
or are afraid
PW: → No, its not that, think about it a minute you've
got a policeman possibly married with children
he's in there in the front line so to speak a::ll
the time okay now (.) its gonna be natural to hang
on a second I wanna see my kids tomorrow I'm just
gonna hang back just that five minutes just to let
them get out of the way=
K: =Ali, it seems to be just from the three things
we've heard now that the police seem to do what
seems to be here they won't go to deal with the
estate with the petrol bombers and th- th- the
thugs terrorizing a hh young innocent family they
→ won't a- deal with a man with a gun hh but they'll
go to the nice safe e- estate which is patrolled
by people like Bertram to deal with a scratched
car. Do the police do enough to protect us?

At line 21, Kilroy produces a cooperative formulation of the gist of the petrol station worker's prior narrative. However, the worker has already embarked on a statement suggesting that he has some sympathy with the police (line 19, "well you've gotta take their point of view"), which Kilroy interrupts with this formulation. Unwilling to accept the worker's progression, Kilroy again reformulates the statement into "they don't take us seriously enough or are afraid" at line 24. This is clearly not how the worker wanted his assertion to be evaluated, as he makes a straightforward denial of Kilroy's presentation of his point of view (line 26). The man eventually frames his narrative in terms of support for the police, but this direction is not allowed to play any further part in the course of the programming. When Kilroy subsequently summarizes the last three lay narratives for the expert Ali (Inspector Ali Dezai of Thames Valley Police), this particular contribution is merely represented as "they won't deal with a man with a gun" (line 38) and is delivered to the expert as support for Kilroy's initial agenda (which began with Michelle) of "do the police do enough to protect us?"

A similar formulation occurs in the next example. After Kilroy's setting an agenda of "are the police overzealous," a father begins to tell a narrative about his son's treatment in police custody. Eventually the son takes over telling his own story but in the process, clearly begins to stray from Kilroy's agenda (around line 6).

Extract 14: [S = son]

S: . . . later on a- a- after that I er was er released
next morning I went straight from custody straight
to um (.) e er main hospital and I had a
fractured cheekbone an the specialist said it
would take between three and five years to heal
→ now (.) if this police officer this lady had been
harassed and has got to get out of the house in't
it you::re job you::re being paid to go on any
call wherever it my be (.) not to decide you're
not the jury or the judge to decide where you go :
o- or who you attend to its not up to you to
decide th[at
K: → [But you're saying sometimes that they're
overzealous
S: Yes
K: Are they overzealous? (**K moves to another selected member of the audience**)

Kilroy's formulation (line 13) clearly is not an accurate summary of the son's contribution because his topic has shifted to the issue of the police deciding to whom they should attend. However, Kilroy will not allow this topic shift and instead appears to formulate the *father's* account about his son's mistreatment while being arrested. Subsequently, Kilroy uses this misformulation as a topic-shift strategy back to his own agenda and presents the question to another selected member of the audience whose story will perhaps fit the framing of overzealous policing.

These examples present another type of formulation than those discussed by Heritage (1985) in his paper on news interviews. Heritage does include a type of formulation that to some extent deliberately misrepresents the gist of the speaker. This he refers to as "the inferential elaborative probe" that is used by the news interviewer to "commit the interviewee to a stronger (and more newsworthy) version of his position . . . than he was initially prepared to adopt" (p. 110). In these instances in the talk show, however, the goal is not so much newsworthiness but rather enhancement of the televisual properties of conflict between expert and lay participants. The motive is to shift the evaluation of the lay narrative into a more contentious and oppositional position to that expected to be adopted by the experts. The point of these misformulations, therefore, is the pursuit of conflict and dramatic tension.

In summary, despite the evidence that a good proportion of the program is given over to the narratives of lay people, it is not the case that in taking primacy over expert discourses, these narratives are produced freely or that lay people develop the agendas for the program in their own way. Rather, through the framing of the question and answer sequences and the careful formulating of what has been said, by the host, these narratives are managed to conform to predefined agendas formatted before the show takes place. These are folded neatly around selected persons' narratives in the pre-production phase of the program.

OVER TO THE EXPERTS

The key point in these framing strategies is that the predefined agendas are designed to heighten contentious issues—police overzealousness, racism, police inactivity, etc. Kilroy's management of lay narratives is therefore about prioritizing televisuality, ensuring that "life-world" experiences are reinforced as potential points of conflict. Periods of argument therefore occur when the contentious topic is handed over for response from the experts. Livingstone and Lunt (1994) suggested that the tension is inherent within the challenge presented to expert discourses by anecdotal evidence authenticated by "real" experience. While this may be partly true, it does not explain the role of the host in the mediation of expert and lay discourses. When Hutchby (1996a) discussed the pursuit of conflict in talk radio, his analysis of the interactional strategies at work provided an understanding of the ways in which the host can wield institutional power. In this talk show, the tension between expert/public and lay/private discourses is exacerbated by the management strategy employed by the host.

The difference between Kilroy's management of the experts' space to talk and his management of the lay narratives is marked. Lay narratives are generally produced with the host sitting close to the speakers, encouraging and clarifying their narratives. Often Kilroy protects lay participants' rights to tell a story through interjections such as "listen" and "let her speak." The experts, on the other hand, must fend for themselves; Kilroy almost never aligns himself with experts by physically sitting next to them. Experts are rarely given long periods of time in which to explain their point of view and are frequently interrupted by the host. Most interruptions of experts are aggressive[3] and the reason for this is mainly that Kilroy establishes the primacy of the lay narratives before passing the formulated problems to the experts. The experts, in this case representatives of the police force, can only respond in accordance with their institutional persona and policy. Thus their responses seem inadequate to the individual and personal accounts of the "real" "life-world" experiences that have been presented.

Interrupting the Expert

In this example, Kilroy presents the problem, "Do the police do enough to protect us?" to the expert, Inspector Ali Dezai:

Example 15: [A = Inspector Ali Dezai, M = Michelle]

A: .h absolutely er I think the:e the police clearly
face a: dilemma we are tasked with (.) the job of
enforcing the law but lets put a common myth to bed
right here we are not the prosecuting agency it is
the crown prosecution service which is an
independent body who decide as to who should go to
court now a lot of lay people don't actually
realise that and when we are reluctant to act its
not because we don't act to act its because our
hands are tied by rules of evidence and quite
rightly so: it is the crown prosecution agency who
actually decides who to take to court=
K: → = it doesn't decide whether you go t- t- te
Michelle's area or not you decide that, Michelle?
M: Well er I actually had three youths caught in my

[3]In this case I refer to interruptions that are power-related and marked by aggressive interjections, rather than interruptions that can be understood as neutral or rapport-orientated (Goldberg, 1990).

premises just after Christmas .hh them three youths
all got off with a caution I've had five thousand
pounds worth of damage things taken from my home my
settee cut up, beds cut up I've got nothing t take
when I move.
A: I have every sympathy with [your case n there is
nothing I can say to justify=
M: [a caution?
A: =that but one thing I can say is that seventy
percent of young offenders who are cautioned do not
re-offend and it is fundamentally im[portant (.) if
I may=
M: [but they have
they
=finish it important that there is a diversion
policy to send young offend[ers-
M: =crimin[al records (.) they
have criminal[records.
K: → [You're not listening, Ali
A: pardon?
K: You're not li[stening
M: [One of the when he was aged eight
was done for armed robbery again at the age of
eleven armed robbery he is now thirteen years old
you're not telling me you're sitting there telling
me nothing can be done.
(K presents issue to the MP)

In this extract, Inspector Ali Dezai takes on an institutional footing to explain that the police do not actually have the powers to prosecute. Ali is clearly addressing his response to Kilroy, as he refers to "lay people" in the third person and does not address Michelle herself. This is typical of the form of news interviews where interviewees respond to the interviewer, not directly to the co-interviewee, in an attempt to avoid direct conflict.[4]

However, Kilroy's interruption at line 13 challenges the expert to respond to Michelle's specific case, which is, in effect, pressure to engage in conflict with the lay speaker. Michelle continues with more evidence from her narrative but although he expresses sympathy, the expert's response is to return to his institutionally oriented discourse that rests on the production of figures of young reoffenders. This is not acceptable to Michelle as it

[4]cf. Greatbatch, D. (1992) "On the Management of Disagreement between News Interviewees." In this essay, Greatbatch described the way in which interviewees maintain their institutional footing by directing their talk not to the disagreed with co-interviewee but to the interviewer. Disagreement is strengthened if interviewees break with this expectation and direct their talk to co-interviewees.

does not address her case specifically and she attempts to interrupt. Ali does not relinquish the floor until Kilroy (in his role as hero) intervenes aggressively on Michelle's behalf and accuses Ali of not listening. Notably Kilroy does not interrupt the expert at the point of an anticipated turn-transition. It is, therefore, according Goldberg's (1990) criteria, an aggressive interruption, which demonstrates his power of control over the floor as the host. Although Ali is accused of not listening, he is not allowed to respond to Michelle because a turn is then given to the Member of Parliament.

Interruptions by the host largely occur when there is conflict between the expert's footing as an institutional representative and the pressure in the talk show to discuss the "real" stories of individuals. Here is another example where Kilroy refuses to let the expert respond to the lay narrative on an institutional footing. In this extract, a woman has just told an emotive story about being arrested with her 3-year-old son and locked in a police cell. The woman is very distressed and Kilroy displays a good deal of "caring" and "sensitivity" in helping elicit her story. The host comforts the woman and holds her hand at points where she is visibly upset. (This takes place on camera as it is part of the liveness and immediacy of the event.)

Example 16 [W =woman, C =Chris Waterton, Chairman of Local Police Authorities]

W: I was knocking at the door begging them please .hh
can I have a glass of wa:ter after fifteen
minutes one of the police officers [.hh
K: [y-you were put
in a
police ce[ll w- w- with your three and a half year
old son you were locked in
W: [cell yes with my hh
K: =you were locked in the police cell
W: .hh I was locked in a police cell
K: Just the two of you
W: Just the two of us
K: Stop the:re (.) What's goin on Chris?
C: Well obviously (.)[this is a very anxious situation
K: → [This isn't right. It's a what
K: situation?
C: A very anxious situat[ion-
K: → [It's a scandal!
C: Well hh l-lets understand this .hh the officer, the
officer at the time (.) may or=
K: → It's not anxious it's a scandal you don't put=
C: =may-
K: =a mother and a three and a half year old son in a

police cell we don't put sixteen year olds in
police cells fourteen year olds in police cells
C: → I'm not condoning bad beha:viour but lets
underst:and what's happened-
K: → this is bad behavior, is this bad behavior?
C: a- it is bad behavior ye::s
K: it is bad behavior

In Extract 16, Kilroy attends to the woman and her narrative sympathetically, formulating the points of issue. However, the expert, Chris, provides an institutional response that Kilroy aggressively interrupts at lines 15, 18, 21, and 23. In line 14, Chris's description of the events as an "anxious situation" is formulated by Kilroy in a much more hostile manner—"it's a scandal." Chris then embarks on a defense of hypothetical officers, but again this is not satisfactory as Kilroy presses the expert to deal with *this* situation. He is in pursuit of a contentious admission of guilt. So Kilroy isolates Chris's statement "I'm not condoning bad behavior," which is detached from the actual narrative, and aggressively interrupts the expert again to insist on his relating this statement to the woman's predicament.

DEVELOPING A ROW

Many extended arguments occur at these points in the process where experts' institutional responses do not address lay narratives specifically on their commonsense terms. Experts are often interrupted by other lay speakers because, unlike the host's "hero-like" protection of the lay speaker, he rarely defends the experts' right to the floor. Under constant pressure from interruptions, a further possible strategy, other than an admission of guilt, is for experts to interact with lay participants in a direct way. This usually involves experts relinquishing their institutional footing. Greatbatch (1992) suggested that in the case of disagreements in news interviews, "The strength of disagreements is determined in large part by the extent to which speakers opt to maintain or step out of their institutionalized footing in producing them" (p. 287).

In Extract 17, a man begins to relate his experience of the police provoking a riot at a demonstration:

Extract 17 [M = Man at demonstration, MP = John Townsend Conservative MP for Bridlington]

M: . . . and we has a li:ne of riot police come and move
us along (.) and we were saying to them "look calm

down this is gonna provoke a riot" and they just
didn't look at us in anyway like we were human
be[ings they looked at us as=
MP: → [the police have a right to
M: =as if we were scu:m
MP: to keep the: roads and our streets open for pe[ople
who wanna go about their=
M: [Do
they have a right to provoke=
MP: =own business and if the- if the- of they- if they
if the police-
M: =a riot Mister Townsend do they have a right to
provoke a ri[ot-
MP: → [No, really who provoked the riot who
riot[ed
M: [they did!
MP: → They didn't riot, YOU riot[ed
M: [Yes they did (.) I- I-
rioted I: was a steward trying to keep the dem[o
peaceful
MP: → [b-but
you said they provoked a riot the police [weren't
rioting
M: [they
steamed into a crowd of peaceful people what do
you expect?
MP: → But who was rioting who was rioting
M: The poli:::ce
MP: The police were riot[ing?
M: [Did you see the police charge
into Hyde Pa[rk in a crowd of women and children?
MP: → [That' not a riot (.) that' not a riot.
(an argument ensues which allows multiple interjections from the studio audience and for a short period of time is clearly beyond the host's control)

Despite originally producing a turn that attempts to address a general issue about the police's role in keeping the peace (lines 8–9 and 12–13), the MP switches his footing to take on the actual issue at hand. This is where most arguments (and televisual dramatic moments) take place—when the expert succumbs to the pressure to address *real* world experiences and steps out of his or her institutional footing to interrogate the terms of the lay narrative. The MP at line 16 begins to challenge the man's account of who instigated the riot by suggesting, "No, really who rioted?" In so doing, the MP is making the most extreme move in terms of relinquishing his institutional footing and abandoning the rules of formal political debate. He even directly contradicts the man's version of events by suggesting, "They didn't riot, YOU rioted!." This accusation leads to dramatic conflict as other lay members contribute by rebuking the MP. It is noticeable that Kilroy does not intevene in this exchange as it presents, arguably, the desired televisual moment.

In the talk show scenario, the expert's direct challenging of his co-interviewee is particularly meaningful because of the privilege already afforded to the lay narrative by the host. Therefore, when the MP declares, "you rioted," he is questioning the truth value of the man's version of events, but the truth of "life-world" experiences is never questioned by Kilroy. In instances such as this, therefore, the expert is challenging the conventional wisdom of the talk show framework—the primacy of the "real" event. Personal experience is the talk show's generic epistemology (Livingstone & Lunt, 1994), and so to question the truth value of the "authentic" provokes most conflict and arguably most televisuality.

CONCLUSION

Thus, the examples provided here of the pursuit of agendas in talk shows reach beyond spontaneous unsolicited talk. They suggest that the management of the turn-taking in talk show discourse is designed to maximize conflict and thus enhance televisuality. It is not simply that the discourses of ordinary people and their "life-worlds" emerge as naturally oppositional to the discourses of institutional representatives, but that the careful management and construction of the discourse makes such heated debate inevitable. Experts' institutional footings are continually tested and the pressure to address issues in terms of lay, commonsense discourse leads to the intensification of conflict. Taking issue with the already authenticated lay narrative in terms of "truth value" is the ultimate point of tension in the drama that unfolds.

What I suggest here is that the triumph of common sense is not simply because experiential narrative necessarily affords some romantic claim to authenticity that is lacking in the discourses of institutional representatives. Personal experience is, after all, as discursive a construction as any other. Rather, interactional conflict in talk shows is highly structured around televisual requirements, and for the most part these are pursued by the host as the agent of the broadcast network.

CHAPTER

4

The Many Faces of With Meni: The History and Stories of One Israeli Talk Show

Shoshana Blum-Kulka

It is the second month of the millenium, February 2000. I turn on the television to watch *with Meni* (called in Hebrew *ecel meni*), Israel's longest running talk show. What I see is a huge elevated podium with an elaborate decor of door-windows, and a second podium for the orchestra. The host walks in through one of the door-windows, is greeted by enthusiastic applause from an audience of a few hundred seated in the auditorium, and the show begins. The guests walk in one by one or in pairs and are seated in light armchairs half-facing the host, who interviews them from behind a desk. Each guest has an exceptional story to tell. The program is a succession of melodramatic and optimistic stories about finding love serendipitously (a caption reading "she found love after being abandoned by her husband" is flashed on the screen simultaneously with the interview) or being cured from a grave illness, interspersed with music and interviews with celebrities. It is all highly glittering, light in tone, and theatrical; the audience is there to applaud only (seen for brief moments during the show) and the guests and the host do their best collaboratively to amuse and move their audiences. This highly Americanized version of the show is the latest of its many incarnations.

In this chapter, I focus on this Israeli talk show from two complementary perspectives. First, diachronically, I trace its history through its various generic transformations, and second, synchronically, I examine the performance of narratives during the midphase of the 1996–1997 season. Diachronically, the show went through five transformations in format in less than 10 years (see appendix). Its history reflects the ways in which institutional agendas of production were reflected in, and reshaped by, changes in the overall scene of Israeli television, by audience reception, and by the producers' accommodation to the shifting concepts of the genre. By examining the transformations the show went through in its short history, we can trace ideological tensions with regard to degree of audience participation, focus on personal stories versus focus on social issues, social engagement versus entertainment, and the choice and enactment of performance genres.

Within this ideological context, I then examine, in some detail, the telling of stories in Israeli talk shows. As is widely recognized, talk show conversations are often structured around the display of oral narratives, and it has been suggested that these are coconstructed between guests and hosts, with varying degrees of orchestration by the host (Thornborrow, 1997; Thornborrow, chapter 5, this volume). As in all unequal encounters, the rights of orchestration are both given and negotiated; they are allocated to the *social role* of being the host in the program, and renegotiated in each instance by the *discourse role* of doing/being host on the program. In this, hosts resemble parents orchestrating the stories told by children at dinner: the social role of parents grants them power over children, yet their discursive roles as monitors of children's stories are fluid and negotiable (Blum-Kulka, 1997). This variation in levels of control in story monitoring and modes of coperformance in dinner talk narratives makes them a particularly rich resource for comparison with talk show storytelling. Stories are a prominent discourse genre in both dinner table conversations and in talk shows. In both contexts, stories of personal experience prevail. In both, storytelling is an interactive accomplishment, jointly constructed among several participants. The quest for the *ordinariness* (Scannell, 1996) of talk show narratives is hence pursued here against the backdrop of family dinner narratives.

GENERIC SHIFTS: THE STORY OF FIVE STRUCTURAL TRANSFORMATIONS

The Golden Age of *ben hakis'ot*

The beginnings were humble enough: The program was launched in the late 1980s in a magazine format, intended to provide light entertainment and practical advice on matters of interest to families. Topics included health issues (with an emphasis on the links "between body and soul"), cosmetics, diets, change of profession in midlife, and exceptional human interest stories (for example, German prince found raising horses in the

Galilee; a woman celebrating the birth of her granddaughter's daughter). According to the producer, Rivkah Sneh,[1] *ben hakis'ot* was the first Israeli talk show to introduce human interest stories: "There was no such slot as human interest stories as is common on all TV programs today. We introduced this approach, we looked for moving stories, exceptional stories. . . ." The show was pre-taped in the studio with guests and experts, but no audience. The guests included ordinary people with topically relevant life experience, but no celebrities, following Channel 1 policy of the time to separate talk show subgenres. The guests on *ben hakis'ot* were people who had first-hand experience connected to the issues raised and the experts on the same issues. The program was highly popular, was aired on prime time television on Channel 1, and most importantly, had no competition. Until the introduction of commercial TV and cable TV in the early 1990s, public television Channel 1 had full monopoly: With the exception of Jordanian television, it was the only channel available to Israeli viewers.

In this first incarnation, the program, in Sneh's words, wished to make a "light statement." It looked for novel and potentially amusing angles on the topics raised. For example, the topic of diets was discussed with an invited audience of "quite fat" people. The dietary experts on the program recommended a specific diet, and the most successful dieters from the original group were rewarded with new (smaller-than-their-original size) clothes. Like traditional women's magazines, but with a wider audience in mind, the program at this stage focused on the mundane problems of day-to-day experience, providing practical advice in a light key.

Paradise Lost: Operating in a World of Multiple Channels

The second phase of the program (under the same name) marks the move into the world of multiple channels with fierce competition from several other talk shows. Several dramatic changes were introduced. First, the program moved to a circular studio that could accommodate a studio audience. Second, the range of topics changed, moving from the relatively narrow world of personal concerns to a broader range of controversial social topics, such as homosexuality and AIDS, how to cope with mental illness in the family, handicapped children, the future of the kibbutz, etc. The choice of topics was motivated ideologically "to expose the public to other [unknown] sides of reality." With the experts seated on an elevated stage

---

[1]Rivkah Sneh was the program's first producer, and she continued to produce it through its various transformations until her retirement in 1998. We had several conversations about the program; all quotes come from a long interview I conducted with her in April 1999.

and all the audience seated in a circular studio, the physical setup at this stage resembled British talk shows like *Kilroy*. As in *Kilroy*, the hosts (and later the star-host) moved constantly around the studio, bringing the microphone to both experts and invited guests.

The shift to a one-program, one-topic format introduced a more serious key to the proceedings. The choice of topics entailed a shift in types of participants, yet kept the original emphasis on presenting topics from a novel angle. For example, the issue of AIDS and homosexuality was discussed with health experts and invited gay guests in the studio at a time when the mere appearance of gay people publicly in the media constituted a novelty. The topic of handicapped children was narrativized from the parental perspective of a well-known public persona with such children.

During this phase, the program also shifted to live broadcasting before large studio audiences. Not by chance, this shift coincided with a well-known entertainer—Meni Pe'er—becoming the sole host on the show.[2] As Sneh noted during the first interview, "Meni wanted it, he needed a live audience." Pe'er's joining the show had a dramatic effect. In Sneh's words, "When we moved to Meni we jumped two steps upwards—from the point of view of professionalism he is first rate." Meni Pe'er's central impact on the program becomes more and more evident with each further transformation.

Transitions: Moving to the World of Stardom

The third incarnation of the show (*ulpan layla*, "night studio") marks the full transition into the world of stardom. The introduction of a well-known public persona in the world of Israeli entertainment as its permanent sole host (replacing several hosts in earlier programs) resulted in the program becoming known and labeled as "his" program ("*ecel meni*," which means "chez Meni" or "with Meni").

In this third incarnation as *ulpan layla*, the undercurrent tensions between a serious versus a playful key for the show were clearly at work on the institutional level. The tension was indicated by the choice of program topics, the range of issues discussed, and the perspectives chosen for their presentation. The topics sought a balance between the light and entertaining (e.g., graphology, the "other lives" of people who believe in reincarnation) and the grave and moving (violence in the family, rehabilitation, adoption). The repertoire thus included serious, debatable topics as well as topics chosen for their potential entertainment value. This wavering be-

[2]Though technically Meni Pe'er already joined the program during its phase as *ben hakis'ot*, his impact on its format became prominent as of the next stage (*ulpan layla*) and continues to be so to this day.

tween two broad types of topics reflects tensions at the production level with regard to the identity of the show as an issue-oriented, audience-participation program versus an amusement-oriented chat show.

Sneh considers *ulpan layla* as one of the best programs she ever made because it "treated human issues in depth." It is the power of TV to expose delicate issues to the public eye that was important: "What was good in *ulpan layla* is that we raised issues normally swept under the carpet and not talked about. We showed that there is nothing wrong in that and we are all in the same boat and it is important to talk about it. This was the power of *ulpan layla*."

mishal am: The Format That Did Not Work

During its brief interlude for one season as *mishal am* (literally "referendum;" see appendix), the program shifted from the realm of the personal (and social) to the realm of the political. The shift can be conceived of as a metaphorical move in location between *backstage* and *frontstage* (Goffman, 1959) in the public sphere. At its earliest phase, as a familial program occupied with health, beauty, and education, *ben hakis'ot* located itself in the backstage, at the periphery of "serious" public attention ("We did not expect intellectuals to watch us," says Sneh). Later versions of the program pushed it forward to the frontstage of popular appeal. As in the case of popular press, the program now tried to appeal to the public at large. However, only during its brief (and not very successful) interlude as *mishal am* did the program venture into the competitive limelight of frontstage prime time political debate talk shows. At this stage, the show focused only on controversial political issues. At the onset of the program, a sample of the home audience was asked to vote yes or no on three questions. These questions were then discussed with experts in the studio, with the results of the polls announced during the program. Of all its incarnations, this was the least popular format of the show and was taken off air after only one season.

ecel meni: When the Host Has the Last Word

The latest incarnation of the program to date, *ecel meni*, has settled yet another tension that was implicit during earlier periods. Who is responsible for structuring the show? What is the role of the producer relative to the host? The history of the program saw a shift from the time when the producer had full responsibility with very little involvement in planning from the host(s), to a full sharing of the host in issues of production. In the early phases, the production team originated the topics for the show, chose the guests, wrote out verbatim the questions to be asked, and was involved in the editing process. At a later stage, when professional journalists became hosts on the show, they became involved in planning and writing questions. The final stage occurred when the show came to be identified with its host, Meni Pe'er, who insisted on having a say in various aspects of production and on writing his own questions. Whereas on *ulpan layla*, the onus of responsibility rested equally between the producer and the host, by the time the show became *ecel meni*, it shifted more and more to the host. The outcomes of this shift are most clearly manifest in the practices of mediated performance on *ecel meni* demonstrated in the next section.

Potentially, because the "serious" topics raised on both *ulpan layla* and *ecel meni* (for the period examined) were tied to timely and important social issues, the program could have provided a forum for public discussion, juxtaposing the personal experience stories illustrating the issue at hand with expert opinion, allowing the studio audience to play the role of tribunal. However, the stance taken toward both types of topics at the level of mediated performance often did not live up to this aspiration. In the transition from *ulpan layla* to *ecel meni*, the perspective taken on social issues tended to become personalized. The overall thrust of the show was more and more to sweep the publicly debatable issues under a highly colorful, sometimes melodramatic, and sometimes simply bizarre carpet of personal stories.

The examination of the discursive process of story coconstructions on *ecel meni* reveals how the narrativization of personal experience by ordinary people is carefully monitored to circumvent its potential as argument, or to present a point of view with broad social implications. This claim is substantiated by the analysis of the 221 narratives told on 10 *ecel meni* shows during 1996 and 1997.[3]

MODES OF PERFORMANCE

Tellability, Tales, Tellers, and Telling

What makes a story tellable at dinner or/and on a talk show? What are the transformations stories go through in entering the realm of mediated discourse? In comparing tales at dinner with tales on talk shows, we are ask-

---

[3]"Stories" were defined broadly as in Blum-Kulka (1997) namely as streches of talk referring to a sequence of events in the past. The coding analysis was carried out by Anat Shelly; 10% of the data was coded by a second coder. Stories were coded for: a. type of guest (celebrity, familiar figure or ordinary people) b. initiator (host or guest) and c. mode of telling (monologic, pseudo-dialogic or dialogic). Agreement between the coders was 69% for type of guest, 79% for initiators and 79% for mode of telling. All examples are translated from Hebrew. I am grateful to Gonnen Hacohen for his meticulous help with the transcriptions.

ing questions about the ways in which stories gain *tellable* status in these two contexts, as well as about the way tellability is made demonstrable in the telling. The issue of tellability encompasses and links at least three dimensions of oral story telling: tales, telling, and tellers (Blum-Kulka, 1997). *Tale* is the stuff narratives are made of. It refers to the two dimensions of narrative captured in the poetics of narrative fiction by the distinction between *fabula* and *sjuzet* (in the Russian formalists' terms) or story versus narrative. The story "designates the narrated events, abstracted from their disposition in the text and reconstructed in their chronological order, together with the participants in these events" (Rimmon-Keenan, 1983, p. 3). In experience-based narratives, the "story" consists of the real-world building blocks used for the construction of the narrative. The *narrative* or *text*, on the other hand, relates to the way in which the story is shaped in the making; the "spoken or written discourse that undertakes the telling" (Rimmon-Keenan, 1983, p. 3). In the actual discourse, events do not necessarily appear in chronological order, and content is filtered through some perspective, sometimes called *focalizer*. In Goffman's (1981) *participation framework*, it is the responsibility of the *author* to select the words in which the *fabula* is encoded in a way that is still retrievable for the audience.

Telling is the act of narrating in real time, the actual performance of a story before an audience. In Goffman's terms, telling is enacted by the role of the speaker as *animator*, the one responsible for the sounds that make intelligible speech come into being. At issue in all oral story telling, family dinner and talk show included, is the nature of the interactional emergence of the narrative performance: How does one enter the telling mode, who has the right to enter, and how are such rights negotiated and renegotiated conversationally and between whom? No less important is the issue of the negotiated rights and obligations of other participants to the event. To narrate "is to make a bid for power" (Toolan, 1988, p. 6); so entering the telling mode raises the issue of narrative participation rights. On talk shows, entry to the realm of telling is highly controlled. Narrative participation rights are institutionally controlled, and the actual granting of telling rights is ostensibly the privilege of the host on the program.

Tellers (performers) may or may not be the persons accountable for the story as its principal, the one committed to what the words say. In personal experience narratives, Goffman's three speaker roles (principal, author, and animator) can merge into one, as when the principal who actually has experienced the events claims authorship for the narrative, acting also as animator. More generally, however, and especially when children are involved, these three speaker roles may well be realized by different speakers. Yet in both contexts we also witness acts of appropriation of the tale, cases when stories are told not necessarily by the party who has actually experienced the events recounted. The relation of tellers to telling raises issues of authorship versus performance: How is authorship defined in the two contexts? Who, in each context, is entitled to tell whose stories? Arguably, the appropriation of authorship rights is one of the practices common to both family dinners and talk shows.

Monitoring Tales and Tellers for Tellability

As noted by Bruner (1986), all notions of tellability rest on some demarcation of the borderlines between the exceptional and the ordinary. The question then is: Are the criteria of demarcation evoked in ordinary talk applicable in any way to media discourse? In other words, what makes a story tellable at dinner or on a talk show? Furthermore, who has the right to monitor stories for tellability and how is this monitoring performed in actual discourse?

Sacks (1992) suggested that we monitor our own experiences for tellability. Personal stories in the family are tellable by virtue of category membership. Tellability is defined through entitlement gained by being a member of the family. Because everybody can tell a story, even a young preschooler, notions of exceptionality will vary at least with the age of the teller.

Extract 1: Jewish-Americans 4; Jordan (8m); Sandra (4f).

1 Sandra: Mommy to who will I tell how my day goes?
2 Mother: Okay, lets hear your day.
3 Sandra: Well (0.5) I (. . . . . . .) played puzzles (. . . . . . .) I made (. . . . .)
4 Father: So what *else* did you do today Sandra?
5 Sandra: umm (. . . . .) beads, puzzles and I played clock
(Blum-Kulka 1997: 115, continued)

Extract 1 illustrates this taken-for-granted notion of entitlement in the family: 4-year-old Sandra knows that her day has tellable status, even though playing with puzzles and making beads (lines 3 and 5) might not seem so exceptional to adults other than her parents. Yet there is a fair amount of monitoring: Sandra is being asked "what else" she did that day (line 4), suggesting to her that one event does not constitute a story. Such "today rituals" are typical of the Jewish-American families, where they are strictly monitored by the parents for both participation and content. All children are being asked to respond to recurring formulaic openings such as "How was your day" or "What did you accomplish today," and their contribution is further directed by questions like "What was the best part of your day." Thus children are entitled to tell through familial membership, and socialized to refine their notions of tellability through parental scaffolding.

Differing from the family dinner, where everybody can tell, including the very young, access to narrative space on the talk show is highly controlled in ways that serve the goals of this particular genre of institutionalized discourse. The thematic world of talk show narratives draws on a different set of underlying notions of tellability, motivated by institutional constraints. These determine a double definition of tellability, applied differentially to celebrities and ordinary people. Entry to the show is granted to both, but for celebrities the entitlement to become a teller rests solely on category membership; no further criterion needs to be applied for the choice of the tales. On the other hand, entitlement for ordinary people needs to be motivated through the exceptionality of the tale they have to tell. Thus celebrities can tell tales as ordinary as those told by young children in the family, but the stories told by ordinary people need to be verging on the borders of normality to gain acceptance to the show. This underlying norm is noticeable already from the way prospective tellers are introduced on the show:

Extract 2: *ecel meni*, 21.1.97

Meni: **a.** Good evening. Well, who is with Meni today. Today with Meni are the pe::ople and puppets of "A Lovely Butterfly"
((audience applause))
Here (0.9) public pressure worked and the program stays on the air.
b. (0.7) With us also is the youngest sports correspondent in the country, Ben Mittleman.
((audience applause))
c. A::nd we shall a↓lso note the fact (..) that tomorrow, the 22nd of January (0.9) e (0.5) people will come to the intersection in Beit Lid (0.8) to commemorate two years to that aw::ful and shocking terrorist attack (0.7) and the erection of a monument (0.8) is to be announced.
(0.6) We chose to host here tonight (0.8) e the two people who were (0.4) at the heart (0.4) of the intersection [of Beit Lid] for many years (0.6) and they are Shimon (0.8) and Bella (0.5) Etzioni, the people who held the kiosk [. . .].

In these extracts, the opening sequence relates to both types of tellers, and we can clearly see the difference in framing devices. Here, the more famous the guest, the less words are needed for providing background information. The people and puppets of *Lovely Butterfly* (a children's program) and Ben Mittelman are each introduced with one sentence, respectively, but the two lay people need to be introduced with a lengthy text providing the background and justifying their appearance on the show. In this example, the underlying norm of search for deviations from normality is brought to its limits. The couple have been invited to the show not because they happened to eyewitness the attack, but because "they were [for many preceding years] at the heart of the intersection" serving customers in their kiosk.

On *ecel meni*, these two distinct types of tale and teller configurations yield *tales of the ordinary told by the exceptional, and tales of the exceptional told by the ordinary*. In the first case, well-known public personae, such as actors, singers, and TV personalities, tell anecdotes from their life history in the course of their conversation with the host. In their thematic choice, these stories satisfy the requirements of tellability in ordinary conversations in that, in Sacks' (1978) terms, it is direct personal involvement in the story that provides the right for its telling. Such stories are usually concerned with a presumably publicly unknown aspect of the teller's life that contributes to the building of his or her image in her or his specific role as a public persona. For instance, a well-known Israeli actress tells the story of her first encounter with theater as a child, when she used to sneak into an apartment that at the time led directly into the theater, and spend hours on the steps leading to the stage watching the show.

In the next extract, a journalist debater well known from his weekly appearances on a political audience participation program tells stories about his experiences as an adolescent newcomer to Israel. He recounts how he met his first girlfriend (whose surprise appearance on the show then becomes the high point of the narrative event) and how he acquired his Hebrew name. The teller is introduced in the first part of this extract as a public persona ("He is a journalist and an editor and a playwright and he has had held many public offices") famous especially for his aggressive role in another program ("terrible Tomi"). The second part focuses on what the host frames as "unimportant details about Tomi Lapid you always wanted to know but did not dare to ask," such as the origins of his name:

Extract 3: *ecel meni* 25.11.97

a.

1 Meni: I would like now to introduce to you (0.7) the one I
promised to I would bring to the stage. He:: is a
journalist and an editor and a playwright and he has
held many public offices. O::↑ne office in our memory is
his role as terrible Tomi from "popolitika."
((applause))
So first of all a selection of moments we shall not
forget. ((showing clips from *popolitika*)) Ladies and
gentlemen (0.9) this is Yosef, actually this is Tomi, e
(0.6) Tomi Lapid.

((audience applause.))
Good evening Tomi.
2 Lapid: = Good evening.
3 Meni: Tomi, maybe it is not fair to show the↑se bits. There were also much more so called more coherent bits in the:: debate, but (0.6) as they say, a show is a show is a show. ((the word *show* is said in English))
4 Lapid: All right.

b.
1 Meni: First of all, (0.5) you are not Hungarian.
2 Lapid: No, I am Yugoslav.
3 Meni: That's it. Maybe there is a Hungarian Mafia but he is not part of it.
4 Lapid: But I speak Hungarian and therefore people think I'm Hungarian.
5 Meni: If you were born in what used to be Yugoslavia why do you speak Hungarian?
6 Lapid: Because my parents were Hungarian speaking because I'm from a Yugoslav region that had many Hungarians.
7 Meni: And in Hungarian (0.5) Tomi is Yosef?
8 Lapid: No. (0.7) My original name was Tomislav.
9 Meni: (0.7) yes,
10 Lapid: = a pure Serbian name. (1.3) After the prince Tomislav who was born the same year I was born.
11 Meni: a =
12 Lapid: And Tomi does not come from English or from Hungarian, it's an abbreviation of a Serbian name.
13 Meni: Lempal was your name?
14 Lapid: Lampel.
15 Meni: Lampel.
16 Lapid: Yes. =
17 Meni: = Tomislav Lampel that's actually your name.
18 Lapid: = That's how I got here yes.

Both of these stories as such could have been told at the dinner table or any other social gathering. They are chatty, gossipy, collaborative, played out as if between intimates, and as if talking is an end in itself. Such stories provide a mediated counterpoint to daily sociable encounters. By making such stories tellable for viewers, television appropriates them, transforming them into public commodities. Thus it is not by chance that celebrity chat provides family talk with topics for sociable moments. Gossip around the dinner table is most sociable when the topic is of no serious concern. Thus the life of TV personalities can be discussed with detached amusement ("Is she pregnant again? Didn't she already have a baby?" asked about the actress playing Lacey while watching *Cagney and Lacey*; Blum-Kulka, 2000).

The second type of stories told on *ecel meni* are unique to talk shows. These are the tales of ordinary people who have gained access to public space because their life history embodies some drama, personalizes a social conflict that can appeal to the emotions of the audience, or because of one single event of their lives defined by media criteria as exceptional. Tellability in this case is defined in terms of the exceptionality of the tale; as institutionally monitored, it seeks out the unusual stories and grants public telling rights to their experiencers. Yatziv (2000) claimed that television's choice of stories needs to be tested against a distinction between deviations from normality (e.g., "man bites dog") and deviations from the normative order (e.g., "homeless found dead on the street"). From his perspective as a "normative sociologist," he faults television for defining news value mainly in terms of the former, eschewing the moral stance presumably required by the latter.

As on many talk shows, stories of ordinary people on *ecel meni* stretch to the limit deviations from normality; yet a subset of the same stories carries the potential of being framed and presented as deviation from the normative order. This polysemy is played out in a double manner: at the level of institutional goals, the explicit criteria mentioned by the producer for the selection of stories reflect sensitivity to both dimensions. Stories are expected to be interesting and moving, but also to provide a new angle, to bring to public attention delicate issues like mental illness or homosexuality and thus potentially contribute to opening up a normatively informed public debate concerning the issues raised.[4]

On the level of performance, the tensions between deviations from normality versus deviations from the normative become a matter of framing. Guest and host co-constructed actual performances tend to dramatize emphatically the personal plight involved, stressing its "abnormality," but by its sheer presentation on the program also imply its incorporation in the normative order (e.g., when for the first time in the history of Israeli television homosexuals appear publicly on the show). On the other hand, the stress on the personal angle in performance tends to suppress the broader sociocultural implications of the issues raised, reconfirming rather than challenging the established order.

For example, a recurrent theme on *ecel meni* in the period examined were stories of adoption. Such stories frequently (as in examples next) demonstrate a "social drama" framing (Turner, 1974). In each case there has been a breach in the social order caused by an individual action, such as the desertion of babies by their mothers. The tellers on the program rep-

---

[4]At its stage as *ulpan layla* the television show was followed by a radio-talk program, hosted by the producer, where people could call in and express their opinions about issues raised in the show.

resent various characters from the drama, most frequently the victims. The show is positioned in narrative time as a stage of remedial action, seeking to restore social order through personal salvation. In the case of *ecel meni*, redressive action is offered in concrete, personal terms. Thus one program looks for candidates willing to become adoptive parents of the child-victim interviewed, and on another, the victim is the mother of five in search of two of her children given away in adoption years ago. The program actually helps bring the stories to closure, as when prospective adoptive parents are interviewed on air during the show.

The Arena of Performance: Entering the Realm of Telling

Comparing story initiations and modes of coconstructions in ordinary talk and talk shows is revealing in two ways: on one hand, it shows the genre specificity of opening sequences, and on the other it further underscores the differences between opening sequences with different types of tellers. Entering the realm of telling during multiparty conversations at dinner is achieved by a rich array of means. Whereas some prospective tellers, especially children, are called on to tell through direct elicitation, other prospective tellers rely on various conversational devices to gain the rights to an extended turn. Prospective tellers use textual embedding, such as justifying storytelling through cohesion, (extract 4: "There is a joke about that. There is this guy . . ."), or by signaling the intent to tell by providing a background statement (extract 5).

Extract 4: Jewish-Americans 1; Simon (13m); Jennifer (15f)

1 Simon: There is a joke about <u>that.</u> There is this guy two guys in
a war they're
about to die, okay?
2 Mother: Okay
[Story]

Extract 5: Jewish-Americans 3;

Observer: You know I'm from Miami, (0.5) There was a huge drug store
on Miami Beach when I was growing up there called
Thrifty's,
[Story]

As 4-year-old Sandra's initiation (Extract 1) clearly demonstrates, one of the central concerns of prospective tellers is the need to align participants for upcoming listenership. Such three-turn format access to telling rights is a prevalent form of story initiation in ordinary conversation, as exemplified in Extract 6:

Extract 6: Jewish American family 1; Jennifer 15f; Simon, 13m.

1 Jennifer: General Hospital was so good!
2 Simon: **Oh what happened?**
3 Jennifer: She's not dead.
4 Simon: I told you.

Entering the realm of telling on talk shows raises an additional set of issues. On talk shows, as in classrooms, discourse management is entrusted to the host or teacher, who serves as the gatekeeper to narrative space. Because talk show narration takes place in public space, however, the moderator also needs to ensure its accessibility to the public, while simultaneously allowing for the ostensible authenticity of conversational storytelling that could emerge in a private setting. We see here how conversational concerns of story opening, such as aligning recipients and local occasioning, are accomplished by the adaptation of ordinary conversational devices to the needs of mediated discourse.

Extract 7, from a different Israeli talk show, illustrates well how such simultaneous accommodation to the two spaces is accomplished: In his opening remarks, the moderator begins with general evaluative statements embracing all his guests ("We have here tonight especially strong women who have accomplished extraordinary things") then introduces the prospective teller, Nitzan, as an exemplar of such women. In the same utterance he turns to her and addresses her directly: "You have conquered the fear the fear to jump without a parachute." Thus the story entry is accomplished in three steps. First, the host greets the two relevant audiences (the studio audience and the audience at home) thereby aligning them for listenership. Second, he announces the unifying theme for all guests on the program and links his first guest to this theme, thereby justifying the local occasioning of her story at this point in time. Third, he provides an abstract of the story as a story alert addressed to the prospective teller, thereby designing it to serve as a turn allocation. The point of the story is thus offered a priori for the public, in tune with the institutional goals of the program as celebrating exemplary cases of individual bravery, yet the story is allowed to emerge conversationally, to be told by its protagonist.

Extract 7: *Dan Shilon Hosts* 26.12.96

1 Dan: Good evening to you. good evening to the audience at home. to (1.0) our guests here in the studio and to all the respectable guests gathered in our circle tonight (. . .) This is a program that has guests (0.5)

a variety of guests, especially women guests (1.2)
e each of whom (0.8) is a story by itself. (0.6)
a::personality by herself (0.9) and is somebody with great deeds, in my estima::te (0.9)
e we have here tonight especially strong women, (1.0) who have accomplished extraordinary things, such as e Nitzan Kirshenbaum, (0.5)
e - that **you have conquered the fear the fear to parachute to jump without a parachute.**

2 Nitzan: [tells the story]

Thus, entering the realm of telling on talk shows is pervasively through elicitation by the host. Nevertheless, the social role of the host entrusted with discourse management on the show can be challenged discursively more by some guests than by others. Three types of guests were distinguished: *ordinary people*; *familiar figures* (e.g., people striving for the status of public persona at the beginning stages of their careers); and *celebrities*, namely very well known public personae from media and politics. The count of story initiators in the 224 stories told in the 10 *ecel meni* programs examined showed that the role of the host as initiator *decreases* with the relative fame of his guests. The host initiated 85% of the stories told by ordinary people (n = 118), fewer (75%) of those told by familiar figures (n = 32), and even fewer (63%) of the stories told by celebrities (n = 45).

Coconstructions: Modes of Telling and the Limits of Sociability

The interplay between macro, institutional considerations, such as who is going to appear, and the microdynamics of the interaction yields two extreme protoypes of talk show narrative events. On one hand there is the chatty, dialogic narrative, evoking the aura of *happy conversations* in ordinary talk (Sacks, 1992), and on the other, the highly controlled, *pseudo-dialogic* narration reminiscent of talk that typically emerges in institutionally assymmetric encounters. As a general trend, the degree to which narrative events on *ecel meni* conform to either one of these protopypes seems highly related to the type of guest interviewed. The *more media-performance experienced, publicly better known the guest, the higher the chances for a dialogic, sociable performance, and vice versa.*

This trend is manifest in the configuration of modes of narration and identity of tellers presented on Fig. 4.1. Three modes of telling were distinguished (conceptualized as a cline with differential emphases for each type, not as absolute categories): (a) *monologic* telling, in which the story emerges mainly through the performance of individual tellers, with the

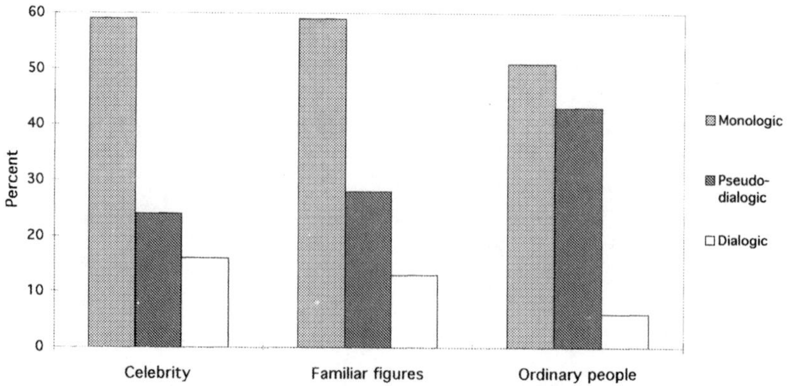

FIG. 4.1. Modes of telling.

host playing the role of the active audience; (b) heavily scaffolded *pseudodialogs*, in which the story emerges through question and answer sequences between the host and the guest; and (c) *dialogic*, or (sometimes) polyphonic telling, in which the story emerges by the accumulation of mutual contributions between the host and one or more of his guests. The configuration of tellers and modes of telling shows that monologic telling is the norm for at least half of the cases even for ordinary people, and in more than half of the stories in the case of familiar figures and celebrities. This trend is not surprising, as it reflects the overall underlying norm expecting the show to enfold as a succesion of stories facilitated by the host. The difference between the groups becomes salient when we consider the relative proportion of pseudodialogs in the three groups: with ordinary people, this controlling mode of telling is quite prominent, typifying almost half of their narrative events on the show (43%), but constitutes less than a third of the cases with the two other groups (24% for celebrities and 28% for known people).

Controlled Coconstructions: Pseudodialogs. It is often autobiographies, in the broadest sense, that are being coconstructed and displayed collaboratively in both family and in talk show contexts. A subset of such stories that is particularly relevant to talk shows is joint recollection of shared events between parents and children:

Extract 8: Israeli 10; Yaron (3.2m); Ruti (11.5 f); Naomi (8.3 f)

1 Mother: Yaron, tell Rachel where we went in the summer, during vacation, where did we go?
2 Yaron: to
3 Mother: To:: well?

		Where did we go? to a place you keep asking me to go to, where do you ask me to go to every day?
4	Rachel:	To the beach?
5	Yaron:	To Eilat.
6	Mother:	Where else do you want to go?
7	Yaron:	To the pool where Eilat is.
		[continued]

When the mother in Extract 8 asks her son, "Tell Rachel where we went in the summer," she sets the stage for the building of memories toward the construction of the child's autobiography (Snow, 1991). Events from the child's past, known to both parent and child, are narrativized in collaboration between several participants, in ways that transform stories into narratives. It is presumably these narratives, in turn, and not the events on which they are based, that will later be remembered and retold on other occasions. Three features in the telling need to be noted. First, telling derives from a shared information state of two of the participants. Second, the adults employ several scaffolding strategies typical of adult–child talk, such as test-questions (turn 1), probing combined with specifications (turns 3, 5, & 6) and check questions (turn 6). Third, the child's contribution (minimal as it is) in turn 7 is attended to and incorporated in the design of the adult's next turn ("Where <u>else</u> do you want to go?"). Furthermore, Extract 8 illustrates the persistence of the eliciting parties (here both mother and an older sister) in the attempt to coconstruct a story with a non-cooperative young child.

Whereas in family narratives the events recounted may or may not be known to other participants in the event, on television the moderator as a rule has some knowledge (from preprogram research) of the story to be told. This shared information state is a prototypical feature of many of the stories told on television, a feature that deeply affects their modes of coconstruction. The host, who has heard at least the rudiments of the story before, can now act as the mediator between the teller and the public, facilitating the best possible performance of the narrative in public space. The striking phenomenon is that the actual practices of mediation are the very same practices adults employ in helping children construct stories of shared events, yielding the same type of pseudodialogs. Systematic scaffolding by the host is particularly prominent in stories of the exceptional told by the ordinary. Consider Extract 9:

Extract 9: *ecel meni* 31.12.96

1	Meni:	We have with us to<u>nigh</u>t Uri (0.4) who is getting <u>mar</u>ried in February and Uri is not coming alone (0.4) he is coming with his <u>bro</u>ther <u>Shal</u>om. (0.9)

And Uri and Shalom (.) are not coming alone (0.5), they are coming with Ruti Assraf their mother (0.6) A mother of five (0.5) children who following a difficult divorce (0.8) two:: of her children were given up for adoption. (1.0)
All they are asking (0.9) for is that the older son (1.0), after he has reached the age (0.9) when he's allowed to:: open the adoption papers (0.9), ma::ybe (0.7) following the program tonight (0.9) he'll open his adoption file.
((other guests are introduced. Following a brief interview with another guest the host turns to the Assraf family, talks briefly to the son Uri, and then turns to the mother))

2 Meni: And between you sits the mother, good evening Ruti.
3 Ruti: Good evening Meni.
4 Meni: (0.7) Ruti Assraf, you are called Assraf by your first [marriage . . .]
5 Ruti: [the second]
6 Meni: You [were Yit]zhak and in the second Assraf=
7 Ruti: [°the second°] = right=
8 Meni: =and you had fi::ve children from the fi::rst marriage a very difficult marriage.
(0.5) And now with good luck you are married again and you have another child, aged?
9 Ruti: Three and three months.
10 Meni: (2.0) But this is not an easy story. (0.8) The:: first marriage was very difficult =
11 Ruti: The first marriage was very difficult. I divorc::ed (0.4) my husband. (0.9) and:: =
12 Meni: = you were left with five children.
13 Ruti: With five children. =
14 Meni: = And you agreed to foster families.
15 Ruti: Right, because I had difficulties raising them, I did not hav::e, no washing machine not anything. Even a home I did not have.
(0.6) Until I invaded and got a flat. .hh and after I moved into the flat, (0.4) diapers, washing (0.4) endlessly.
(0.8) I asked for help and that they'll be taken to foster families.
16 Meni: Throughout the program we show our phone numb-throughout the program our tele::phones numbers and our fax.
(0.8) You ((plural you)) are looking tonight,

(0.8) [for a brother and a sister.]
17 Ruti: [brother and a sister.]
{continued}

In his opening remarks, as his guests enter the studio and are seated, the host firmly anchors the discourse in the here and now by the use of verbs in the present, and builds up the dramatic effect through the chaining of repeated phrases. By naming the characters of the story—the two brothers and the mother—he provides some of the orientation for the story, completing it with an abstract (following a difficult divorce, etc.) that hints at the complicating action. It is in the nature of the program that one of the resolutions to the story is to be offered as the direct end result of the program itself—"Maybe he will be allowed to open his adoption papers." As we shall see, the interview with the mother leads to a second, even more dramatic resolution.

Though these opening remarks seem to bear all the hallmarks of mediated, public discourse, oriented as they are to the audience at home, their framing is not alien to family discourse. As in the family when a parent tells the whole family a story about something that happened to a child in the presence of the child, here, too, the host is appropriating authorship rights for a story experienced by the protagonist of the story, in the presence and later with the collboration of that other participant.

As the dialogue with the mother opens, the host takes up five turns to further establish the background to the story, acting as the main teller. He is making statements related to what Labov and Fanshel (1977) called A–B events, namely events known to both participants, relying on the conversational norm that if A makes a statement about an event from B's biography, B is then called on to confirm or deny this statement. This is also a typical elicitation procedure in the family dicourse, when parents tell stories about the children in the presence of the child, and the child is asked to confirm. As in ordinary conversation, such confirmation checks in the media can act theoretically both to support or to challenge the respondent, but are typically used supportively in human interest interviews such as the one here. Used with experienced interviewees, such statements are often interpreted as turn allocations, providing a slot for an elaborate response. (Thus when an interviewer says to an actress, "You began your career in. . . ," she responds by providing a story about the beginning of her career.) Here, as happens with young children, respondent elaborations are slow to emerge: in turn 5, Ruti offers a correction that, overlapping with the host's statement, cannot count as a response; in turn 7, she whisperingly offers a brief confirmation and in turn 9 provides the age of her son, but no more information.

At this point the host changes strategy. The relatively long pause that precedes this utterance signals that a response is expected; when it is not provided, an informative assessment is offered in turn 10 as an elicitation device: "But it is not an easy story (0.8) The:: first marriage was very difficult =". Still no narrative emerges; instead, the respondent ratifies the host's assessment through repetition, echoing his utterance in the same rhythmic pattern, then begins to provide some information but then trails off, inviting yet another prompt from the host. It is only following a further repetition, in turn 13, and a further prompt, that finally in turn 15 Ruti takes up the extended turn, offered much earlier, to tell her story. There is an interesting role reversal here in the use of repetition: We would normally expect echoing, or in therapeutic language, *mirroring* (Ferrara, 1994) to signal supportive listenership in the language of the more powerful party in an unequal encounter, such as the teacher, the parent, or the therapist. Indeed, echoing is regularly used by the hosts on talk shows as confirmation of previous talk for the benefit of the audience. The use of repetition here is different. Coming from the respondent, it halts the emergence of the story, filling the response slots without providing substantive answers, casting the host in the role of the parent attempting to elicit a story from a reluctant child.

Thus, giving voice to the public participator in this presumably new public space (Livingstone & Lunt, 1994) may on some occasions appear more controlling than sociable, drawing as it does on the expressive modes of unequal encounters more than on those of ordinary conversations between equal partners.

Breakthrough to Performance: The Dialogic and Monologic Modes. Talk with celebrities on *ecel meni* exhibits all the features of televised chat (Tolson, 1991). Consider again the second part of Extract 3:

1 Meni: First of all, (0.5) you are not Hungarian.
2 Lapid: No, I am Yugoslav.
3 Meni: That's it. Maybe there is a Hungarian Mafia but he is not part of it.
4 Lapid: But I speak Hungarian and therefore people think I'm Hungarian.
5 Meni: If you were born in what used to be Yugoslavia why do you speak Hungarian?
6 Lapid: Because my parents were Hungarian speaking because I'm from a Yugoslav region that had many Hungarians.

The conversation between the host and the guest in this extract opens with a B-event statement ("First of all, (0.5) you are not Hungarian") from Lapid's biography, typical of opening moves in supportive interviews.

However, although this first statement bears the hallmarks of double articulation (informing the public while addressing the guest), by the second question (turn 5), the host seems to pose "true" questions for which he does not have the answer. Because this is a performed conversation between members of the same media community with equal discursive rights, it does not seem to matter who asks the questions and who provides the answers. Furthermore, only such "celebrity talk" can incorporate the type of other-directed humor (turn 3) that might have come off as offensive with another type of guest.

Monologic telling on the show can vary in length from brief one or two utterances to lengthy performances; the format as such does not mark the narrative as more or less sociable. As the next extract shows, it is the quality of the performance that can make a difference in this regard:

Extract 10: *ecel meni* 14.1.97

1 Meni: .h Tahel, an actress, appearing these days in (. . .).
(0.8) But I think people remember you from the television
program made by I believe *fredi gruber*, right?
(0.5) In *yoman hashavua*, ((the weekend news magazine on
channel 1)) (0.7) where he took you to the orphanage where
you grew up?=
2 Tahel: = Right. =
3 Meni: = From the age of (..) ten days, (1.0) you did not have
your biological parents by you. (0.6) from the age of ten
days, right?
4 Tahel: Yes. =
5 Meni: = You remember this period of time where (0.9) Na:talie
(0.5) e (0.7) is in now, the period one stands by the
gate and wants a family would finally come, (0.9) to take
me?
6 Tahel: I every day remember this period. As if (0.4) everything
happened yesterday. You can say, the memories did not get
sour.
(0.8) .h And when Natalie talked, (0.8) .h I actually
felt her longing and her hope. (0.5) .h and if one talks
of forces, then I think that as a child (0.7) .h
the::hope for love, the hope that somebody outside, (0.7)
.h will listen, hear, (0.9) take me, take us, me and my
sister this hope I think kept me alive. and-=
7 Meni: = You were with your sister in the institute=
8 Tahel: = I was with my sister.
9 Meni: (0.8) [and th-]
10 Tahel: [And I] remember that in the soccer yard,
every afternoon we would circle the yard as with a
mantra. Regularly. At four o'clock hand n hand in a

recurring mantra, I was the big sister, I would say to
her (0.4) you'll see some one will take us, (0.5) we'll
find a dad and a mom, (0.5) somebody that won't leave us.
Natalie talked about getting angry when somebody leaves.
(0.6) I think it's a very very (..) private agony. And
also there are many families who want to take and have a
heart, (0.5) but sometime↓s they don::'t understand that
in that moment the significance of what they are doing
and the responsibility they are taking upon themselves.
And I think that what's important, because sometimes you
take a small puppy and you get excited (0.9) about how it
wags its ka- tail and is so small. and then it grows, and
has its needs. (1.0) .h And I think that- I- I can
actually feel Natalie that waits and believes [somebody
will take her.]

11 Meni: [You remember yourself] waiting by the gate of
the institute?=

12 Tahel: = every day. = = every hour. every Shabat (0.7)
standing with

13 Meni: = ex =

14 Tahel: my ten years at the iron gate (0.7) me and my sister
waiting (0.4) looking at the long road. It was empty.
only in our imagination, like when you're in a desert and
you imagine water (1.2) .hh I imagined tha- that people
are passing by, and some woman will come. Whenever I saw
a small creature, does not matter if it was a mart↓en
wildly crossing the road, .hh I would imagine it is
somebody who came to fetch us, somebody in America,
somebody from the Carmel, somebody from the village.
And and rem I think that that's what kept me.

15 Meni: Maybe somebody like that is now on the telephone line.

Extract 10 represents a liminal case between stories told by the ordinary and stories told by celebrities. Though Tahel, the teller, is an actress, she is inteviewed on the show because of the topical relevance of her story to the overall institutional framing of the program, not because of her personal fame. The timing of her story at this particular point in the program is orchestrated carefully: Following a brief interview with Natalie, a young child looking for adoptive parents, Tahel is brought in to give voice to the distress of a child in such a situation. The overall structure of the program's macronarrative goes beyond this particular story: The first interview provides the setting and the complicating action (child with no parents), whereas the resolution (namely finding such parents) is set up as the overall goal of the program, bridging between story-worlds and life-worlds. In this overall narrative scheme, Tahel's story dwells in a highly evaluative fashion on the stage of the complicating action. We are never told if she herself was adopted, but are invited to infer she was by several hints in the introduction and the text, as well as by the mere fact of her impressive performance on the show at that particular moment in its sequence.

Coconstruction proceeds first along the lines of supportive scaffolding noted earlier. At the onset of the narrative, the moderator presents Tahel with a B-event statement from her own biography (turns 1 to 3), which she confirms, and then asks her to recollect a particular moment of her life history. As the narrative enfolds, his contributions serve to display information thought important to the audience (turn 7), to direct the teller even more to the emotive aspects of her story (turn 11) and finally, and typically, to translate the coda provided by Tahel (end of turn 14—"that's what kept me"—bridging past and present) into instrumental terms, narrowing the time frame to the here and now of the program, and reminding all concerned indirectly that the function of this narration was to underscore an appeal to the public to come forth and adopt Natalie (turn 15).

The lack of narrative development in Tahel's story stands in stark contrast to the competence she shows in the act of telling. In Hymes' (1981) terms, we witness a true breakthrough to performance, unparalleled or at least rare in ordinary conversational storytelling. In essence the story is about waiting, namely a nonevent. In Bruner's (1986) terms, it is focused on the plan of consciousness, not on the plan of action. The narrator freezes a specific moment in time, reconstructing its mood in a plastic and poetic fashion. In a language rich in emotive terms like longing, hope, and agony, Tahel draws the dramatic picture of the children waiting by the gate through vivid detail (turn 10: every afternon at four, they circled the yard "hand in hand," she remembers "standing with my ten years at the iron gate"), rich figurative language (children are like small puppies, the mood is that of the thirsty wanderer in the desert) and dramatization through direct quote (telling her sister "you'll see someone will take <u>us</u>"). The effectiveness of the emotional appeal is further aided by a skillful use of repetition (turn 12: "waiting and waiting", "<u>every day</u>, <u>every hour</u>, <u>every Shabat</u>") and emphatic lists of three (turn 14: "somebody in America, somebody from the <u>Carmel</u>, somebody from the village"—cf. Atkinson, 1984).

Thus a program that begins with a highly controlling key in the interview with young Natalie is transformed for a fleeting moment to a purely sociable event through the dramatic skills of Tahel. The way the transformation takes place can be understood through the way the three levels of narrative positioning posited by Bamberg (1997) are acted out in this program. On level one, the storyteller positions the characters vis-à-vis one another in the tale-world. On this level, television as storyteller (enacted by the host) positions the little girl Natalie as the protagonist, granting her the role of the victim, and Tahel as the helper who can install hope and enlist helpers from the real world.

On level two the story teller positions herself as the speaker with regard to the audience in the act of narrating. It is on this level that Tahel's minor role as helper in the tale-world, constructed institutionally by the program, is being transformed by the storyteller herself to a major role as the protagonist of another, related story. Because she is so good as a performer, her story takes precedence, and at least for its duration, she becomes the only protagonist.

Level three is the achievement of the former two levels, namely the positioning of tellers vis-à-vis themselves. The storytellers at this level make claims that they hold to be true and relevant above and beyond the local conversational situation. The only acceptable coda for both Natalie's and Tahel's stories will be finding an adoptive-parent rescuer for Natalie. For our second story teller, namely Tahel, there are general claims to be made and she attempts to make them, but allowing for these claims to be made could potentially undermine the level one positioning of her narrative and hence they are discouraged.

The last point is demonstrable through the tension between the discourse of narrative and the discourse of argumentation in Tahel's performance. Emotive appeal through narration is not the only speech genre in this performance. In turn 10 the discourse of storytelling is replaced by the the discourse of argumentation: Tahel is using her personal experience to offer an opinion, to construct an argument concerning the responsibility of adoptive parents. However, the argument is never completed (note the trailing off following the last "I think that"), perhaps because it does not seem to be the preferred genre of the program. Thus the host's responsive behavior typically focuses either on emotion (turn 9) or on eliciting memories (turns 5 and 11), ignoring completely Tahel's attempt to offer an opinion.

Differing from the British and American audience discussion programs (e.g., Thornborrow, 1997), the melodramatic framing of *ecel meni* in its last incarnation suppresses the use of talk show narratives as a key interactional resource in the production of mediated public debate. In the terms used by Livingstone and Lunt (1994), romance wins over debate in the generic struggle between debate and romance conventions. Unlike programs such as *Oprah*, stories of personal experience on *ecel meni* often do not seem to play a central role in the construction of opinions. Their emphasis may shift instead to that of pure emotional appeal, as acting out in the excessive style of true melodramas the unhappy fate of struggling victims in a romantic narrative, where television, represented by the host, undertakes to solve their personal problems. Notably this is a historical development; the generic struggle on the level of performance reflects institutional tensions at the level of production, paralleling the shift in the onus of responsibility for production from the producer and her production team to the star-host and his production team.

SOCIABILITY REVISITED

This chapter demonstrates two points with regard to sociability: sociability as a form of talk and sociability as a feature of talk possibly at odds with television as public forum.

The first point concerns sociability as a form of talk in ordinary talk and mediated discourse. Sociable gatherings, granting equal status and equal discursive right to all participants, played out in truly dialogic discourse with no specific goal, are only one (and probably not a highly frequent) manifestation of ordinary conversations. Arguably, ordinary conversations encompass a wide range of variation in levels of sociability as linked to given and negotiated social power, collective and individual goals, and forms of interaction in both institutionalized and noninstitutionalized discourse. Thus, in examining how mediated discourse draws on the interactional resources of ordinary talk, there is no "ordinary conversation" to which it can easily be compared. Rather, forms of talk in mediated discourse echo generically forms of talk in nonmediated conversation, enriched in each context by the discursive features of the talk that are the specific outcomes of the context in which they are produced.

Our quest for such "echoes" led to the identification of two prototypical forms of talk on talk shows: the dialogic talk echoing sociable gatherings, and the pseudodialogical, controlling talk typical of many assymetrical encounters. In the context of the show examined, the first mode was found to typify mainly talk with celebrities, the second, talk with ordinary people. In the first mode sociability is at its highest when the talk enfolds as if naturally, when the discourse roles of the host and guests as interlocutors are seamlessly woven into their roles as presenters on the show.

This is when the program satisfies Scannell's requirement for sociability in broadcasting: "A sociable occasion, then for broadcasters, should exhibit the following characteristics: it should be an 'event' that is original and particular to broadcasting. It should be an event whose object is nothing more (or less) than to produce an interaction between people for its own sake, as something enjoyable and interesting for listeners" (Scannell, 1996, p. 96). But woven through the programs is another, less sociable form of talk. This pseudo dialogic mode, by its similarity to parent–child talk at the dinner table, highlights the role of the host as the facilitator, the one whose scaffolding is needed to transform stories to narratives. The degree of scaffolding provided may depend on the competence of individual tellers, and yet in both contexts it always involves a certain appropriation of authorship rights from the child or the guest whose experience is being narrativized. The way authorship is divided in the actual telling signals in both contexts whether the talk comes through as more sociable and chatty, or more controlled and orchestrated.

The second point concerns the possible tension between the sociability of talk shows and the potential of talk shows as public forum. From this perspective, "sociability" is related to the keying of the interaction on the cline from the playful to the serious and to its choice of genres as narrative or debate. As we saw, at the level of insititutional goals as seen from the perspective of the producer, throwing light on dark corners of society seemed to be at least as important as the power to excite and entertain. On the other hand, from the perspective of the host, Meni Pe'er, as formulated during an interview with a journalist in 1997, admittedly the topics chosen have to have a social, cultural, or aesthetic value, yet for him the main criterion of selection is novelty and the power to excite and entertain. The tension between these two framings reflects the ongoing debate between those scholars who claim that talk shows give voice to the expression of opinions by private people (Livingstone & Lunt, 1994; Thornborrow, 1997), and those who claim that, through narrativization, talk shows act to depoliticize social issues, returning them to the private sphere (McGuigan, 1992). Historically, the Israeli case examined seems to lend support for the claim of depoliticization: no matter how central or poignant the social issue topicalized; at the arena of performance, giving colorful as possible narrative versions of private experiences seems to have become with time an end in itself, overriding all other concerns. Yet as long as the narrativization of human experience unfolds in a dialogic and therefore "enjoyable and interesting" manner, it still may serve a point, have serious implications, underscore an argument in the public forum. Thus the public forum potential of talk shows arguably rests not on the preference of narrative over argument, and not even in the shunning of the serious for the playful, but rather on the degree of sociability in which narratives emerge and unfold in real time on the show.

APPENDIX: FORMAT TRANSFORMATIONS: FROM *BEN HAKIS'OT TO ECEL MENI*

	Between the chairs 1 [ben hakis'ot 1]	*Between the chairs 2 [ben hakis'ot 2]*	*Night studio [ulpan layla]*	*Referendum [mishal am]*	*Chez Meni [ecel meni]*
Dates and times on air	1988–1993 Prime time	1993–1994 Prime time	1994–1995 Prime time	1995–1996 Prime time	1996–Now Prime time
Production format	Variety of topics; magazine format Pre-Taped	Topic centered; issue-oriented Live	Topic centered Live	Topic centered Live	Nontopic centered Live
Audience	None	Limited; only topic-related guests	Participant*	Extended to home audiences	Large but silent**
Type of topics	Familial and personal	Controversial social issues	Social issues & human interest stories	Political & social issues	Human interest stories; Celebrity chat***
Competition	None	+	+	+	+
Guests	Relevant people**** Experts	Relevant people; Experts	Experts Relevant people + studio audience	Experts Relevant people + studio audience Politicians	Celebrities Relevant people + studio audience

*The studio was changed to a bigger one; the audience at this stage consisted of guests who were invited specifically with relation to the topic as well as a general studio audience. The individually invited guests were seated in the first row. The program encouraged participation from the studio audience.

**From the stage examined (1996–1997) to date, the role of the audience was transformed from an active to a passive one. The audience has been allocated the role of a theatre audience, reacting by applause only and shown for brief moments during the show. With larger studios, its size has grown considerably from the period examined to date.

***People individually invited in relation to the topic.

****Two features typifying the last stage in the history of the show were introduced by the host: the systematic inclusion of the presentation of personal problems solved on air during the show and the systematic inclusion of chat with celebrities.

CHAPTER

5

"Has It Ever Happened to You?": Talk Show Stories as Mediated Performance

Joanna Thornborrow

As several academic commentators have noted, one of the distinguishing features of television talk shows is the narrativization of lay experience. In most programs within this genre, varied as they have become over the past 2 decades, it is certainly the case that participants regularly tell stories of their own personal experiences. However, some recent research into the structure and organization of talk show discourse has shown that these stories do much more than simply provide a core of commonsense experience that, it has been claimed, such shows counterpose against "expert" institutionally based knowledge (Carpignano et al., 1990; Livingstone & Lunt, 1994). They also serve important interactional purposes and function as a resource for participants to accomplish a range of different discursive actions. For example, speakers frequently use stories as a rhetorical device in the production of opinions (Hutchby, 1999b) and as a resource for constructing their position with regard to the issues under debate (Thornborrow, 1997). Talk show hosts can also construct the evaluative elements of personal experience narratives as contentious statements, thus sustaining the interactional dynamic of the debate (Thornborrow, 1997). So narratives, in the broadest definition of the term, from brief anecdotes to personal accounts and reports, form a rich discursive resource for talk show participants to present their personal experiences, construct their positions within a debate, and argue their points of view.

In this chapter I focus on a specific aspect of talk show narratives: the ways in which personal experience stories get transformed into public discourse, that is, how participants' personal narratives become interactionally mediated narratives. In other contexts for storytelling, such as in conversational narratives between friends or within families (Blum-Kulka, 1997; Coates, 1996, in press; Norrick, 1998; Ochs & Taylor, 1992; Schiffrin, 1984a), or in folk-story telling (Bauman, 1992; Leith, 1995), a defining feature of the way stories get told is that they are always sensitive to their contextual telling. Discourse analytic work on the structure of oral narratives has found that a story is never a self-contained object. In conversational contexts, a story is always locally produced and designed for the audience of the moment, embedded into the ongoing talk, negotiated as worth telling, and often assessed by its recipients in some way (Jefferson, 1978; Sacks, 1992). Some stories are coproduced, that is, there is more than one teller (Blum-Kulka, 1997), and the same story can be told by the same teller in different ways on different occasions for different audiences (Leith, 1995; Norrick, 1998). In talk shows then, I am interested in what effect this mediated context has on how the stories are told, how they are embedded into the talk, and how they might be designed for the participating studio audience.

In an account of an earlier broadcast context for the narrativization of lay experience, Montgomery (1991) has argued that the handling of the story materials in their broadcast mode was accomplished largely through certain forms of empathetic orientation by the narrator towards the story protagonists. He describes *Our Tune*,[1] a radio feature that involves the retelling of a listener's story by the DJ, as "a manifest clash between the private confessional letter and the public narrative" (p. 174), and he shows how the specific mediated context, and the relations between the story, its teller and its recipients, produce conditions for the story's telling in which a personal, "real life" story gets to be transformed from its original format (in this case a letter), into a public narrative event.

In the following analysis, I explore how the local production of personal experience narratives is managed in the context of talk shows, and how these narratives are designed and "performed" as public discourse. In particular, I show how the host's role contributes to the production of the narratives as a performance.

DISCOURSE CONTEXTS FOR NARRATIVES

In naturally occurring, conversational data, stories are negotiated events that are "carefully and appropriately situated" by their tellers in sequences of talk (Sacks, 1978, p. 261). Typically, a story is preceded by a first turn

---

[1]For many years this was a regular slot in a popular morning show hosted by DJ Simon Bates, on BBC Radio One, where listeners were invited to write in with stories about difficult episodes in their lives.

in which a story preface is produced, where a speaker announces that a story is available, a next turn where one or more coparticipants align themselves as recipient of the story, and a third turn where the story gets told, as in the following example:

Barbara: My aunt died
Martha: Died, what happened.
Barbara: *((tells story))*
(Goodwin, 1990, p. 235)

Jefferson (1978) describes how "a story is 'triggered' in the course of turn-by-turn talk" and "a story is methodically introduced into turn-by-turn talk" (p. 220); in other words, there is an observable relationship between the telling of a story and what has occurred immediately prior to the telling of that story. Goodwin (1990) also argues that narratives have to be examined not as free-standing linguistic or discursive entities, but as elements within the wider context of the speech event in which they occur. It is this wider social context that she claims is "consequential for the construction of a story by speaker and its interpretation by hearer" (p. 238).

One such social context for storytelling is within family interaction, which Ochs and Taylor (1992) have described as "political" activity. Based on data taken from mealtime talk in two-parent American families, they identified the participant roles of family narrative discourse: story introducer, narrator, conarrator, protagonist, primary recipient, "problematizer," and "problematizee." Problematizers produce critical evaluative commentary on the story events; problematizees are the characters whose actions are thus critically evaluated. Typically, Ochs and Taylor found that mothers most frequently took on the roles of story introducer, fathers those of primary story recipient and problematizer, and children those of protagonist and problematizee.[2]

In the context of talk shows, the distribution of narrative participant roles also proves to be a relevant framework for describing how many of the stories are produced, problematized, and received by hosts, participants, and audience. Through an analysis of these stories, I suggest that a further participant role, that of *dramatizer*, emerges as a significant category for describing hosts' contributions to the narratives as a performance.

[2]Ochs and Taylor found that mothers often took up the role of story elicitor because they were already familiar with the story events and that the children often resisted being positioned as narrator. They were clearly aware that telling stories in which they are the protagonist is a politically sensitive event, exposing them to the evaluatory, or "problematizing" role of the adult. Ochs and Taylor compare this scrutiny of children's activities through narrative to the panopticon (Foucault, 1977), their exposure to the powerful gaze of adults, and their resistance to that power.

TALK SHOWS AS A NARRATIVE CONTEXT

In conversational narratives, speakers often open up the space to tell a story by presenting it to potential recipients as news (as in the extract from Goodwin, 1990). In talk shows, hosts are normally already familiar with many of the stories that are going to be told on their show through the process of planning and structuring the broadcast. Consequently, these stories are not news to them in the conversational sense. Also in contrast to conversational narratives, where the space to tell a story is locally negotiated by the teller and aligned to by the recipient, in talk shows many of these stories are elicited by the host at relevant moments. On these occasions, the teller does not have to do the interactional work of building some narrative space; rather, it is the host whose business it is to ensure that these stories get told to their primary recipients: the studio audience and the wider, viewing audience.

One interactional feature of the production of news for an overhearing audience is that news elicitors (e.g., interviewers) tend to withhold third turn receipt[3] of news stories in order to maintain the noncopresent viewers or listeners as primary recipients of that news (cf. Heritage, 1985; Heritage & Greatbach, 1991). In TV talk shows, however, the context for telling personal experience narratives is more immediately public for participants. The storytellers are present in the TV studio, and the story recipients are not simply the "absent" audience (although they clearly exist as viewers of the program), but also the copresent studio audience. Their stories are therefore told first hand, not just to the host, but also to that copresent audience. It is likely, therefore, that there will be ways in which hosts work to maintain that copresent audience as corecipients of the stories, even though they may not be the storytellers' primary addressees.

ELICITING THE STORIES

The stories presented here are a sample taken from a larger corpus of recorded data from a variety of talk shows.[4] They are all elicited narratives, in that they are produced in response to a host's prior turn in which some kind of prompt to tell a story has occurred. These prompts can take various forms, and range from the very explicit "tell me about *x*" to rather

---

[3]Third turn receipt of "news" typically involves the recipient giving some form of assessment of what he or she has just been told, such as "How wonderful!" or "How dreadful!." These news receipts are mainly absent in the institutional context of media news discourse.

[4]This data corpus includes programs from the USA, Australia, and the UK, broadcast between 1995 and 1999.

more indirect invitations to tell a story, as the following extracts from the data show:

tell me about your son
(Denise's Story//Sally/11/99)
has it ever happened to you have you ever had that sort of attention from the paparazzi
(Paparazzi//Esther/08/97)
what did your mother do to you
(The Break In//Montel/09/97)
so it's insecurity is that right Simon
(Tesco's//Esther/08/97)

For each story, the host has selected the next speaker as a likely storyteller, opened up access to the floor, and given them the discursive space in which to tell their story.[5] Occasionally, and for various reasons, the selected speakers may not respond to hosts' story prompts with a fully-fledged narrative, as the following instances show:

Begging in London// Frost//5.95

1. Host: That's given us a very good picture of your situation
2. What about your situation=
3. Beggar: =well er (.) I didn't choose to
4. be on the streets right (.) it was family conditions
5. (1.0) but like you talk about like (.) all these hostels
6. yeah you're taking them off us (.) you're closing them
7. down

Here, although the speaker is prompted to give a personal experience story, he doesn't really tell it. There is a marked pause at line 5, where he makes the shift from a brief account of his situation into a much more political point about the closure of hostels for homeless people. In this case, the speaker resists the host's positioning of him as narrator, protagonist, and potential problematizee, and pursues his own agenda. In the next extract, it seems simply that the speaker does not produce her story quickly enough, and the host tells it for her:

Jealousy//Esther//8.97

1. Esther: tell us what's happened to you madam

[5]Of course not all stories occur in this way, and often participants have to negotiate their own access to the floor, but it is elicited narratives that I am concerned with here.

2. Woman: uuhhm=
3. Esther: =now you've been arrested (.) by the police for kicking,
4. Woman: I couldn't help myself
5. Esther: your boyfriend's girlfriend's door down--

This speaker prolongs her take-up of the floor for slightly too long, perhaps understandably given the delicacy of her story, and in the third turn, the host takes on the role of narrator. The speaker's second turn is a defensive statement, where it seems she has moved into the role of problematizee. In most cases, though, some form of personal experience narrative *is* forthcoming, and it is the design and production of these elicited stories that I am concerned with here.

As I have suggested, in talk show narratives the work of the host (among other things) is to make sure that a story gets told. Once a story is underway, however, there are various other things that hosts do. One particularly noticeable feature of the elicited talk show narratives is the degree to which hosts intervene in their telling, and the form that intervention can take, particularly in relation to the type of participant roles that hosts assume. Because hosts have reasonably detailed prior knowledge of who is going to say what when (i.e., of the content and sequential ordering of the stories they want to build into their shows), their position is somewhat similar to that of story introducer in family narratives (Ochs & Taylor, 1992), where the story has to be reproduced in its current context for new recipients. The stories in my corpus tend to fall broadly into two categories: those that are produced with minimal host intervention, and those where the host plays a significant role in their production. I start with the first category, then look at the (larger) second category.

TELLING YOUR OWN STORY

The following three stories were produced during two different episodes of the British talk show, *Esther*. The three participants (in Extract 1, an ex-politician turned writer; in Extract 2, a key "platform" participant; and in Extract 3, a member of the audience) each tell a personal story after a host's prompting turn. One is about a recurrent problem, the other two are about specific incidents. All three stories told are complete, in the sense that they contain all the oral narrative components identified by Labov and Waletsky (1967). They also have some similar structural features in their opening sequences, but the level of interaction between host and storyteller is rather different in each one. Here are the openings of these stories:

Extract 1: Paparazzi//Esther//8.97

1.	Esther:	has (.) it ever happened to you have you ever
2.		had that that sort of attention from the paparazzi
3.	Currie:	oh I I beat them once (.) I had a wonderful time
4.		actually (.) sort of (.) I don't know whether it
5.		was you but .hh after I left uh the government
6.		it was in fact Christmas time=

The speaker here is a well-known British public figure, Edwina Currie, an ex-MP who is taking part in a discussion about the intrusiveness of the press.[6] The "you" in line 5 refers to press photographers who are also key participants on the show. In her response, Currie provides an abstract of the story she is about to tell: "oh I beat them once," an evaluation of her own role in that story: "I had a wonderful time actually;" and a comment on the possible significance of her story for her coparticipants: "I don't know whether it was you," before shifting into telling the story proper in line 6. In so doing, even though the host has done the work of giving her the space to tell her story, she is engaging in some preliminary framing of her story, giving the recipients information about what the story will consist of, and displaying it as relevant and tellable in this context (particularly for some of its immediately copresent recipients, the photographers).

In Extract 2, Simon also does some preliminary framing. After providing an evaluatory response to the host's question about insecurity in lines 2 and 3 ("my biggest worry in the whole world . . ."), he sets up his story about going to the supermarket Tesco with his girlfriend, and its relevance to the issue under discussion:

Extract 2: Tesco's//Esther//8.97

1.	Esther:	so it's insecurity is that right [Si]mon=
2.	Simon:	[yes] =my biggest
3.		worry (.)in the whole world I think is losing her (.)
4.		I mean (.) we used to go to Tesco's (.)
5.		all the time to do our shopping like everybody else (.)
6.		but now we have to go sort of just before closing time
7.		[because] there's so much hassle=
8.	Esther:	[(so)]
9.	Marie:	=((laughter))
10.	Simon:	like y'go I go to the - - -

[6]This was recorded shortly before the death of Princess Diana and Dodi el Fayad in a car accident in Paris in September 1997, where press photographers were implicated as possibly causing the accident because they were following the car when it occurred.

In Extract 3, "The Party," Marie frames her story in a very similar way to Simon. Her response to the host's question "Has he changed . . . ?" generates a response of laughter from the audience and simultaneously a further story prompt from the host: "in what way?" (line 4). Once the laughter has subsided (and the loud response from Marie's daughter Kelly), Marie then sets up her story: "well we can't go in a pub . . ." before moving into the narration itself about an incident at a party (line 8).

Extract 3: The Party//Esther//8.97

Esther: do you- has he changed over the years
Marie: yeah he's got worse (.) actually
Aud: [((laughs—))]
Esther: [in what way]=
Kelly: =((screeches))
Marie: well we can't go in a pub (1.0) like we could
never go to a night club (.) could never go in a pub
.hh like we went to a party (.)

In each case, although all the storytellers provide categorical answers to the host's prior question turn, they also show that they treat that question as a signal that an appropriate moment to tell a relevant story is being offered by producing a preliminary frame for the story they are about to tell.

In conversational narratives, Sacks (1992) has described the way in which speakers use story prefaces to inform recipients what it will take for the story to be over, and to give indications of how it should be received (Vol II, p. 11). Although in this context it is not necessary for participants to negotiate their own story telling space with a story preface, once they have the floor, they still provide recipients with some information about how their upcoming story is going to be relevant and what it will take for the story to be over.

Edwina Currie's story comes closest to this notion of what gets put in a story preface when she says, "I beat them once," so we know the story we are going to hear is likely to be about *how* she beat the press, and what the teller thinks of her story: "I had a wonderful time." (As we will see later, she also designs her story ending very clearly, so we are in no doubt about when it is over). The other two speakers also give the recipients some idea of what makes their story relevant at this juncture, by producing a preliminary frame: "I mean we used to go to Tesco's . . .", "well we can never go in a pub. . . ." before telling the story proper. So although acting as story introducer, the host refrains from taking on the role of conarrator or giving any indication of what the story will be about. It is still the participants who design their prestory telling turns with some form of preliminary frame, even though they don't negotiate their own story telling space.

There is a varying degree of host intervention in these stories. Currie is an experienced public speaker, and her "Paparazzi" story is constructed with high levels of rhetorical structure and narrative skill. The complete transcript of this narrative is given here:

Extract 4: Paparazzi//Esther//8.97

Esther: has (.) it ever happened to you have you ever
had that that sort of attention from the paparazzi
Currie: oh I I beat them once (.) I had a wonderful time actually
(.) sort of (.) I don't know whether it was you
but .hh after I left uh the government
it was in fact Christmas time=
Esther: =when [the salmonella=
Currie: [and I- =1988
over the salmonella thing and we wanted to get home for
Christmas=
Esther: =you put me off boiled eggs for life
Audience: ((laughter))
Currie: no boiled eggs are all right it's raw ones you shouldn't
touch .h erm and I contacted my local police
and they said well actually there's about 30 (.)
of these cars sitting on your lawn
if you come home now (.) they're (.) just gonna be
taking lots of pictures an' they'll be here (.)
right through the holiday an' they'll make your (.)
life a misery=
Esther: =but couldn't you have done what you
suggested Princess Diana did n'just (.) go there
smile=
Currie: =well what what we did was we hid in a friend's
flat for a little while (.) until we hel- we felt
that the (.) story should have moved on .hh an'
then I contacted the police again they said
they're still here (.) so I said (.) hang on (.)
now let's see what we can do .h I phoned our local pub
.h in the pub was a er an ex police officer who's a good
friend (.) I told him the problem an'he said (.)
leave it to me Edwina uh an' very ostentatiously
'cos by then these guys were all in the pub having a
drink 'cos they got a bit bored waiting .hh um
he said um I'm going to fetch them from the station (.)
got in his car and drove off an'of course the pub emptied
all the paparazzi got into the cars an' they drove off
into rural Derbyshire .h er er very late in the evening
.h he drove them until (.) he had almost run out of petrol
(.) an'then abandoned them in a field

41. Audience: ((laughter))
42. Currie: by which point we had got home an' we were in (.)
43. the gates were shut the doors were locked
44. the curtains were drawn (.) an' they didn't get any
45. pictures=
46. (?) =(he hey)
47. Audience: ((applause))
48. Esther: yes but if you'd been the Princess of Wales (.)
49. i- there would have been a second lot---

Currie tells most of this story with minimal host intervention. As well as a having fairly rapid speed of delivery, the narrative contains episodes of direct speech (lines 15 to 20 and 27 to 30), a highly structured three-part list resolution sequence (lines 42 and 43) and a very clear coda ("they didn't get any pictures") that brings the story neatly back to the current issue. The host interrupts the narrative (line 7) with a turn that provides more orientation detail, probably to situate the story more clearly for the members of the audience who might not know the background to the events. This interruptive move, however, also gives rise to a short digression on the topic of the "salmonella thing":[7]

6. Currie: it was in fact Christmas time=
7. Esther: =when [the salmonella=
8. Currie: [and I- =1988
9. over the salmonella thing and we wanted to get home for
10. Christmas=
11. Esther: =you put me off boiled eggs for life
12. Audience: ((laughter))
13. Currie: no boiled eggs are all right it's raw ones you shouldn't
14. touch .h erm and I contacted---

After a short overlapping stretch (lines 7 and 8), both speakers stop, then Currie takes the next turn to confirm the detail "1988 over the salmonella thing." Esther makes the most of the humorous potential of the topic, generating laughter from the audience at the next available transition point with her comment about boiled eggs. Currie then has to resume her story, but she does not do this without first dealing with the occurrence of the joke and the audience's reception of it. Her next action is a squash where she neatly puts down the host before moving back into her narrative (lines 13 and 14). As well as intervening with extra background information, the host also acts as problematizer of this story on two occasions, when she produces a critical evaluation of the actions described by

[7]This is a reference to Currie's resignation from her ministerial post in 1988 after exposing the high levels of this bacteria in British poultry.

Currie in her story of evasion tactics (lines 21 to 23 and 48 to 49). Her main narrative roles are therefore introducer and problematizer, but she also produces a humorous episode that provokes a response from the audience.

In the next extract, Marie also tells her own story. Once again this is a highly structured oral narrative, with an abstract orientation, the complicating action involving Kelly and the telephone number, Tony's reaction, and then the resolution, having to leave the party. Like the previous example, it is told with minimal host intervention, and when she does intervene, the host's turn at line 22 is a question directly addressed not to Marie, but to Kelly, in which she evaluates the incident as "upsetting." Marie finishes off her story with a coda ("n'Kelly missed out on the boyfriend") in overlap with Kelly's response (lines 24 and 25). Here is Marie's story:

Extract 5: The Party//Esther//8.97

Esther: do you- has he changed over the years
Marie: yeah he's got worse (.) actually
Audi: [((laughs—))]
Esther: [in what way]=
Kelly: =((screeches))
Marie: well we can't go in a pub (1.0) like we could never
go to a night club (.) could never go in a pub (.hh)
like we went to a party (.) and there was a bit
of an incident .hh like Kelly (.) that's my daughter
in the blonde hair (1.0) .hh a young chap (1.0)
had fancied her n'asked for her telephone number (1.0)
hh n'it caused a bit of an argument over it
Tony thought (.) that I was taking the young chap's
telephone number (1.0) so it was quite embarrassing (.)
n'we had to leave the party .hh (1.0)
we didn't have a row at- we had a f-few disagreements
at the party .hh but when we had come out (1.0)
I was in tears n'Kelly was in tears (.)
it caused so much disruptions at the party (1.0)
that we had to leave=
Esther: =was this a bit up[setting] for you=
Kelly: [((clears throat))]
Esther: =Kelly too
Kelly: [yes] [yes] it was
Marie: [n'Kelly] missed out on the boy [friend]((laughs))

Although it may lack the rhetorical finesse of "Paparazzi," Marie tells a good story. In lines 9 and 10, she identifies her daughter among members of the audience, foregrounding her presence in the studio as well as in the story, which turns out to be consequential for her, too. In contrast to the previous story, rather than taking up the role of problematizer, the host aligns herself with Marie's own evaluation of the incident as embarrassing and disruptive when she says to Kelly, "Was this a bit upsetting for you Kelly too?" (line 23). Despite the host's direct address to Kelly, it is Marie who also takes the next turn, overlapping with Kelly's response. Her story isn't done yet and she provides a coda, where the upshot of these events for Kelly is brought out as centrally relevant to Marie's telling of them. The host's role in the production of this narrative is again one of introducer and of problematizer.

"Tesco's" is a rather different story. Simon's account is not about a specific incident, but about a recurring problem, and although he is still the principal narrator, the host intervenes more frequently at particular points in the production of the narrative:

Extract 6: Tesco's//Esther//8.97

1.	Esther:	so it's insecurity is that right [Si]mon=
2.	Simon:	[yes] =my biggest
3.		worry (.) in the whole world I think is losing her (.)
4.		I mean (.) we used to go to Tesco's (.)
5.		all the time to do our shopping like everybody else (.)
6.		but now we have to go sort of just before closing time
7.		[because] there's so much hassle=
8.	Esther:	[(so)]
9.	Marie:	=((laughter))
10.	Simon:	like y'go I go to the (.) pick some strawberries
11.		and I turn around an' there's s- couple of blokes sort of
12.		going (( ))and I s- suddenly I just wanta (1.0)
13.		ram my trolley into them or=
14.	Aud:	=[((laughter))]
15.	(?):	=[(xxxxxxxxxx)]
16.	Simon:	or I make I make eye contact and (1.0)
17.	(?):	(xxxxx)
18.	Simon:	I try to (.) I mean I (.) I haven't yet (1.0)
19.		done anything physical but I have been=
20.	Esther:	=so these

The host attempts to take a turn straight after Simon's preliminary story frame, but he holds on to the floor and continues his narration. He gets appreciative audience feedback (laughter at line 15), and there is also some indecipherable but audible murmured response from members of the audience (lines 16 and 18). He finishes the story, moving back into the issue at hand with a reference to his fear of resorting to physical violence, but at that point the host intervenes and an extended closing sequence ensues that is jointly accomplished between host and narrator:

20. Esther: =so these
21. aren't people talking to [Amanda these]
22. Simon: [no not at all]
23. Esther: are people just looking at [her]
24. Simon: [just] looking
25. Esther: over the strawberries=
26. Simon: =just-(.)
27. or over anything=[(xxxxxxxxxx)]
28. Audience: =[((laughter))]
29. Esther: washing powder or anything [and you] cannot bear it
30. Simon: [anything]

Looking more closely at what happens here, we see that the host takes up a specific detail in Simon's narrative and reformulates it "so these aren't people. . . ." Simon then starts his next turn very close to a moment of possible transition in the host's turn: "talking to [Amanda]." Here he confirms the point made in the prior utterance, but in overlap with the host as she completes her reformulation with "just looking at her." After this he again confirms her reformulation with a repeat of "just looking," once more slightly overlapping with the end of the host's prior turn. The next exchange between them prolongs what has now become a tightly patterned sequence, where Simon self-repairs his turn start after "just" to continue the series of parallel utterances:

Esther: over the strawberries=
Simon: =just(.) or
over anything=[(xxxxxxxxxx)]
Audience: =[((laughter))]

At this point the audience responds to the exchange with laughter. The host picks up the pattern one last time with "washing powder or anything," again Simon parallels it, "anything," and it is the host who finally closes off the sequence with an evaluation turn, "and you cannot bear it."

This story differs significantly from the other two in the degree of host intervention. In the first two narratives, we saw the host take up the participant roles of critical problematizer ("Paparazzi") and sympathetic evaluator ("The Party"), but in "Tesco's," her role functions more as a dramatizer of certain aspects of the narrative. This dramatization is produced jointly by host and teller, as we saw by the way Simon deals with her contributions to the telling. However, in the "Paparazzi" story, we can also see that the host's interventions produce moments in the talk where the potential for humorous performance of a story is maximally exploited. In the one case, this occurs in the detail of orientation, in the other, in relation to aspects of the story events themselves. It is at precisely these moments, I suggest, that the narration of personal experience becomes transformed through the interplay between host and storyteller into public performance. These are the moments where the talk becomes displayed for the audience as a performed version of events, a display that is recognized and responded to as such by that audience through laughter. I return to this notion of host as dramatizer later, but now I look at stories where the host does more work in terms of actually getting the stories out on the floor and intervenes to a greater extent in their telling.

COPRODUCTION OF STORIES

In the three narratives just discussed, each speaker tells their own story as a bounded event, with clearly structured beginnings and endings. In the next two stories, the host is more actively involved in the telling. The following example is taken from the British talk show, *Trisha*. Lyn, a key participant, has been invited to talk about her difficulties with her husband, Adrian. Here is the initial elicitation sequence:

Extract 7: The Ring//Trisha//2.99

1. Trisha: so Lyn (.) tell us I said (.) a ring a flash car and
2. [six children]
3. Lyn: [(that's right)]
4. Trisha: so l-=
5. Lyn =and six children yeah
6. Trisha: ok so the ring what's that about because we're saying (.)
7. you know you've got the ring but you're having (.)
8. [some doubts]
9. Lyn: [he's uh-] (.) we got married about eight months ago

The host acts as story introducer with her prompt to Lyn, "tell us," but there then follows a six-turn exchange in which orientation information gets produced, but no story. Lyn's first two turns (lines 3 and 5) deal with confirming some details given in the host's opening turn, but it is the host who does some preliminary framing work (lines 6 and 7): "because we're saying (.) you know you've got the ring but. . . ." Lyn begins her next turn (line 9) with what looks like a candidate statement about her husband, but then repairs this to a statement that ties in closer to the host's prior topicalization of the ring "so the ring what's that about." Again, she supplies a narrative event, "we got married," but she is not yet telling the story. Over the next few turns, some more specific details emerge, but the key moment comes in line 13, when we find out what the story is really about:

10. Trisha: how long have you been together
11. Lyn: five years
12. Trisha: five years [okay
13. Lyn: [and um (.) he's cheated on me (.) three times
14. (1.2)
15. Lyn: [um-
16. Trisha: [what you know this for a fact [or (youxxx)
17. Lyn: [yeah I've caught him as
18. well
19. Aud: oooo[oohhhhh

The story that we eventually get is not, as we might have first thought, Lyn's account of what her problem is, but an account of a very specific incident. Once the three-turn sequence about how long they have been together is completed, Lyn moves into the first stage of her story "and he's cheated on me," with a marked pause before upgrading her claim with "three times." After another noticeable pause, there is a moment of overlap as both host and Lyn self-select as next speaker, but the host continues to build up the drama of this moment with "you know this for a fact?" The story set-up is now nearly complete, as Lyn produces the final element in the sequence: "I've caught him as well." Over this six-turn sequence, host and teller have coconstructed what amounts to an extended story preface (Jefferson, 1978), at which point the audience responds with a collective "oooohhhh." This provides the occasion for the host to align herself and the audience as story recipients in the next turn with "what happened?"

In this stretch of talk, the host is acting as story elicitor, but through her orientation questions, she is also participating in the dramatization of Lyn's upcoming account. Here again, I suggest that the upshot of the host's intervention in this story's production is to maximize the performance potential of the story. It is precisely at the end of this sequence that the audience takes their collective turn, as it were, as they actively display their role at that moment as story recipients, and their alignment in evaluation of Lyn's "news" as it has been produced for them up to that point. Here is the final episode in the telling of this story:

20. Trisha: [what happened you say you cau- what happened
21. Lyn: he was in a ca- he said he was going to work
22. Trisha: [yeah]
23. Lyn: [I] rang up his works (.) to ask him to bring something
24. home when he finished
25. Trisha: [right]
26. Lyn: [his] boss said he wasn't at work

27.	Trisha:	yeah
28.	Lyn:	so I went down (.) an'I caught him in the car with a girl
29.	Trisha:	you caught him
30.	Lyn:	yeah (.) [or-
31.	Trisha:	[did he make an excuse
32.	Lyn:	no
33.		(1.0)
34.	Trisha:	not at all=
35.	Lyn:	=no=
36.	Trisha:	=so you [(xxx)
37.	Lyn:	[just laughed at me and told me to
38.		shut up an' go away
39.	Aud:	((disapproving noises))

We can observe how the host continues to actively participate in the production of this story, first through her three back-channeling turns "yeah," "right," "yeah," where she maintains her role of story elicitor, moving Lyn through each narrative event until the climax of the story at line 28: "I caught him in the car with a girl." In her next turn, she repeats the phrase "you caught him," emphasizing this as the dramatic moment, which Lyn confirms. After a slight pause, she moves on to the next question of a possible resolution: "Did he make an excuse?" Again the two speakers collaborate to maximize the impact of this moment. There is another marked pause between Lyn's answer "no" and Trisha's next turn, in which she pushes the relevance of this answer (and, by implication, the chance of some minimal redemption for Adrian!) in her question, "not at all?" The host then attempts to round off the episode with what sounds potentially like the start of a summarizing action (similar to that in line 20 in "Tesco's"): "so you-," but the story isn't over yet. Trisha abandons her turn while Lyn goes on to produce the actual resolution (line 37 and 38), which confirms Adrian as the villain of the piece. This story ends with the audience's response, clearly displaying its reception with audible noises of shock and disapproval (line 39).

The telling of this story is, then, very much a coproduction between host and teller to a far greater degree than the first three, and the story itself is only one part of the wider contextualized narrative. From its initial elicitation, the buildup to this story spans a long stretch of talk, during which time host and teller engage in its dramatization, creating a maximally performed telling for the recipients, the studio audience. The episode continues with a similar coproduction of another part to Lyn's story, this time about how she got married:

40.	Trisha:	so okay you- but you got married to him
41.	Lyn:	I got married to him=
42.	Trisha:	=what he asked you to marry him.

43. Lyn: well he kept asking me to marry him (.) marry [me]
44. Trisha: [yeah]
45. Lyn: you know n'he kept going away for months (.) on end
46. n'then coming back=
47. Trisha: =he took off n'come [back]
48. Lyn: [he took off]
49. n'come back
50. Trisha: yeah
51. Lyn: n'he said will you marry me [n'I] just went out and=
52. Trisha: [yeah]
53. Lyn: =booked the registry office n'everything (.)
54. and dragged him there basically ((slight laugh))
55. Trisha: you dragged him there to [marry] marry you (.) okay]=
56. Lyn: [yeah]
57. Aud: [((murmurs---------------))]

In this narrative sequence, the host resumes with another key event, "but you got married to him," confirmed by Lyn with a repeat in her next turn. In her next turn, the host pushes for more information with her question, "what he asked you to marry him." (line 42). Although the syntactic form of this utterance is interrogative, the marked falling tone on "him" makes it hearable as a prompt for Lyn to continue, rather than as a request for information that is new to the host. Although she is aligned as primary recipient because of the highly interactive telling of this story, the host is also maintaining her role as story elicitor, getting the story she already knows out for the studio audience. In subsequent turns (lines 44, 50, 52) she provides more back-channel prompts at appropriate pauses in Lyn's story, but she also repeats chunks of the story as it unfolds (lines 47 and 55). The repeat of the phrase "took off n'come back" (lines 47 to 49) lasts over three turns, and the resolution of the story "and dragged him there basically" is also picked up by the host in a repeat turn:

Lyn: =booked the registry office n'everything (.)
and dragged him there basically ((slight laugh))
Trisha: you dragged him there to [marry] marry you (.) okay]=
Lyn: [yeah]
Aud: [((murmurs---------------))]

The host's work in getting this narrative told results in her alignment as primary story recipient, but also, through her repeats of significant elements of Lyn's narrative, as story dramatizer, replaying those elements and displaying them as in some way salient for the wider recipiency of the studio audience. The audience responds to this story after the host's repeat of "you dragged him there . . ." with a low but clearly audible murmur of what could be either surprise or disapproval. In terms of this analysis, the important point is that an audience response does occur at this moment. The narrative is complete, and the host's intervention in its telling has contributed to its production as a dramatic one.

Finally, I turn to a narrative where the host's intervention in the telling results not just in the dramatization of the story, but in a dramatization that is also highly evaluative and problematizing for the teller. The topic of this show is teenage girls who have problems with parental authority, particularly with their mothers. Here is the opening sequence of the story:

Extract 8: The Break In//Montel//8.97

1.	MW:	what did your mother do to you
2.	Ang:	.hhh well (.) she kicked me outa the house
3.		because she took away my keys (.)
4.		n'so I had to break in to get clothes out of my house (.)
5.		while they were out of town .hhh=
6.	MW:	=while your Mum
7.		and Dad were outa town (.) you broke in to their house

The host's first turn is an explicit story prompt in the form of a question, and the teller goes straight into her story without any preliminary framing. Angel tells how her mother kicked her out, took away her keys, and how she had to break in to get her clothes. As we saw in previous stories, the host then reformulates an element of the narrative in his next turn. However, this reformulation does not provide an exact or even partial repeat of Angel's story, although he does restate some of the story events. The marked stresses on "broke in" and "their house" clearly contribute to the evaluatory nature of this turn, as Montel not only dramatizes these events, but in doing so, produces a skeptical assessment of Angel's version of them. In the next four turns, the host takes over the role of narrator, expanding Angel's story to include an invitation to her friends:

6.	MW:	=while your Mum
7.		and Dad were outa town (.) you broke in to their house
8.	Ang:	[huh - wu- (xxxxxxxxxxxxxxx)]
9.	MW:	[and to get some things and you said well]
10.		so now I (already) broke up may as well have a coupla
11.		friends over
12.	Aud:	((laughter))
13.	MW:	so the friends came over had a little party
14.	Ang:	(w)ell no (.) three friends I wou[ldn't call]=
15.	MW:	[three friends]
16.	Ang:	=that a party but

Angel begins to contest his version (line 8) and there is a stretch of overlapping talk, but the host holds the floor, not only telling the story but moving into direct speech (line 10): "and you said so now I (already) broke up. . . ." Here he takes on not just the role of storyteller, but the role of protagonist too, and this discursive move produces laughter from the audience in the next turn (line 11). He then shifts back into the role of coteller (line 13), but Angel in her next turn contests what has now become the host's telling of her story around the issue of what constitutes a party: "well no (.) three friends I wouldn't call that a party."

Again, the host picks up on the detail, repeating "three friends," but with no acknowledgment of Angel's prior contestation of his account. He produces another party component: "little beer," while Angel continues to make her point that this was not a party:

14. Ang: (w)ell no (.) three friends I wou[ldn't call]=
15. MW: [three friends]
16. Ang: =that a party but
17. MW: little beer=
18. Ang: =they they acted like it was a party
19. [(yeah)]
20. MW: [little beer]
21. Ang: a little beer [yeah]
22. MW: [little] pizza
23. Ang: little pizza [yeah]
24. MW: [what] else did you do

At line 20 the host repeats his offered party component "little beer" after the overlap with the end of Angel's turn (line 19), and this time she repeats the phrase in confirmation. The same exchange pattern occurs in lines 22 and 23 with "little pizza," and at that point Montel hands back the story to her at line 24:

24. MW: [what] else did you do
25. Ang: erm nothin' we just watched movies (.)
26. stayed there for a little while (.)
27. pizza man came an' (.) went n' (.)
28. snitched on us for not paying him (.)
29. a dollar that we owed him .hhhh [and-]
30. MW: [then] they called
31. back up and told your mother that,
32. Ang: yeah (.) and she freaked out about it like always (.)
33. 'cos (0.9) s'just how she is I guess she's a little
34. church lady
35. Aud: (xxxx)
36. MW: and she pitched you outa the house
37. Ang: yeah

The host once again reformulates part of her story (lines 30 and 31), but without the evaluatory features of his previous reformulation of the break-in. In her next turn Angel confirms this event, then produces an evaluation of her mother's actions. There are two clear pauses before and after "'cos" (line 33) that precede the next part of her turn, as the speaker highlights what is coming next (a negative evaluation of her mother) for the recipients, and the audience at this point can be heard to produce a collective response (murmuring and slight laughter). The host then completes the story with the coda in line 36 "and she pitched you out of the house," and Angel confirms this.

What we find in this sequence, then, are two moments of dramatic display, when first the host, then the teller, produce talk that is maximally audience-orientated. Montel's evaluatory take-up of the story at line 6, followed by his move into the role of narrator (lines 10 to 12) produces a next-turn response of audience laughter. In the final stages of the narrative, the action of the pizza man is first dramatized in a reformulation by the host, the mother's reaction is negatively evaluated by the teller, then the audience produce their response.

CONCLUSIONS

The narrativization of lay experience in talk show discourse, then, is not simply a matter of giving lay participants a public voice, a space in which to tell their stories; it involves the transformation of that experience into a public performance. Stories are coproduced, dramatized by the host in collaboration with the tellers, and can also be evaluated or problematized through the host's intervention, as we saw in the high degree of Montel's participation during Angel's story of "The Break-In."

Where a story is already produced as a performed narrative (as in "Paparazzi"), the role of the host was to act as problematizer; however, she also intervened in its telling through making the most of a potentially humorous moment. Where the stories are less rhetorically structured by their tellers, then the host's role as dramatizer is more active. This dramatizing work can be jointly accomplished by hosts and tellers, as we saw in some of the highly structured sequences in the data presented here, and when this collaboration occurs (e.g., with Simon in "Tesco's" or with Lyn in "The Ring"), it is at precisely these moments that talk show narratives are most clearly displayed as performance. These are also the moments that tend to trigger clear responses from the audience as story recipients and where we can observe the specifically public nature of this form of narrative discourse.

Through this analysis of personal experience narratives, I have discussed how host-elicited stories come to be produced as performed narratives within their mediated context, particularly through the dramatizing actions of the host. To summarize the points I have made here: I have shown that in talk shows, as on all occasions for storytelling, the elicited narratives are not simply told, but are carefully embedded in and designed for their public context. The presence of a participating studio audience, who have to be maintained as recipients of the stories, clearly affects how they are produced, often jointly, by the tellers and the hosts.

In the telling of these personal experience stories, talk show hosts can and do take up a range of narrative participant roles. They act as story introducer, primary recipient, and co-narrator; they do the story-eliciting work to open up participants' narrative space; in some cases they participate in the story's telling; and on occasions, they also act as problematizer. However, I have argued that we also need to add the role of dramatizer in order to fully account for hosts' contributions to the design of these stories. It is in this role that their interventions are most functionally oriented to producing the narrative as a performance and thereby to maintaining the studio audience as story recipients.

CHAPTER

6

"It Makes It Okay to Cry": Two Types of "Therapy Talk" in TV Talk Shows

Raina Brunvatne
Andrew Tolson

As we previously noted, in the literature on talk shows there is some discussion of different practices of presentation. There is a tendency to focus such discussion on the personal characteristics and/or communicative styles of individual hosts. Thus Masciarotte (1991) makes critical observations about the appearance of Phil Donahue (a "gray-haired White man" who represents "phallic privilege") as opposed to the "full-bodied Black" feminism of Oprah Winfrey. Peck (1995) distinguishes between the communicative styles of Winfrey and Sally Jesse Raphael, suggesting that Winfrey "relies more on empathetic identification and direct confrontation" whereas Raphael comes across as "authoritative, somewhat detached, consciously employing 'caring skills' " (p. 65). The tendency here, then, is to discuss talk show hosts as television personalities where personal style embodies cultural or sometimes ideological connotations (cf. Langer, 1981). As Shattuc (1997) reminds us, however, these styles are not just personal characteristics; they are promoted as marketable personae, as brand names for cultural products: "There was no authentic Winfrey; there was the image of Winfrey's authenticity" (p. 57).

In this chapter, we explore two different practices of presentation in the light of concepts developed through the study of broadcast talk. These practices are illustrated in an analysis of two shows that both engage in forms of *therapy talk*, or "social issues in a personal perspective," as Haarman defines this subgenre in chapter 2. We argue here, however, that differences of presentational style cannot be understood simply as a feature of personalities, but more precisely as functioning within the particular formats of the shows, or their "contexts of situation," in Haarman's words. That is to say, as discursive functions, practices of presentation can be analyzed in terms of their performative components, particularly modes of address and the performance of footings by various participants (not just the hosts). Together, within their formats, these components construct different orientations to audiences, and ultimately amount to different subgenres of therapy talk.

Before we turn to the analysis of particular shows, it will be useful to make a couple of preliminary points about therapeutic discourse in broadcasting. The first point is simply that it is ubiquitous and by no means restricted to talk shows. White's (1992) survey of therapeutic discourse on American TV ranges from game shows and drama series to the more novel experiences of home shopping and televangelism. White also makes a second, crucial point that echoes Scannell's (1991b) observation about the "double articulation" in all forms of broadcast talk: that is, that such talk involves both the immediate and copresent participants (including studio audiences) and an address to the unseen, distant listener or viewer. As White (1992) argues in her discussion of the TV sex therapist, Dr. Ruth, her programs "strive to confirm that on a routine basis the advice given to individual callers in fact extends to many viewers" (p. 40). She goes on to suggest that the appeal of such programs lies first in their catering for "voyeuristic pleasures," but second, in their construction of a position of "authority" for the viewer: "One can choose to believe oneself as an authority among all the competing confessional voices" (p. 51).

As such, mediated therapy is never simply therapeutic. In view of the extensive claims and counterclaims made in the feminist debate about talk shows, it is important to insist that therapy, as such, cannot be their primary concern. This caveat is necessary not only for the feminist discussions that discover positive therapeutic experiences in some talk shows, but also for the counterargument that sees the genre as a Foucaultian disciplinary practice (see chapter 1). As we have seen, some feminist writers (such as Lupton and Shattuc) themselves point out that talk show confessions are never just confessions, they are also public performances. While it might be possible to suggest that the credibility of the host bears some resemblance to the "authority" of Foucault's confessor, it must be remembered that this is always subject to the further judgment, and approbation, of the TV audience.

TOPICS AND TITLES

In this context then, we compare and contrast the practices of presentation on two talk shows that engage in *therapy talk*: the British show *Trisha* (which transmits weekday mornings on ITV) and the American show *Sally*

Jesse Raphael (which can be seen in Britain daily on the satellite channel, Sky One). *Trisha* is hosted by Trisha Goddard, a trained counsellor with a background in Australian broadcasting. Trisha, a Black woman, can be seen in some respects as the British answer to Oprah Winfrey. On the other hand, Sally Jesse Raphael, the White American presenter, now has a global reach. Sally graduated from a radio advice show, through a TV celebrity show, to the current talk show, with its focus on personal issues, that began to achieve a national audience in the United States from the late 1980s (Shattuc, 1997, p. 39).

Both programs conform to the broad definition of therapeutic discourse that is offered in Haarman's discussion, as they operate "through the solicitation of free-flowing talk around deeply personal matters, but also in the general focus on psychological and sociopsychological issues." In actual fact, however, if we pause to reflect on this quotation, it is apparent that there might be two rather different inflections to the topics of these shows. "Deeply personal matters" might involve the exploration of personal problems by the individuals concerned, albeit with a wider relevance for the audience. On the other hand, "sociopsychological issues" suggests that some topics are already perceived to be general social problems. There is some degree of overlap, but this distinction does begin to identify a basic difference between the two programs: whereas *Trisha* is engaged in an enactment (actually, a preliminary form, as we shall see) of therapeutic counseling, *Sally* is more generally concerned with issues defined by a social, and sometimes sexual-political, agenda.

To some extent, this difference is reflected in the titles of the shows. The two episodes of *Trisha* selected for detailed analysis in this chapter are entitled "Your broken heart is tearing me apart" (11/3/99) and "My body is my business, so butt out" (11/5/99). Clearly the former is dealing with emotional stress and the latter, though it does relate to sexual–political issues, in the end focuses on personal adjustment and the acceptance of body shape. Alternatively, the *Sally* programs had the following titles: "I was jailed for punishing my teen" (11/12/99) and "Lose weight or I'm leaving you" (11/13/99). Here the first program is concerned with issues of parental authority and discipline and in the second, the question of body shape is explicitly defined as a gender issue, in a problematic personal relationship.

However, the titles of these shows are also interesting insofar as they indicate an approach that is taken to the problems and issues they introduce. It is evident here that topics are announced in the forms of dialogic statements from a particular subject position. Topics are thus defined by personal experience, often in the context of an interpersonal relationship. Furthermore, it is also the case that it is frequently possible to infer a gendered subjectivity in these statements. We can anticipate that the individuals adjusting to their body shape in *Trisha* will be female, whereas the accusatory voice in the second *Sally* program is clearly recognizable as male. It might be assumed from this that the programs are speaking to a target audience for which gender is a salient issue, but more to the point is the question of the cultural criteria that make such gendered interpretations possible. For it would seem that the titles of the programs also suggest an implicit normative framework within which topics can be discussed.

As we said, in the first instance this is interpersonal and dialogical, but the form of the dialogue is also often argumentative, even confrontational. Where does the confrontation lead? Some programs, especially on *Trisha*, are about working through personal problems by "being honest" and confronting the self. More often on *Sally*, interpersonal confrontation leads to a debate about the social norms that govern personal conduct. What are the moral, as distinct from the legal, obligations on parental discipline? How much personal abuse can a woman take from her judgmental male partner? Note that in these scenarios what is firmly in place is a familial, heterosexual, normative framework for moral conduct. We suggest that if it is the aim of this subgenre to explore and debate such areas of personal morality, then it seems to be the intention of the "trash" subgenre (see Hutchby, chapter 7, and Myers, chapter 8) to dramatize them.

MODES OF ADDRESS

In this context, different forms of therapeutic discourse are enacted and displayed. We can begin to explore the differences between *Trisha* and *Sally* if we first examine the different strategies adopted by the hosts in their modes of address to the audience. Both hosts, as is standard practice, introduce the programs in direct address, defining the topic and positioning the viewer with the studio audience in its first encounter with the guests. Where the topic has the status of "newsworthiness," it might be introduced with video footage (e.g., *Sally's* use of a news clip of Angel who was jailed for beating her child), but more often it is presented as a general scenario with which we, as anyone, can identify:

Extract 1

T: Hello (1.0) all right, well getting over a tragedy in your
life is a painful process, (0.3) you fee:l as if you're
getting over it, then wham (0.4) you hit a brick wall. (0.3)
And even when you are beginning to feel better, .hh you
can look around and find the rest of your life's fallin
apart. .hhh well my first guests say (0.3) they love their
sister, (0.4) but her grief (.) is splitting the family in

two, .hh so say hello to Wendy and Julie.
((XXXXXxxxxxxxx))

The discursive strategy for constructing this initial identification is, of course, the shifting use of personal pronouns. The second person plural alternates between a direct reference to the immediate audience (incorporating greetings and response demands) and the more generalized use of the exemplary, inclusive "you," as subject of an imaginary scenario. This strategy is a routine feature of "conversational" discourse in advertising as well as broadcast talk (Fairclough, 1994; Myers, 1994).

From here, however, Trisha proceeds to engage in an interpersonal dialogue with her guests. Once they have been introduced, Wendy and Julie tell us about their sister Susan, whose husband Paul has died. What is noticeable here is that Trisha asks open-ended questions that invite the guests to recount their experiences in their own terms (we will appreciate the significance of this in a moment). Thus: "Julie . . . can you tell me a couple of things she's actually done?"; "What about you Wendy, what's she said to you?" To be sure, there is a degree of prompting in some of the questions (line 7) and Trisha manages Wendy's talk by completing her utterance (line 23), but essentially this is a dialogical interview in which guests are enabled to tell their stories:

Extract 2

T: so I mean you you
[loved him and obviously you love your si[ster?
W: [very much [yeah
T: and you both what're trying to help her?
W: mm
T: and she's biting back so I mean how do you feel about that?
(0.6) Julie how do you how do you feel about that [does it
make you ↑angry with her, do=
J: [it really
T: = you argue back with her?
J: it really does hurt (0.7) a lot (0.8) [to see (0.3) that
she's going through=
T: [and are you
J: =what she's going through.
T: Wendy what about you (0.5) what do you, what do you want to
say to her today, what do you want to work out today?
W: hh we, we, we're fightin a battle here because we're tryin to
show Susan (0.4)[.hh that we love her we're hurtin (0.5) we
T: [mm
W: don't want to upset [her at=
T: [yeah,=
W: =the same time

T: =but you've got your own problems. All right well Wendy and
Julie say their sister can't love (0.4) and won't let anyone
near enough (0.3) to love her so let's actually meet her. Say
hello to Susan.

The dialogical character of these exchanges is reinforced by the fact that Trisha frequently discloses aspects of her own personal history. Thus, in response to Susan's story about how her husband died, Trisha follows up with reference to the death of her own sister: "Did you go through that at all?" More extensively, the conclusion to this program begins with Trisha mentioning how she has experienced similar tragedy, as a preface to a metastatement about the importance of grieving. Note how in this extract Trisha shifts from personal reference (lines 2 and 3) through a disclaimer (lines 3 and 4) to a form of advice giving that again begins to stretch the use of "you" (lines 10 and 11). We return to this strategy later in our discussion of footings. Here we simply observe that the advice is very much a product of an interpersonal exchange in which all participants engage in self-disclosure:

Extract 3

T: Well you know I think .hhhh I mean it takes your breath away
(.) but really I mean (0.6) as I've said to everyone before
I've been through (.) my own sort of hell .hhh and I can't
presume to tell any of you (0.5) how you should and shouldn't
grieve (0.4) but you can all talk to each other as you said
indeed Beryl, talking about it is the very first thing and as
you said as well .hh it takes you that step forward .hhh so I
know you're gonna keep talking, and we've got a counsellor,
so we're not gonna just drop you into thin air .hhh you know
(.) you can celebrate the life of your loved ones .hh by
talking about them, and it doesn't matter if you get angry or
cry or whatever (0.5) but you can work through this (0.8) all
right you can (0.6) really work through this . . .

In contrast, the exchanges in *Sally Jesse Raphael* are more explicitly and continuously addressed to the studio audience. That is, not only does the program employ the standard introductions, but also Sally continually interrupts guests' narratives to clarify or repeat key points for the audience. Furthermore, it is notable that in these utterances, the guest is referred to in the third person. In the following exchange, Angel describes being taken into custody following a friend's complaint to the police that she was hitting her son:

Extract 4

S: You had never done this before (.) [what else did they charge
you with?
A [never em they told me on
the way to em to the to the what they call central booking
that em (0.4) I could be looking at eight more charges (1.8)
.hh .hh could not imagine (0.4) why this was happening.
→ S: She was handcuffed, she was put in a ho:lding cell for thirty
hours
A: thirty hours my son was taken [away from me
→ S: [taken away from her and put
in foster care which is supposed to help him out right [and
Angel had never been in=
A: [no
S: =trouble before, what was it like in jail?

It might be possible, up to a point, to characterize these third person references as "formulations" for the overhearing audience (Heritage, 1985). That is, the clarification "furnishes the gist" of the prior statement and reinforces the drama of the experience being described. Only up to a point, however, because if we look carefully, we notice that Sally is not only reinforcing prior statements, she is also adding to them. The details about handcuffs and the holding cell (line 7) and the mention of foster care (lines 10 and 11) introduce further information not previously provided by Angel. In addition, there are several points, not just at the start of Angel's story, where Sally herself assumes the position of narrator, introducing details that Angel's function is now simply to confirm. In such moments, it is as if the guest is not so much telling her story, as being reduced to a character in a story told to the audience by the host, and where the utterances the host produces, far from being open questions, presuppose and direct the line the guest's response will take:

Extract 5

S: hh how bad was his behaviour?
A: hh (.) his behaviour is terrible. (0.5) He he (0.5) .hhh he's
so bad (.) that
S: he'd bit, he's bit [you through your skin
A: [yes he's bit me through my skin [he's
blacked my eye
S: [he
points a gun [at=
A: [yes
S: =you a toy gun [he keeps saying I wish you were dead (0.4)
((XXxxxxx))

[a he hit=
A: [yeap
S: =you so hard we're talking about a three year old now at this
time he hit her so hard he leaves bruises. (0.4) Now (0.3) a
(0.4) a lot, you've done everything you conceivably c-can do

In short, in her third person links to the audience and in her tendency to assume the role of narrator, Sally directs the performances of guests much more explicitly than does Trisha. However, the guests are not diminished by this; on the contrary, they, too, at certain key moments in these programs, are able to lay claim to similar privileges. Here, the guests refer to each other in the third person, but to appreciate the import of this point, it is necessary to distinguish between two levels of third person characterization. It is routine and unremarkable, in all types of "panel interview," for guests to refer to each other indirectly, or "through the chair" as it were (Greatbatch, 1992). At this level, guests refer to each other in the third person because they implicitly acknowledge the position of the host/interviewer as primary mediator. Such unremarkable behavior is illustrated in "Lose weight or I'm leaving you" by James' comments on what he sees as Mary Ann's slovenly attitude (lines 2 to 4, extract 6). However, the use of the third person by the guests on *Sally* moves to another level when they, like the host, start to address the audience directly. What is not apparent in the verbal transcript is the fact that Mary Ann then turns to face the audience (line 5). On this basis her story generates audience reaction (line 12) and Sally invites a further restatement of Mary Ann's position (lines 15 and 16), thereby generating an extensive further response (line 18):

Extract 6

S: Lo:ve is not love which alters when it alteration find[s
→ J: [She
doesn't even try though, that's what I'm saying (1.1) she
does not try one bit [(I've bought=
→ M: [What is it about him I I get up with
him at four o'clock at four four thirty in the=
J: =her) I've bought her tapes
M: =morning, and fix his lunch, make sure his breakfast is made,
and make sure he is up up ready to go to work in the mornings
at four four thirty in the morning he has to be at work at
five thirty .hh I get up w[ith him.
[((XXXxxxx))
J: Right so go back to bed (.) I mean
M: I don't always go back[to bed.
S: [Mary Ann you said you have an
ultimatum for James what is it?

(1.1)
→ M: He either straighten up and like the way I look (.) or get out.
((XXXXXxxxxxx))

In these various ways, *Sally Jesse Raphael* appears to be much more of a performance for the audience than does *Trisha*. *Trisha* is an enactment of therapeutic dialogue, which is clearly designed to be overheard, but which does not seem to be entirely prescripted. Trisha herself engages with her guests by sharing personal experiences with them. *Sally*, on the other hand, is much more overtly aware of its studio audience, where the shift to third person reference by both host and guests constructs participants as characters and invites audience reaction to them. Moreover, these characters function within the prescripted stories that Sally herself narrates. At least, the lay persons do, for as we shall now see, it is also crucial that *Sally* also makes use of experts who have another kind of discursive function.

FOOTINGS

The hosts of these programs, Trisha and Sally, also differ in the kinds of footings they are prepared to perform. *Footing*, we recall, is the concept introduced by Goffman (1974, 1981) to refer to speaker alignment in the "participation framework" of spoken communication. Speakers may thus perform as *authors* of their own words, as *animators* of the words of others (as in quotations or scripts), or they can adopt the *principal* footing, where they speak on behalf of an organization or an authority. As we discussed, Goffman's concept has been usefully applied to talk shows by Livingstone and Lunt (1994), where the distinction between lay persons and experts is evident in the different footings (author vs. principal) they perform. This difference seems to be particularly marked in the audience discussion format (shows like *Kilroy*; see chapter 3) where it is staged as a confrontation between commonsense and expertise. However, it is less clear that footings are always as clearly marked in the kinds of therapy talk discussed here.

Of the two shows, *Sally* is the more conventional in this respect. As Shattuc (1997) notes, the program has a structure consisting of four segments: first, guests are invited to tell their stories (with Sally's substantial prompting); second, they are interrogated by the studio audience; in the third and fourth segments, experts are introduced to deliver their pronouncements. Guests speak as authors of their own experiences and experts speak as principals, with Sally herself animating the script. However, as Shattuc again points out, experts are not simply selected for their professional expertise, but also for their ability to perform their role in an acceptable way. They are not just spokespersons and they are not subjected to the kind of populist interrogation we find in programs like *Kilroy*. A regular expert on *Sally* is Dr. Gilda Carle, who appears in the program on parental discipline:

Extract 7

→ GC: And it is a funny thing about adolescence psychology the more
you say no no no believe it or not that's the more they
understand that oh (.) mom and dad must love me (.) they push
you to the limit just so that you can say no and they
interpret that as love (0.4) it's it's not to be understood
it's just to be accepted
S: No wait wait wait let me understa:nd something, because
that's a little (0.5) strange to me (0.4) are you saying that
in studies of adolescents or in adolescence psychology (0.5)
ah you love your child, but disciplin:e says to the child I
love you
→ GC: yes

What is noticeable in this extract is that although Carle is speaking for "adolescence psychology" on a principal footing, the language she uses is colloquial and conversational. That discipline can be understood as love is a "funny thing," and it is animated in this scenario through the words of the child (line 3). In this context, Carle again shifts to the generalized "you," which establishes the scenario as exemplary for the audience. For her part, Sally, as narrator and moderator, interrupts with a question that also contains a cooperative formulation (lines 8 to 11) explicitly reinforcing Carle's claim to expertise.

On the other hand, basically, Trisha is her own expert. This is quite a complicated role to play, and it is performed in a different type of program structure. Each episode of *Trisha* presents a series of separate segments (usually three, sometimes four) that function, in a sense, as case studies. Trisha herself begins each segment on stage, interviewing the first guest(s) to establish the problem; but then as further guests arrive, she moves into the audience to interrogate them (with audience members making occasional comments). There is, thus, the familiar triangular pattern in many audience participation programs where guests talk to each other on stage but are talked back to from the floor by host and audience. Toward the end of each segment, Trisha then tries to sum up, and it is here that the footings become complex. We have already seen (extract 3) how Trisha concludes the program on broken hearts, drawing various threads together into a metastatement about the need to grieve. Here is how she reaches that position:

Extract 8

T: Let me come to you Susan (0.5) .hh I mean (0.6) strong people
you I I I must say I feel very much (0.3) like you I might be
totally out of order here, but I was eldest sister in my
family and I was always strong (0.4) .hh and I don't cry I
don't do that stuff (0.7) but I do (.) and one of my first
step forward was learning how to cry (0.6) in front of (0.3)
I haven't learned to cry in front of my family yet (.) I'm
sure they are all watching this at home saying you hypocrite
(0.6) .hh but I hhh d-did learn how to cry in front of my
daughter (0.6) that's where I did it, (0.9) and I think
that's the most powerful (0.5) thing is to share your tears
with someone else (.) and it makes it okay to cry (.) yeah.
((XXXXXxxxxx))
Wendy (.) Wendy what about you, (0.6) I mean (0.3) can you
back off a bit.

Clearly Trisha is not just a narrator and she is more than a colloquial expert. In sharing her own experiences, she too performs *authorship* in Goffman's terms; but then, this is also self-consciously characterized as a performance and, thus, as an *animation*. That is to say, on lines 2 and 3, the disclaimer ("I might be totally out of order") indicates the prior assumption of an authorship footing ("I must say I feel . . ."), which the subsequent aside on lines 7 and 8 ("I'm sure they're all watching this at home") questions in terms of its authenticity ("you hypocrite"). In this combination of authorship and animation, Trisha establishes a self-reflexive persona where she also becomes a character, or perhaps a "case," in the drama of the show. With this credibility (suffering plus self-awareness), Trisha can then move on to deliver her metastatements. These are not only couched in the generalized "you," they can also be presented, as in this example, as quasi-intellectual propositions: "I think that's the most powerful thing . . . [that's what] makes it okay to cry."

Trisha's role is performed, therefore, in a complex alternation of footings. As a trained counsellor herself, she sometimes refers to her professional experience and some of her authored statements have an intellectual legitimacy. However, she doesn't simply speak for the profession in the language of expertise; rather, it would seem appropriate to relate her performance (as exemplified here) to Goffman's (1981) concept of "fresh talk," which he suggests "*commonly* presents congruence among animator, author and principal" (p. 229, his emphasis). We must acknowledge here that Goffman is making broad distinctions between recitation, scripted, and unscripted speech in the context of an essay on radio talk. Nevertheless, with its disclaimers and reflexive interpolations, Trisha's expertise is performed as the spontaneous product of an unscripted exchange, rather than as some kind of expert pronouncement. "Authorship" becomes "authoritative," we might say.

TWO TYPES OF THERAPY TALK

Taken together, these variations in audience address and the performance of footings on *Trisha* and *Sally* amount to two different types of mediated therapy talk. In *Trisha* the talk is more conventionally therapeutic, and indeed, as Extract 3 reveals, there is a counselor waiting in the wings. The program also advertises helplines and agencies for personal support. In this context, the purpose of the show seems to be to act as a rehearsal for proper therapy, where guests are invited to work through their problems to the point where this becomes a subsequent possibility. The intimate, interpersonal exchanges Trisha has with her guests seem not simply to be concerned with personal storytelling, but also directed towards moments of introspection and self-analysis:

Extract 9

T: But then he was on the list for a kidney transplant wasn't
he?
S: He was yeah he was on the-e short list hh
T: So you've known him since you were seven[teen sixteen [so
you've been=
S: [sixteen [mm
→ T: =through (0.4) a <u>hell</u> of a lot with him. (0.7) Was it always
hanging over your head the fact that he might die one day.
(0.7) Do you think it was always there.
S: He used to say it. (0.6) He used to say he wasn't gonna live
past thirty (.) but I used to tell him be strong
(1.4)
T: You didn't believe it
S: No I I roughly thought about (0.4) fifty.
(0.7)
→ T: Yeah, which seems a long way. All right so you were pregnant
with your baby . . .

In this extract, we see Trisha using follow-ups to Susan's narrative statements (lines 4 to 7, 16), which have a dual function. First, they act as formulations of the gist of Susan's experiences ("so you've been through a hell of a lot"). Second, however, in their colloquial articulation, but particularly in their affiliative alignment, they function as supportive reformulations in the manner of classic therapeutic discourse (Labov & Fanshel, 1977). In these moments, then, the audience is invited to share in the drama of a quasi-therapeutic encounter, a mediated enactment of what Foucault (1982) describes as the form of power that makes the individual a subject: "tied to his own identity by a conscience or self-knowledge" (p. 212).

On the other hand, some exchanges in *Sally* seem to have a rather different emphasis. In Extract 10, from "Lose weight or I'm leaving you," Sally is engaged in her usual practice of eliciting Mary Ann's narrative. The main concern seems to be with driving the narrative forward, without the pauses for self-reflection that might be provided by reformulations. For her part, however, and this is not easily represented in a transcript, Mary Ann performs differently from Susan on the *Trisha* show. At line 4, Mary Ann bursts into tears (to sympathetic applause) and she subsequently answers Sally's questions in a "teary voice"—indicated by the asterisks (lines 10, 18, 20, 24, 27). This is supplemented by hand gestures in line 27. Feelings are therefore on display, rather than under discussion, in this type of performance:

Extract 10

S: We want you to meet Mary Ann (0.3) ehe (0.5) Mary Ann (0.3)
is engaged to be married ah but instead of being happy she is
kind of a nervous wreck. (0.5) She has a fiancee, his name is
James, and he will not marry her until (0.7) oh Mary Ann
until she loses the weight. (1.4) ((Mary Ann starts
crying))
((XXXXxxxx))
Mary Ann (0.6) what does he say about the weight tell me what
he says.
M: *He calls me a fat bitch, a lazy bitch, (0.7) a (.) .hh big
ass
((XXXXxxxxx))
he won't marry me until I loses my weight [(.2) I just don't
know what=
S: [Why would you want
to marry him, would you want to marry him?
M: =why else to do.
M: *I've been with him for so long.
S: How long have you been with him?
M: *Fourteen years
((XXXXxxxx))
S: How does it make you feel?
(1.3)
M: *How was he or how was I?
→ S: How (.) has this made you feel?
(0.8)
→ M: *It's made me feel real little. ((indicating with fingers))
(0.8)

S: But you've been with him fourteen years, and all you want is
to get married, and all he wants is for you to lose weight
[It's one of those stand offs, is=
M: [right
S: =that right? [Now he has postponed the wedding three times.
(0.8) What=
M: [yeahhh
S: =does he say when he postpones the wedding?
→ M: He says it's because of my weight. (0.6) If I lose my weight
he will ↑marry me

If therefore, in *Trisha*, "It makes it okay to cry" is a proposition, in *Sally*, at least in such exchanges, it is a performative act. To some extent (though with less initial resistance) this is reminiscent of the incident from *Oprah Winfrey* described by Masciarotte (1991, p. 97), and it can be theorized in the same way. That is to say, the public display of the suffering body, represented by the uncontrollable voice, offers a guarantee of the authenticity of the experience—if we suspend our disbelief in its melodramatic performance. Mary Ann is acting a melodramatic role in a conventional domestic scenario, where, as we have seen, she functions as a character in a story narrated by the host. If the therapeutic orientation of *Trisha* offers the possibility of real counselling beyond the confines of the show, the therapeutic value of *Sally* is more an effect of the types of melodramatic experience the show itself provides.

To define this type of "therapy," we finally turn to the coda to the story of Mary Ann and James. This is delivered by Julia Griggs Havey, whose expertise is located first in the fact that she has had similar experiences of personal abuse due to body shape, but second that she has written an "inspirational" book on how to overcome this. Havey is therefore introduced by Sally as someone who can "understand what's going on 'cause she went through it," and she responds by saying "every name they've been called, every tear you've shed, I've been there . . ." She then produces a narrative about gaining weight, suffering verbal abuse from her husband and the discovery that he was having an affair, and then going through an apparently instantaneous moment of self-realization resulting in a newly disciplined regime consisting of healthy eating and plastic surgery. Finally this leads to remarriage to "the finest man who walks the planet." Melodrama thus meets the technologies of the self in this all-too-familiar kind of account. Finally, prompted by Sally, Havey concludes her contribution as follows:

Extract 11

S: In in case (0.5) case you were wondering if this was
important you would know from her but we're here today to
validate how important it is and and we have hundreds and

hundreds of cases unfortunately .hh like this ah well
she has written a book a very inspirational book about this
em I'd like to get all of you a copy tell me what you'd say
to the guys.
(0.8)
→ JH: I would say (0.5) when you married your wife (0.5) you told
her that you loved her (0.4) and in your heart I hope you did
(0.5) if your wife had been in an accident and lost a limb
would you've loved her any less (0.5) her weight is merely
(.) merely (0.5) weight on her body it's not her soul it's
not who she is if you love this woman start taking her out
(.) get her an appointment at her local beauty salon to get a
facial or something to show her that you care about her (.)
and the weight will come off when she feels good about her
which if you love her (.) you can help do that every day tell
her I love you today let's both make healthy choices for
ourselves. You can help her.
((XXXXXXxxxxxx))

We suggest that Havey's display of expertise here takes therapeutic discourse into a distinctive speech genre (Bakhtin, 1986). We define this as a type of *homily*, and suggest that what is distinctive about this genre is that it recasts a personal narrative as the pretext for a moral lesson (cf. in chapter 8, this volume, Myers' discussion of Jerry Springer's "Final Thoughts"). It is, of course, the speech genre favored by the (Protestant) sermon, which provides further support for the argument that there are affinities between some types of talk show and nonconformist religious activities. Here Havey's expertise is not provided by any professional qualification, and she does not use her experience to share therapeutic insights. Rather her experiences, via her authorship, serve as the basis from which to deliver a set of moral imperatives to men. Perhaps this can be seen as populist rather than professional expertise, for we can see that it generates substantial audience support (line 21).

As a speech genre, the homily belongs to a class of popular forms of talk where narrative serves as a pretext for cultural generalization. This class includes some types of joke, for instance those that reaffirm cultural stereotypes, and it certainly encompasses the anecdote, in which an exemplary incident confirms the truth about a person, or more generally about "life" (Tolson, 1985). It is crucial that the truth here is easily recognized; in fact, it can be delivered in the form of a maxim or proverb which assumes a cultural consensus. You cannot argue with a proverb, just as you cannot quarrel with a joke or anecdote (or else be accused of having no sense of humor). These speech forms can therefore be regarded as consensus-producing techniques—in the sense that not only is the truth universally affirmed, but also its form renders it uncontrovertible. In the homily, such truth takes the form of a universally approved moral lesson: "Show her that you care."

CONCLUSION

In the conclusion to her discussion of Oprah Winfrey, Shattuc (1997) suggests that she performs a combination of our two types of therapy talk:

> It is no wonder that Winfrey as a self confessed victim of child abuse, drugs and self hate is the most highly paid woman interlocutor. The private has become public. The personal is political. And the ability to confess publicly has become a sign of power and control. Such public therapy is an ideology that combines the negative hermeneutics of Freudian subjectivity with the affirmation of the active individual within a shared community. And that tension is ultimately the therapeutic power of talk on TV. (p. 136)

From our point of view, however, much hangs on the reference to "tension" here; we suggest that these two rather different therapeutic practices are not very easily synthesized. Clearly, we have not studied the *Oprah Winfrey Show*, so we would have to concede that Shattuc may well be correct, but from our analysis of *Trisha* and *Sally*, we conclude that the orientation to self-analysis is rather different from the construction of a communal identification. This is not so much an ideological matter, however, as a question of two quite different "contexts of situation" with different kinds of communicative intentionality. In the first context, problematic experiences are presented as personal projects for individuals to work through beyond the confines of the show. In the second, experiences are recreated and performed, in melodramatic fashion, on the show itself.

Accordingly, the slogan "It's okay to cry" has two different meanings because it is constructed differently in the two contexts that define these programs. Indeed, we also suggest that other familiar propositions such as the "private has become public" and "the personal is political" are also inflected differently, because in these two types of therapy talk, the private attains public visibility in two very different kinds of verbal performance. In the final analysis, then, what determines the performance of all participants in talk shows, but particularly the hosts, is a perceived relation to the overhearing audience. However, this is not just a matter of chasing audience ratings, nor is it simply that the hosts perform in marketable personae for product identification. Rather, as our analysis demonstrates, these programs offer different kinds of discursive experience, in the way they announce their topics, address their audiences, and, as participants, act out particular roles and footings. Our two types of therapy talk are two kinds of verbal performance, offering two different forms of entertainment, in the institutional context of contemporary broadcasting.

CHAPTER

7

Confrontation as a Spectacle: The Argumentative Frame of the *Ricki Lake* Show

Ian Hutchby

In the mid-1990s a new strain of talk show emerged, led by the American shows *Ricki Lake* and *Jerry Springer*. This type of show is guest-based, rather than being an audience participation debate on pertinent social issues, as for example the long-running shows *Donahue* and, in the United Kingdom, *Kilroy*. The topics or themes of the show center not around questions of wider public concern but "everyday life dilemmas," and the guests, who do most of the talking, are ordinary members of the public, usually with a bone to pick with each other. The show's discourse routinely revolves around confrontations between ex-lovers, family members, friends who have fallen out, neighbors who are in dispute, and so on. In this sense, such shows create what could be called *confrontation as a spectacle*, in which guests are encouraged to air publicly disputes that ordinarily would be confined to the private sphere of everyday life.

The *Ricki Lake* show, like its precursor *Oprah Winfrey* and its competitor *Jerry Springer*, has developed its basic format over time. This partly has to do with the sheer number of shows recorded in a typical season and is partly because of competition from other shows that seek to up the ante by being more controversial. During the period when recordings were being collected for this study (1997–1998), the show focused almost entirely on broadcasting revelations and resulting confrontations among friends and family members. More recently, in response to *Jerry Springer*'s more extreme controversialism (see Myers, chapter 8, this volume), the show has often adopted a lighter presentational style. Yet although *Jerry Springer* has subsequently gained a wider notoriety, even leading, in the UK, to the emergence of attempts to copy its format (such as *Vanessa*), it is worth remembering that the format itself, in which ordinary folks confront each other over private life issues and revelations, was pioneered by *Ricki Lake*. At the time of its emergence, this show presented a wholly novel form of televisual discourse, in which audience members, both at home and in the studio, could find themselves looking in on an argument played out between the participants on stage.

The interfacing of the private and the public has long been noted as a key feature of audience participation talk shows in general (Carpignano et al., 1990; Livingstone & Lunt, 1994). Indeed, many writers have begun from the idea that audience participation shows can be seen as a means of providing private citizens access to the public sphere represented in large part, in modern society, by broadcasting. As Tolson points out in chapter 1, the notion of an "oppositional" public sphere has received considerable endorsement not only from writers on TV talk shows, but also in the analysis of political communication. In addition, Crittenden (1971), Avery and Ellis (1979), and Verwey (1990) all explicitly addressed the "democratic functions" of talk radio, by examining the degree to which talk radio discussions come to permeate the wider population of the overhearing audience, or evaluating the extent to which different talk radio hosts facilitate open debate between themselves and members of the public.

In this chapter, I focus on a different aspect of this private–public interface. Following on from recent work in which the characteristically argumentative and often confrontational talk found on talk radio shows has been subjected to analysis in its own right (Hutchby, 1996a), I examine the nature of confrontational talk on the *Ricki Lake* show as a form of public argumentation. Public argumentation is not a new phenomenon in itself; there is a long tradition in democratic societies of debating fora in which large-scale audiences are copresent with the debaters. However, televised versions of argumentative debate are novel in the sense that, by being broadcast, the debate becomes accessible to a further audience, one that is absent from the debate's physical arena and is both geographically and temporally distributed. Broadcast forms of public argumentation involve a set of participants (the audience at home) whose very involvement is enabled by virtue of the televisual medium. One of the questions that thereby arises is: What forms of argumentative discourse occupy this distinctive public arena?

This chapter offers some observations on the properties of that new form of televisual discourse. For the most part, throughout its history as well as in the present, television (leaving aside dramatic output) has sought to produce forms of talk that address the "overhearing" audience more or less directly (Scannell & Cardiff, 1991). This is so even when the talk that is broadcast is ostensibly a conversation between two people face to face in a radio or television studio, such as a news interview (Heritage, 1985). What kinds of address formats come into play in contexts such as the *Ricki Lake* show, when a routine feature is that guests turn to address each other directly in the course of arguing about matters in their private lives? Specifically, therefore, I am interested in how confrontational or argumentative talk is produced in a setting where there are (a) multiple (more than two) participants, (b) an array of possible forms of address and "targeting" for contributions to a confrontation, and, significantly, (c) various kinds of audiences, from the participants in the confrontation, through the host and the studio audience, to the audience at home.

We might imagine that the mere fact that these confrontations are played out in front of a studio audience and broadcast to be heard and observed by a wider audience suffices to make them spectacular, that is, a spectacle that is played out in front of, and (like other forms of broadcast talk) specifically for the benefit of, an overhearing audience. However, close observation reveals that there are specific characteristics of the structures of talk and of participation in this show that work to facilitate the kind of confrontational talk that occurs, and that play an important role in an audience's ability to hear it *as* spectacular. What is of interest here is not individual audience members' reactions to the show as a "spectacle of confrontation" (on the lines, for instance, of Livingstone and Lunt's [1994] work on TV talk shows), but the indigenous organizational structures through which the show allows itself to be heard and experienced as such. I look at a number of aspects of this, including the overall structure of the show and the range of different participation dynamics within which the talk is produced.

I address *Ricki Lake* as a form of "mediated interaction." This interest can be traced back to the classic article by Horton and Wohl (1956) in which they described some of the basic techniques of what they called *para-social interaction* (cf. Haarman, chapter 2, this volume). They discussed the ways in which broadcasters give the impression of relating to audience members directly, and not as indistinguishable members of a "mass." These included direct address to the camera, beckonings or asides directed at the camera that situated it (and hence the viewer) as a confidante, and many others. However, Horton and Wohl (1956) paid little attention to the way in which basic structures of talk-in-interaction themselves underpin the forms of communication by which broadcasting addresses its audience. It is only more recently that conversation analysts have begun to address this issue, starting with the work on news interviews (Clayman, 1988, 1992; Heritage, 1985) and spreading out to other areas such as radio phone-ins (Hutchby, 1995, 1996a, 1996b, 1999a) and panel debates (Hutchby, 1997). In this work, one key interest has been the question of precisely how the routines and resources of face-to-face conversation are utilized and transformed in order to address the overhearing audience appropriately.

Elsewhere I have described such work as revealing the *interactional substrate* of broadcast discourse (Hutchby, 1997). This notion refers to the interactional dynamics of the live copresent talk that forms the basis of the program as it is eventually edited and broadcast—the interactional structures underlying what comes to be transmitted to the viewer. Certainly, the process of editing itself cannot be ignored in this. My focus here, however, is on the interactional dynamics of the broadcast itself, the phenomenon as it is ordinarily accessible to television viewers, and to which I as an analyst have equal access through making a recording of that piece of media output. If we were to consider what anyone watching *Ricki Lake* (or any other example of "live" broadcast talk) actually observes, then clearly it is, on one level, a pre-constituted, talk-instantiated relationship between shifting categories of speakers and recipients. However, the patterns of interaction that are observed as part of the program can be seen as unfolding within the course of the talk itself. In order to analyze that unfolding, it is necessary to find some way of moving inside the broadcast talk. As Heritage, Clayman, and Zimmerman (1988) argued:

> [I]t has become increasingly unrealistic to analyze the structure and content of [media] messages independent of the interactional medium within which they are generated. For, although the medium may not be the message, the interactional structures through which broadcast [talk] is conveyed must necessarily contribute to [its] content and appearance (pp. 79–80).

In short, the discourse of broadcasting has its own frameworks of participation and dynamics of address that operate within, and necessarily shape, the transmission that reaches the audience at home. This is what I call the interactional substrate of a show.

In what follows, I examine some aspects of the interactional substrate of the *Ricki Lake* show, and discuss the role this plays in the show's hearable character as a spectacle of confrontation. I focus on two principal dimensions: structures of turn-taking, and participation frameworks. In previous work, conversation analysts have focused mostly on the first of these. For instance, a key factor in the accomplishment of an interactional event as recognizably a "news interview" lies in the way the participants orient to more restricted patterns of turn-taking than are characteristic of ordinary conversation (Clayman, 1988; Schegloff, 1988/9). This is also a

significant factor in the particular form of cc
Ricki Lake. A richer description of the producti
context is possible, however, if we also take int
of manifold shifts in participation frameworks,
and recipiency between the participants (Go
1999a). It is by a combination of these means th
Lake achieves its hearable character as a spectac.

FRAMING CONFRONTATION TALK

The data consist of a small, randomly selected set of installments with titles such as, “If You Have Something To Say . . . Say It To My Face!” and “I’m Not Fat . . . I’m All That!.” These shows take similar forms, in which aggrieved guests get a chance to give their account of how they have been victims of some complainable behavior—such as being the butt of malicious gossip, or having a mother who so objects to their physical appearance that she refuses to be seen in public with them—before the accused are brought from backstage to join their accusers center-stage and give their side of the story. The host remains standing throughout, positioned within the audience, who sit in rows facing the stage. Shortly before the end, an “expert” (who could be anything from a psychiatrist to a magazine columnist) is brought on and seated in a large armchair to give advice to each pair about what they should do to resolve their problems.

The show has much in common with other audience participation broadcasts. For instance, it involves a studio audience in live copresence with the host and the main speakers; the host, as we will see, tends to play a role that fluctuates between mediation and advocacy; and there is some participation by an “expert” (see Livingstone & Lunt, 1994). However, the structure of the *Ricki Lake* show also has much in common with a game show. Guest participants are introduced as if contestants, within a discursive structure in which the audience are openly invited to take sides in the dispute-game. This feature is a key factor in the recognizably public character of the show’s confrontations.

The shows are divided into segments, and each segment begins with the first guest being introduced by Ricki Lake. However, first guests are introduced not simply as guests, but as particular *kinds* of occupants of the show’s discursive arena. Specifically, they are framed from the outset as the possessors of “complainable matters.” The standard format is for the host to describe the matter the guest is to complain about, before inviting the guest’s own comments. For instance:

Extract 1

	VERBAL TRACK	VISUAL TRACK
Ricki:	This is Erin. (.) .hh	*Close up on guest*
	Erin now you're having problems	.
	with your boyfrien:d Doug's	.
	best friend Michelle. (.)	.
	What's goin' on.	.

Here, Ricki categorizes the guest explicitly and solely as someone who is "having problems"—in this case with her boyfriend's "best friend"—before inviting the guest to comment on the matter. This way of categorizing not only invites but entitles the guest to speak (cf. Hester & Fitzgerald, 1999). That is, through being situated as the possessor of a complainable matter—and, for present discursive purposes, nothing more than the possessor of such a matter—the guest's presence at this point in the show is justified.

More than that, however, the introduction projects a sequential space of conditional relevance (see Schegloff, 1991): What is said next is to be heard as a complaint, one that involves another (named but as yet invisible) participant. Note, also, that in an important sense, it is the audience (the studio audience and the audience at home) who are being situated as the principal recipient of this next move, the complaint. Though the host does not say, "Tell the audience what's goin' on," the fact that the guest is named at the turn's outset ("This is Erin") implicates the audience as principal recipient of the guest's upcoming turn.

Following this introduction, the first guest is framed in close-up as she tells the story behind her complaint, prompted by the host. The talk at this point is thus produced in an interview-like framework. However, there are some important differences with the forms of broadcast interview talk previously studied in news interviews. One is that the interviewer (that is, Ricki Lake) does not refrain from reacting to the tellings of the interviewee. In fact, she not only produces reactions, but those reactions exhibit a clear stance on her part. Consider the following example, in which the host produces an emphatic reaction to the guest's remark about how long the complainable behavior of her coguest has been going on:

Extract 2

	VERBAL TRACK	VISUAL TRACK
Erin:	It's been goin' on fer a	*Shot of female audience member*
	year now and I j[us' want-	*Close up on guest*
Ricki:→	[A YEA:R?	.
Erin:	Just a- [just abou:t.	.
Audience:	[° wwuuuhuhuho°	.

Ricki:	And you've never confronted her on this issue.	*Switch to shot of host*

One thing to notice here is that the guest, Erin, appears to accord no especially remarkable status to her revelation that, "It's been goin' on fer a year now." That is, she refrains from doing anything that would serve to draw attention to the length of time itself, for example by emphasizing the length of time through placing stress on the word "year," or pausing for some kind of reaction following the announcement that the behavior has been going on "fer a year." Rather, without any noticeable pause, she goes on to the next part of the utterance, "and I jus' want-" before withdrawing from the turn in overlap with the host.

Instead, it is the host herself who draws attention to what could be described as a *particularly* complainable matter. By this I mean that if one can describe some form of bad behavior as having been going on for a year, then it can be said both that the behavior is particularly bad, and that the victim of it is being particularly victimized. This illustrates how the host monitors the guest's talk for matters that can be picked up on in pursuit of controversy or confrontation. More significantly, however, in picking up on those matters, she makes them visible for the audience, and hence, available as objects for audience (which is to say, public) reaction.

This represents a major difference with work on broadcast news interviews. As Heritage (1985) showed (see also Clayman, 1988), news interviewers tend to refrain from verbally reacting to an interviewee's talk in the course of the interviewee's answers to interviewer questions. The reason for this is that by doing so, the interviewer avoids acting as the primary recipient of the interviewee's talk (even though he or she is both the questioner and, usually, physically copresent with the answerer). That role is thereby preserved for the overhearing audience.

In the present case, by contrast, Ricki Lake acts precisely to frame the audience's role as recipient, providing the studio audience with the opportunity for reactions that are appropriate both in terms of their placement (in this case, in overlap with continuing talk that is moving on from the controversial point) and in terms of their content. Notice, then, that her utterance, "A YEA:R?," which overlaps the guest's talk, is closely followed by an audible gasp from the audience. Both these actions are designed to do a form of "negative affiliation" with the speaker—affiliation through an exhibition of dismay at the reported behavior. There is a sense in which the host and the audience are heard to be collaboratively aligned against the reported activities of the complained-about guest.

I noted earlier that Ricki Lake always stands within the part of the studio occupied by the studio audience, and it is often the case that her reactions to the talk of speakers on the platform are closely coordinated, both temporally and in terms of content (that is, the action they are designed to do), with those of the audience. The host at these points is not only situated within the audience physically or spatially, but also stands *with* the audience in a discursive sense in relation to the confrontations being played out on stage. In later extracts, I look at other ways in which the reactions of host and audience to the talk of the platform guests can be closely coordinated in terms of the host's role in actively promoting a confrontational discourse among the participants.

Returning to the overall structure: These complaints are always produced first in each segment of the show, and are always presented precisely *as* complainables. In the foregoing examples, the complaint is that someone has been talking behind the complainant's back. In other shows, as noted, it may be that the complainant's mother disapproves of him or her being overweight and refuses to be seen in public with him or her, or some other, similar kind of matter. Regardless, the complainant always speaks first.

Once the complainant has given his or her account, the respondent is introduced, typically in the following kind of way:

Extract 3

	VERBAL TRACK	VISUAL TRACK
Ricki:	Are we ready to meet Michelle gang?	*Ricki turns to side, towards audience*
Audience:	Ye:[::a::hhh A:::::hh	*Close up on guest*
Audience:	[xx-XXXXXXXXXXXXXXXXXXXXXX=	*Guest looks stage right*
Ricki:	[Michelle, come on out	.
Audience:	=[XXXXxxxxxxxxxxxxxxxxxxxxxx	.
Audience:	[↓ w:ooh BOOOOOOOOOOO ↑ wooh	*Guest 2 enters, right*

In this extract, the audience both applauds and jeers as the second guest emerges through a door and walks down a short staircase to a seat next to the first guest. Clearly, through the first speaker's telling about the complainable behavior of these second guests, the latter are already constructed in a negative light, but the very way in which they are announced reinforces this construction, and does so in a way that points up the specifically public nature of the event.

In three important senses, these second guests are presented as someone who has been or is being *revealed*. First, there is the sense that their disagreeable actions, previously confined to the private sphere of the guests' everyday lives, are now being brought to public attention. Second, there is the sense that they are now being physically revealed in order to be called to account; hence, the host typically uses formulations such as "[Guest], come on out" or "Let's bring out [guest] now." Third, and most significantly, that bringing to account is something that the audience is hearably implicated in. Notice in extract 3 how the host turns slightly toward the audience as she asks them, "Are we ready to meet Michelle, gang?"

Looking at the first few moments of the show thus begins to illustrate the important role played by the sequencing of actions in constructing an occasion for the bringing to public account of complainable actions by "ordinary" people. It is not just that these people have engaged in actions that may readily be condemned, and now they are, indeed, to be (very publicly) condemned. The organization of the talk—particularly the way in which the host both introduces, and manages her responses to the talk of, the guests—represents a key factor in the way in which confrontation on *Ricki Lake* is framed from the outset as a recognizably public spectacle, that is, an event in which the public finds available to it opportunities for involvement in both the revelation and the condemnation of complainable actions. In the next section, I turn to look in more detail at how those opportunities for responsive involvement may be actively fashioned by the principal participants.

PARTICIPATION FRAMEWORKS AND THE PRODUCTION OF CONFRONTATION

The previous section offered a very general account of the way in which confrontation on this show is framed, in the sense that participants—both studio guests and audience—are discursively and spatially situated in particular agonistic roles during the opening phases of each segment. I now ask: What are the ways in which confrontations are played out within that basic interactional framework? As we will see, the production of confrontation as a public spectacle on *Ricki Lake* is intimately bound up with the organization of talk-in-interaction on a much finer scale.

A key factor involved in this is the range of different participation frameworks that are involved in the talk as each confrontation progresses from its opening segment. As was previously discussed (Tolson, chapter 1, this volume), the notion of participation frameworks was introduced by Goffman (1974, 1981) to refer to the way in which any utterance in conversation furnishes a certain range of possibilities for recipients to situate themselves in relation to the speaker. For instance, the way in which an utterance is phrased may enable a hearer to situate himself or herself as its direct target, an indirect addressee, an overhearer, and so on. However, the term *participation framework* can refer not just to the ways in which people in different speaker categories address one another—that is, the lexical content of addressing turns—but also to the *sequential* formats in which their talk is produced.

The *Ricki Lake* show is a form of multiparty confrontation: It is not just two disputants who are involved, but a whole array of categories of participant. In this sense, there are similarities between the *Ricki Lake* show and other forms of disputatious interaction involving multiple participants in an institutional setting, principally, the professional dispute mediation hearings analyzed by Garcia (1991) and the panel-based news interview–discussion shows examined by Greatbatch (1992). In all three settings, persons with competing views on an issue are invited by a host or mediator to express and argue over their views, usually in the presence of an audience (whether consisting of other participants, a studio audience, and/or an absent audience of listeners or viewers).

A common theme of Garcia's and Greatbatch's work on these settings is that the turn-taking format itself plays a key role in whether confrontations occur or not, or at least, in the degree of confrontation that is allowed. Briefly, the presence of a central mediator often means that disputants' turns are required structurally (and also normatively) to be addressed to the mediator. This is because disputants can only legitimately speak in response to the mediator's questions. Therefore, there is a systematic bias against the possibility of direct address between the disputants (though, of course, it may still occur) and this results in an attenuated form of argument.

On the *Ricki Lake* show, by contrast, disputants routinely address one another—in fact, they may be specifically invited to do so at certain points within their segments—and the host plays a key role not just as questioner, mediator, and the target of appeals from one or both of the disputants, but also as an advocate and a key facilitator of alignment and counter-alignment within the dispute. Thus, the structures of address within the show's participation frameworks represent an important means by which confrontation may be accentuated, rather than attenuated, on *Ricki Lake* (see also the similar patterns in some exchanges on *Sally Jesse Raphael* as discussed by Brunvatne and Tolson in chapter 6).

At first sight, four principal categories of participant seem to be involved in these shows: host, studio audience, guests, and viewing audience. In fact, there are at least five, because the guests, as noted, play quite different roles, and in a highly structured way. One is always the complainant or aggrieved, whereas the other is the offending party. There may also be other guests on the platform, usually associated with one or the other side in the dispute, the presence of whom adds further dimensions to the structures of participation in the show.

These are the eight basic participation frameworks that routinely come into play on *Ricki Lake*:

Basic patterns of address on *Ricki Lake*

1. Host addresses viewing audience (talks to camera).

2. Host addresses studio audience.
3. Studio audience member addresses host.
4. Host addresses platform guest.
5. Platform guest addresses host.
6. Platform guest addresses studio audience.
7. Studio audience member addresses platform guest.
8. Platform guest addresses other platform guest.

Within each of these frames, there may be a great deal more going on than these basic descriptions suggest. For example, within any one of them, the viewing audience may be addressed overtly or covertly; and although each of them has been characterized here as dyadic, there may actually be a wide range of addressees (or *targets*, to use the term adopted by Levinson [1988]) being addressed in a wide variety of ways.

For present purposes I focus on just two of the frameworks mentioned: the host addressing platform guests (framework 4) and platform guests addressing each other (framework 8). In these two dynamics of talk on the show, we find some of the principal ways in which this form of talk is produced, or performed, not only as hearably confrontational, but as confrontational in a hearably public sense.

BETWEEN PRIVATE AND PUBLIC

One of the key themes in previous research on broadcast talk has been the question of how that talk is designed so that its audience(s) may encounter it as produced primarily for them. That is, although a great deal of talk broadcast on radio and television is, on one level, an interaction between two or more copresent speakers (such as an interviewer and an interviewee), how is it that those speakers produce their talk so that the audience can unproblematically "overhear" it? As I mentioned earlier, Heritage (1985) suggested that, in the case of news interviews, the fact that interviewers routinely refrain from producing back-channel items—or to use Schegloff's (1981) term, *continuers*—such as "mm hm," "oh," or "right" during the talk of interviewees represents an important way in which they avoid acting as the primary recipient of the interviewee's answers to their questions, leaving that role open for the listening audience. From a slightly different angle, Montgomery (1986, 1991), looking at the talk of radio disk jockeys, explored a number of ways in which this overtly monologic talk is designed so as to address the audience in subtly differentiated ways both as listeners and as participants. Hutchby (1995) brought these two

how experts on radio advice phone-ins system- such that it is hearably designed for both the a specific piece of advice, and the various ab- ening audience, through using techniques such he question" and "proxy advice-giving" (in stensibly naive questions that function to en- to provide increasingly generalized advice).

A common feature of all these studies is that broadcast talk simultaneously exhibits features characteristic of "private" talk (casual conversation) and expressly "public" talk (talk directed at a listening audience). It is in part by virtue of its being thus between the private and the public that broadcast talk achieves its qualities of sociability and utterly ordinary accessibility (Scannell, 1996). However, another way of viewing it is that the talk can often be seen as exhibiting ambivalence between whether it is designed primarily for the audience or primarily for the copresent participants. Indeed, in Hutchby (1995) I spent some time looking at one example where that ambivalence was clearly at the root of interactional problems that arose between the advice-seeking caller and the radio expert.

On the *Ricki Lake* show, this ambivalence can play an important part in the spectacular character of the confrontations between guests. I illustrate that by looking at two quite differently structured examples from the show.

Extract 4 ((Gisela is Guest 1, Tanisha is Guest 2))

	<u>VERBAL TRACK</u>	<u>VISUAL TRACK</u>
Tanisha:	Your first daughter has three, thr:ee fathers, your second one got [two.	*Two shot guests 1 & 2*
Gisela:	[↑<u>WHAT</u>?	*Close up guest 1*
Tanisha:	An' th<u>e</u>:n- the one-=	*Two shot guests 1 & 2*
Gisela:	=You don't even know anything a<u>bou</u>t me=	.
Tanisha:	=[(	.
Gisela:	=[<u>I'M</u> <u>NOT</u> pr<u>e</u>g[nant. I'm not pregnant.	.
Ricki:	=[W<u>ai</u>t. [Wait.	*Close up on host*
(?):	[( )	
Ricki:	[Tanisha how does that work, a daughter has three fa:thers?	*Brief shot of guests, then back to host*
Audience:	Ha ha ha . . .	

Here we find a good example of participation framework 8—guests addressing each other. As a result of the direct address between Gisela and Tanisha—most clearly indexed in the transcript through the repeated use of "you," but in the video also shown by the bodily orientations of the two disputants—the talk in the first few lines exhibits the same features as arguments in nonpublic, nonmediated settings. Remember that there are a number of participant categories involved in the show as an occasion for talk, yet in this particular segment of talk, it is unclear, or ambivalent, what the recipient status of the other participants is. Is this talk designed for the speaking participants alone, for the audience, or somehow for both? In an important sense, it seems, by virtue of the directly addressed exchange of argumentative turns, the audience (both in the studio and at home) is able to "look in on" a confrontation played out as a spectacle in front of them.

Of course, as in the forms of third-party mediated disputes analyzed by Garcia (1991) and Greatbatch (1992), this type of two-party, directly addressed talk only occurs on certain occasions, even though it is a much more routine, even invited, feature of these talk shows than of other examples such as panel-based interviews. As in those other settings, the host frequently intervenes in the dispute, yet there are notable differences in the kinds of interventions made and in their interactional functions.

The intervention seen in extract 4 illustrates something of this. Ricki Lake's utterance, "Tanisha how does that work, a daughter has three fathers?" has very similar features to the case in Extract 2. First of all, it picks up on a controversial point that appears in danger of falling below the conversational horizon of relevance. Note that although Gisela has initially reacted with some incredulity to Tanisha's claim that Gisela's daughter has "three fathers and your second one got two" ("WHAT?"), the argument almost immediately proceeds to a next point apparently having to do with whether Gisela is currently pregnant. (It is very difficult to hear what Tanisha says on this issue because her point is loudly overlapped both by Gisela denying that she is pregnant and by the host shouting "W<u>ai</u>t. Wait.").

The key thing about Ricki Lake's intervention is not just that it picks up on the apparent absurdity of Tanisha's claim (how could a child have three fathers), but that it picks up on it in such a way that the joke can be a joke *for the audience*. In order for the audience to take sides by reacting to this claim along with Gisela, a space needs to be provided within the rapid flow of the argument on stage to enable it to do so. Ricki's intervention succeeds in providing that space. Thus, again, we find the host standing figuratively with the audience, actively working to pick up on points of contention in order to further the audience's opportunities to take sides in the dispute being played out on stage.

This gives a sense of what I mean when I suggest that these arguments take place in—or constitute—a discursive space between the private and the public. Extract 5 offers a slightly different angle on this:

Extract 5 ((Laurie is Guest 1, Reynold is Guest 2))

	VERBAL TRACK	VISUAL TRACK
Ricki:	Are you paying child support for	*Shot of host*
	this child?	*Two shot, guests 1 & 2*
Reynold:	I haven't given her money- I've not	
	given her money, in, y'know about	
	th:ree weeks=.h=But I	*Close up on guest 2*
	have [receipts	
Laurie:	[TH:REE W:EEKS?	*Close up on guest 1*
Reynold:	I have receipts (.) fer- for all	*Two shot, guests 1 & 2*
	the money I have given her. And	.
	I've just uh the job I'm working	.
	right no:w um I've spoken with them	.
	and I told her this about a week ago.	.
	before I even knew about this show,	.
	that I've spoken with them they've	.
	taken forty dollars a week outta each	.
	p:ay ch:eck, a:nd they're gonna put it	
	in a check in h:er name sent straight to	
	h:er house.	
Ricki:	Alright.	
Laurie:	OK. We'll see it [when it happens.	
Ricki:	[What abo:ut when the	
	child got sick?	
	(.)	
Laurie:	↑O:h. OH OK, I can tell you [this part.	
Reynold:	[↓ O:H pss.	
Laurie:	OK she was sick for like three weeks and	*Close up on guest 1*
	I took her, I have the doctor bills,	*Close up on guest 2*
	they were over three hundred dollars.	*Two shot, 1 & 2*
	He told me, I ain't givin you no money	
	you shoulda taken her to the health	
	department cos it's free.	*Close up on guest 1*
	(0.5)	
Audience:	O:o[oh	
Reynold:	[↑ Isn't it? (.) Isn't it free?	*Close up on guest 2*
Audience:	[O:ooh	
Ricki:	[REYNOLD. REYNOLD.	*Close up on host*
Reynold:	↑ NO=no=no=no=[no=no:.	*Close up, guest 2*
Ricki:	[Reynold, this is your	*then two shot, 1 & 2*
	child we're talking about. Don't you	*Close up on host,*
	want the best for yo:ur ch[ild?	*moving toward stage*
Reynold:	[Yes. Yes.	*Close up on guest 2*
	I do.	
Ricki:	Well, the best is not free:.	

One way in which this extract differs from Extract 4 is that the guests do not address each other. Rather, we find two different participation frameworks in play at the same time. Whereas one of the disputants, Reynold, addresses all his talk to the host and the audience, his girlfriend shifts between directing her talk at the host/audience and directly addressing him (for instance, at the point where she says 'TH:REE W:EEKS?' she turns in her chair to face him).

The extract clearly shows the way in which the host acts not only as mediator, but as facilitator of the disputes being played out on stage. Ricki works to elicit a story about the defendant (Reynold) from the complainant: "What about when the child got sick?" Of course, on one level, this turn illustrates a certain level of pre-preparedness about the disputes that occur; that is, it is not just that the disputants are invited to play out their disputes in front of the host and audience, but the host herself evidently already knows a good deal about the key points of contention. This makes it even more clear that the host spends at least some of her time monitoring the talk for those points that can be picked up in order to provide the audience with an opportunity to react.

There are some other things of note about the utterance, "What about when the child got sick?" First, it seems unclear precisely who the target is; it could be addressed to Reynold, to Laurie, or to both of them. Yet the overall structure of the show's discursive arena, as outlined earlier, enables Laurie to hear it as addressed to her and to respond to it in the particular way that she does. In this segment, Laurie is the "first guest"—the complainant—whereas Reynold's behavior is the subject of her complaint. Ricki's utterance introduces a fresh complainable matter into the dispute. Whereas both guests potentially know about this issue and so Reynold, conceivably, could go straight into a defense of his behavior, Ricki's utterance does not provide enough information for the audience to be able to judge that behavior. This utterance thus needs to be oriented to as an invitation to tell the story rather than to respond to what is already implicitly known by those involved.

Of course, gaze direction could also be involved here as a speaker selection technique. This is a feature that we do not have access to on the basis of the video-recorded data because the camera is on Ricki at the point where she asks about the child, and it is not possible to establish exactly where her gaze is directed from the perspective of the guests on the platform. But it is noticeable that Laurie responds by nominating herself as the speaker able to tell this story ('↑O:h. OH OK, I can tell you this part'), rather than as the speaker who is specifically being selected to tell it. There is thus evidence that Laurie hears this not only as an invitation to tell the story, but as an invitation properly aimed at her, even though we cannot say whether gaze direction was also used by the host. This, along with the way the invitation is responded to by Reynold expressing his irritation at yet another issue being brought up ('↓O:H pss'), illustrates how participants themselves orient to and thus preserve the overall structures of participation already outlined.

A second point is that once again we find the host actively involving herself in the audience's reaction against the defendant's villainy. Yet here, in contrast with earlier examples, the audience's reaction (a collective, low-pitched "Ooooh") precedes that of the host. In response to the audience, Reynold himself, maintaining his earlier practice of addressing himself to the audience, speaks ("Isn't it? Isn't it free?"). Note that this utterance could just as well have been addressed directly to Laurie, but the reaction of the audience means that a three-way argument structure comes into play, in which (a) Laurie addresses the audience, (b) the audience then address themselves to Reynold, and (c) Reynold in turn addresses his response to them. This is reinforced on the video where it is possible to see that Reynold (somewhat exaggeratedly) orients himself bodily to the audience (that is, frontally) and not to Laurie, who is sitting next to him.

It is within this three-way structure that Ricki Lake now involves herself, as before, in line with the audience. Moreover, her utterance, "REYNOLD. REYNOLD," has a similar character to the audience's "Ooooh" in that both utterance types point to the sense of Reynold's (reported) actions as being "beyond the pale." In this way, once more, we observe the spectacular nature of confrontation being produced in the details of a momentary collective alignment of complainant, host, and studio audience against the actions of the defendant. Although there may be a gross sense in which this pattern of alignment is built into the show as a discursive arena, it is actually produced as relevant for the course of interaction in the local context of turn exchange in the real time unfolding of talk.

CONCLUDING REMARKS

My aim in this chapter has been to examine the interactional dynamics of the studio talk that forms the basis of the *Ricki Lake* show considered as an example of "live-event" broadcasting: a show that involves a substantial amount of spontaneous (as opposed to scripted) talk and that, in its broadcast form, effectively preserves a sense of liveness and immediacy about the events unfolding on screen. The analytic focus has been on the interactional structures underlying what is transmitted to the viewer: the indigenous frameworks of participation and dynamics of address that operate within, and necessarily shape, the "message" that reaches the audience at home. It is this that I have called the *interactional substrate* of broadcast discourse.

Part of this has been to suggest that the confrontational and controversial character of the talk is not a pre-existing factor that shapes people's participation in the show, but a practical accomplishment of the participants in local occasions of talk. This represents the standard perspective in conversation analysis on the question of institutional or otherwise "special" forms of talk-in-interaction (Schegloff, 1991). However, it is equally important to avoid the implication to be found in that perspective, that such practical accomplishments are somehow generated *ex nihilo*. In line with the sociological position that individual agency and social structures are reflexively intertwined and mutually informing (Giddens, 1984), my position is that the regularities of institutional forms of talk, whether they be actively enforced or otherwise sedimented in practice, reflexively inform the conduct of interaction for different categories of participants (Hutchby, 1996a).

This has particular implications for how we might best study the products of broadcasting. It is inadequate to view *Ricki Lake* as broadcast discourse in the simplistic sense of media analyses that focus on the mediation of "messages" between the "encoding" institutions of broadcasting and the "decoding" or receiving audience at home. As Scannell (1991b) observed, media studies continues to be dominated by such a model, mapped onto which is "a text-reader theory, derived from literary studies of written texts, to account for the relationship between the products of radio and television and their audiences" (p. 10). As he pointed out, "The combined effect of these positions is to make it well-nigh impossible to discover talk as an object of study in relation to broadcasting" (p. 10).

Concentrating on talk itself, on the other hand, leads us to treat as the focus of our attention the particular dynamics of live interaction in the studio. Although the viewer has access only to a form of reconstruction of this actual situation (albeit one that effectively reproduces its sense of liveness), as a member of the culture or language community, the resources he or she relies on to make sense of the talk are the same as those involved in the production of that talk in the first place. Focusing on these resources and their deployment reveals the interactional substrate of media messages. By looking at how the talk itself is organized, we gain insight into the very interactional production of one aspect of a mediated public event.

Audiences for broadcast talk may be either absent from or present at the site of the talk's production. Analysts have observed in the first kind of case how talk is designed to display the orientations of speakers to the "presence" of a distributed set of recipients (Heritage, 1985; Hutchby, 1995; Montgomery, 1986). In forms of broadcasting where there is a studio audience in place, however, the interaction between studio participants and the studio audience represents another, and perhaps more primary, dynamic. In an important sense, the viewing audience "looks in on" an interactive event that occurred elsewhere, but that is now being transmitted for wider public consumption.

The upshot of this is that if we want to understand the mediated, or what I have called spectacular, nature of confrontation in the genre of audience-participation talk shows, we have to study the phenomenon itself, that is, the structures of opinion formulation, disputation, and alignment building that constitute the show in and through the ongoing course of talk. These structures are only instantiated in, and made sense of through, talk itself. Certainly, that talk is broadcast, and so consumed by a wider audience than the one involved in its immediate arena of production, but it is first and foremost through the interactional substrate of mediated discourse that viewers gain access to the "spectacle of confrontation."

CHAPTER

8

"I'm out of It; You Guys Argue": Making an Issue of It on *The Jerry Springer Show*

Greg Myers

Talk shows that take personal conflicts as their topics, such as *Ricki Lake* or *The Jerry Springer Show*, have been accused of blurring the line between public and private, leading participants into insincere performances and viewers into voyeuristic spectatorship. These criticisms assume that the kinds of issues available (or not) for public discussion are already determined, and that the scenes of public and private are already defined. In this chapter I analyze the way a topic is made into a public issue, and intimate and mediated scenes linked, in one episode of *The Jerry Springer Show*. I outline four stages: (a) defining and representing stances; (b) making the stances controversial and seeking alignment; (c) making the controversy dramatic, a story with a build-up of tension and a climax; and (d) making the controversy meaningful, by generalizing from the particulars of the story. I focus on the sequential organization of turns by the host, guests, and audience, and the articulation of frames between the stage, the studio, and the broadcast. On the basis of this analysis, I argue for a reconsideration of issues of performance and sincerity of the participants and the spectatorship of the viewers.

TALK SHOW TOPICS

Academic commentators have had some difficulty keeping up with the rapid mutations of talk shows and their spin-offs. No sooner had Livingstone and Lunt (1994) published their study of the British day-time talk [illegible] diated public sphere, than the show itself began deal- [illegible] nds of personal issues usually found on the problem [illegible] ne example of a wider change, from *Donahue* (Car- [illegible] *i Lake* (Shattuc, 1997), or from early *Jerry Springer* [illegible] ocal program dealing with party political debates) to [illegible] *ger*, famous for its on-screen revelations and punch-ups. The earlier forms persist, but much of the attention has shifted to the new forms, where the following developments can be seen as an underlying change in the genre:

- from public issues ("What is poverty in Britain?" on *Kilroy*) to private issues ("You're too fat to be a drag queen" on *Ricki Lake*);
- from a focus on celebrity guests and experts (psychologists, politicians, academics) to a focus on people who were unknown before their appearance on the show and whose special entitlement is in their experiences;
- from discussion in front of an audience to a spectacle of conflict in which the studio audience is a key participant.

Fortunately the rich work on interviews, talk shows, and broadcasting during the last 10 years provides approaches that help us to understand these changes, by focusing not on the titillating topics, but on the complex interactions in which these topics are developed. It is possible to characterize the new form of talk show as a subgenre (Haarman, chapter 2, this volume) that specializes in what Hutchby (1996), writing about talk radio, called *confrontation talk*. A key question here, according to Hutchby, is why anyone wants to watch strangers argue about their own affairs. Something is engaging about argument for its own sake. Sacks (1992) touched on this point in responding to Gans' claim that controversial topics close down group conversation:

> It is regularly the case that the way one gets people participating is to have an argument. Argument may not shut down conversation, it may make for "the best conversation." The circumstances under which, when arguments occur others talk, and when arguments occur others don't talk, may have to be differentiated. And it may well be that various characterizations of who participants are, is specifically relevant to the usability of argument as a technique for generating happy conversations. (Vol. I, p. 707)

Talk shows present a genre in which topics that might end conversation, with other participants and in other settings, instead open it up.

---

[1]Robert Kilroy-Silk said in a recent interview with Michael Parkinson that he had been responding to pressure from producers to make programs on more personal topics, and he had since moved the program back to more public issues.

I argue that the proper topic and the proper scene for talk shows are not given, but have to be constructed in the course of a program. Talk shows elaborate on topics to make them something participants—and audiences—can talk about. To show this, I focus on four moments from one episode of *The Jerry Springer Show* entitled "I Won't Let You Get Married." A pregnant girl and a disapproving family are certainly matters for drama, but they are not matters for public discussion until they are made into an issue, with stances, controversy, conflict, and meanings. (Similarly, "You're too fat to be a drag queen" would seem to be a matter between the particular drag queen and his potential audience, until it is transformed into an issue for discussion).

The devices involved in the process of making an issue include Jerry's uses of interrogation, formulation, withdrawal, and generalization; the guests' responses to assessment, disagreement, or blame; and the relationships between guests' turns and responses from the studio audience. Different elements of turn-taking are crucial at different stages in the development of the issue:

- in the introduction of stances, the host's questioning, and the audience's response of "oooh" and the guest's response to the audience;
- in the development of controversy, the guests' use of silence and repetition;
- in the dramatization of conflict, the guests' pursuit of the audience's laughter and applause;
- and in the closure, the host's use of plurals, collective pronouns, and commonplaces.

At each stage, the responses are not simply determined by the format, but are worked out moment to moment, by host, guests, and audience. The slightest variation in timing or relevance can transform the way a participant is viewed.

Of course, talk shows are not just talk: there are visuals, participants' actions, camera viewpoints, and editing structures. One way of making sense of this complexity is to see the show as involving three different frames—stage, studio, and broadcast—with their own conventions of involvement, rules of interpretation, and norms of evaluation. On stage there are the guests, having their family argument and relating to each other, on one level, as family. This is the audience's way of seeing what the conflicts are, but more important to *The Jerry Springer Show*, it is the audience's chance to see the conflict enacted. It is not enough for the guests to say what the difference of opinion between them and another guest might be; they have to act out this difference. Goffman (1974) captured this ambiguity in discussing theatrical performances: "The occurrence on-stage of a verbal quarrel is not merely a verbal means of providing indirect evidence of bad relations; it constitutes a direct presentation of an event" (p. 554). For this enactment, a second frame is essential, a frame in which audience and host are watching and responding to a family drama. However, I argue that the relations are more complex than this duality might suggest. The complexity arises partly because the studio frame is sometimes bracketed off (e.g., when the host tells guests to talk to each other, not to him), and partly because it is emphasized by the interplay between backstage and frontstage (figuratively, or in *The Jerry Springer Show*, literally). Finally, the broadcast frame is emphasized at the beginning and end of the show, in the juxtaposition of camera angles that gives the broadcast audience a different view from that of the studio audience, and in the editing that constructs a whole development out of the scattered performances. These three frames have been noted before (Haarman, 1999); my point is that they are constantly articulated throughout the show, in the sense that participants' words and actions distinguish one frame from another, and also in the sense that they constantly link one frame to another.

These observations, that the issue is developed in talk, not given, and that the frames are constantly articulated, not inherently distinct, have implications for the way we understand and evaluate participants and audiences. The way a performer projects sincerity has been discussed in other genres (Montgomery, 1999; Myers, 2000a; Scannell, 1996); here we see sincerity as a matter of maintaining the proper frame for one's performance. The effects of bringing intimate and personal responses into public space has also been discussed in other contexts (Liebes, 1998; Meyrowitz, 1985); here we see that the articulation of different frames involves the broadcast audience in a complex and two-way process. The talk within the stage frame may generate further talk in the studio and broadcast frames. To refer to the Sacks quotation, "the various characterizations of who participants are" clearly govern the argument in the stage frame, where the participants come with labels attached; less obviously, in ways that remain to be explicated, they also govern the possibilities for engagement or disengagement on the part of the broadcast audience.

ESTABLISHING STANCES

The episode of *The Jerry Springer Show* analyzed here has as its title (which remains at the bottom of the screen throughout the show) "I Won't Let You Get Married." Presented like that, the story of the young girl and the unsuitable suitor is as old as Shakespearean comedy and as new as soap opera, and we may think we know all the possible roles to be played, and indeed, all that there is to be said on the topic. It is not obvious what the sides in such a debate would be, besides "Oh yes you will" and "Oh no I won't." The show has to introduce various possible stances, embody these stances in participants, dramatize their conflict, and draw a meaning from it.

Unlike an episode of such a show that might have two parties confronting each other (see Hutchby, chapter 7, this volume), this episode has a proliferating cast. There is of course the girl, Diane, or as the identifying caption on screen has it: "DIANE, 17, ENGAGED TO AND PREGNANT BY A MAN ALMOST TWICE HER AGE". There's her sister and her sister-in-law (Tina and Christina), the man (Kenny), her uncle (Jim), and her mother (Estelle). They are introduced in this order, each at a moment of tension in the discussion, and each presented as relevant to the discussion at that time. Each is associated with a stance, as suggested by the caption on screen; I consider how this stance is built up for Diane.

The title of the show gives us one stance on the situation, that of the parent who says, "I Won't Let You Get Married." Jerry's[2] introduction gives an opposing stance, that of the potential bridegroom in such a family dispute:

MS (medium shot) of Jerry in front of audience, turns from chatting to them		[applause]
	JS	very much . thank you . hey welcome to the show .what can you do when you fall in love with a teenage girl who's half your age . what if her family was willing to do anything to get you out of her life . we:ll my guests today say they'll stop at nothing to be with the girl they love

The introduction of Diane both presents her case and makes it problematic, first by the way the audience responds to Jerry's framing of the issue, and then by the way Jerry questions her:

Extract 1

MS of JS in front of audience	JS	I'd like you to meet seventeen-year-old Diane .
MS of D in front of a brick wall with house plants and books		she's engaged to a man she met . at the age of ten
	Aud	/ooo(3.0)/
	D	/[hhhhh(3.0)]/
	JS	um .

[2]I call the persona as performed on the show "Jerry," and the public person outside the show "Jerry Springer," to emphasize that the host, like the guests, is enacting a role.

MS of JS		tell us about your/
MS of D - raises hand and waves it horizontally	D	/ wasn't with him that long

Why is there this audience response? The pause after "met" is part of the signals to the audience that what follows is shocking, and they respond with an exaggerated, stylized version of an "oh," which signals that they take this as new information. That this "oooh" can be heard as stylized, like the boos at a pantomime, is suggested by Diane's first response, which is to laugh. However, before Jerry can complete his question, she interrupts, suggesting that she (belatedly) hears the emphasis on her age then as carrying an implication that must be denied without delay. She responds after the implication that she could also be seen as a victim: "the age of ten" selects one of the possible issues. The first part of Jerry's questioning establishes the possibility of stances different from hers:

Extract 2

MS of JS	JS	how old . you're seventeen now
	D	uh huh
	JS	ok . when did you start really dating him?
MS of D	D	July '96
	JS	and how old were you then?
	D	sixteen
	JS	is that a little .
MS of JS		too young to be dating an adult?(3.0)
MS of D - tosses head and smiles	D	. not in my opinion . my parents' opinion and my sister-in-law obviously yeah but . not in mine

Note the way Jerry's questions are divided up like those of a legal cross-examination; each question calls for a short answer (yes, no, or a number) and no further response or comment, and each is made the basis for a further question. He remains within the conventions of the broadcast news interview (Heritage & Greatbatch, 1991), not providing any third turns that would indicate affiliation with Diane or response to the audience.

Diane responds by reframing the issue; the age for such behavior is not a matter for reference to some shared, absolute conventions of conduct, but is a discussable matter of opinion. The phrase "not in my opinion" serves two functions, signalling both that opinions can differ and that her own opinion can be offered as hers without further support. Typically, participants in such a discussion use such an expression in what is their last turn on a topic, to signal the topic is closed (Myers, 1998). Of course, if there is just a difference of opinion, and everyone is entitled to his or her own opinion, this show would be over very quickly: it would then be a matter for a survey, not a discussion. The development of the issue depends on different stances, with further participants, being brought together in controversy.

MAKING IT CONTROVERSIAL

Each new participant is presented as being relevant to the discussion at that particular point. Jerry notes the relevance, whereas the visual juxtaposition of the participants sets up the sense of conflict. Here it is the cut to Kenny, as well as the audience response, that signals the conflict to come:

Extract 3

MS of JS Kenny is shown in an inset with the caption OUTSIDE STUDIO	JS	ok . when you started dating him you were sixteen he was how old?
MS of D	D	twenty-eight
	Aud	ooo(4.0)
MS of JS - looks at cards	JS	let's bring out your sister Tina and your sister-in-law Christina
T and C shown from side, walking onto stage. Applause continues until they are on stage	Aud	xxxxxxx
MS of Diane from front	C	how could you do this?
LS of T and C from front		look how pretty you are . he's twenty-nine he doesn't own anything
MS of D	D	do you think I care?

Christina's first turn would seem odd, out of the context of this kind of show. How can this encounter begin without the rituals that mark the opening of nearly all focused engagements (Goffman, 1971), without greeting or nod or even a turn to Diane? Why do they make no acknowledgment of the cameras and studio audience? What makes Diane's relationship and marriage available to everyone at this point as "this"? Typically, an argument requires a minimum of three moves, as Antaki (1998) outlined them: (a) speaker A makes some utterance; (b) B orients to a disputable meaning of that utterance; and (c) A confirms that disputable meaning (p. 64). Christina starts with the second of these moves, however, without responding to anything Diane has said.

All these discontinuities make sense if we see the participants as embodied stances brought together in the frame of the stage. No greeting is necessary when Diane was visible to all the other participants on monitors all during the show. The "this" is available in this situation, just as "this" is a complainable matter when one comes into a room and finds the occupant has dropped a cookie jar. Christina presents two arguments without needing to say what they are arguments for: "look how pretty you are. he's twenty-nine he doesn't own anything". This dispute is framed within the world on stage; the participants maintain a boundary that excludes the studio audience and seems to ignore their responses, even as they leave time for those responses. They are not developing their stances on an issue for a new audience; in Goffman's (1971) terms, they are enacting the dispute about which the audiences can then have opinions.

The audience, though not directly addressed, plays a key role in the development of this conflict, with laughter and applause. The audience does not simply respond, but takes sides. The talk show is, like the radio phone-ins studied by Hutchby (1997), an "alignment-saturated" forum, and all remarks are interpreted in relation to taking one side or the other. A single laugh can be heard as refusal to accept what is said:

Extract 4

T and C from behind stage, so C is facing camera as she faces D	C	Diane he doesn't own nothing . you've been living with me . look at me I'm twenty-three look at everything I own . he's twenty-nine he doesn't own anything but clothes Diane . look how pretty you are
	Aud	hh[a laugh]
	C	Diane go on look how pretty you are
T sitting	T	you could find someone your own age
	Aud	(2.0) xxxxx [pause then applause]
Christina sits down between Tina and Diane		

Christina has to go on to repeat "look how pretty you are," not because Diane failed to accept it, but because someone in the audience laughed. Laughter, as Anderson (1999) pointed out, is an ambiguous response that could mean laughing with or laughing at. Here the audience is not yet taking sides. Then Tina, sitting separated from Diane, asserts a more general rule and elicits applause. The delay in this applause, however, suggests a moment's uncertainty about recognizing this as an applause line, before a collective audience response is forthcoming. This need not mean, however, that the audience, or the whole audience, is taking this participant's side in the debate; they could simply be responding to a point scored, a telling remark, a turn-around. They are responding to the immediate interaction, not voting in a debate on an abstract issue. In a similar way, they respond to the sorts of "clap-traps" Atkinson (1984) identified for political orators; three-part lists, polar oppositions, delayed conclusions, or extreme case formulations.

The oddity of this entrance is that Tina and Christina orient physically to the frame of the program, but their words are those of a family dispute. Diane has the choice between looking forward and confirming the frame of the studio, or looking at the other participants and confirming the family fight on stage. She responds by addressing no one, looking away and remaining silent. However, silence does not work in this frame as it does in a family argument; the one thing one must do on a talk show is talk. Challenged again, her second response is to attack Tina and Christina, and this response does work to treat the issue as controversial. Again the audience responds to the form of turns as much as to the content:

Extract 5

JS walking through the audience		
front MCU	C	what does he have to offer you (2.0) what does he have to offer you . what
D looking away		does he have to offer the baby (4.0)
	Aud	hhhh(4.0)
	C	huh?
MS of JS	D	you two laughing at me you don't know [beep] [beep] [beep]
CUs of audience members	Aud	hhhoooo(7.0)
JS turns and walks across set	JS	I'm sorry . we'll leave
LS of stage from front	Aud	xxxxx(6.0)
MS of JS	JS	ok
	Aud	xxxxx(4.0)
LS from front showing T, C, and D	JS	what if she says . what if she says back to you . you know what . I love him
C faces JS	C	but we love her and that's why we're trying to talk some sense into her
	Aud	xxxxxx

The shots of individual audience members responding (almost the first in the show) focus on their response to the unbroadcastable words; that is to say, to their awareness of the broadcast frame as much as to the argument itself. In this context, Jerry's comment here represents a common move for him, disaffiliating himself and the audience from the conflict on stage. If the obscenities mark a breaching of the broadcast frame, an apparent "flooding out" of emotion (Goffman, 1974), the disaffiliation reestablishes the broadcast frame and brackets off the interaction of the guests as private. Jerry then restarts the discussion with his own hypothetical speaking for one of the participants. To speak for another is to assume established positions in the controversy; if one knows the available stances, one can provide the appropriate words (Myers, 2000b). Christina responds to him, not only in her gaze and orientation, but in the way she echoes the structure of Jerry's remark. It is this echo, this verbal turn on an apparently critical question, that signals the applause.

There is, then, a constant slippage between the internal conflict, confined on stage between the characters, and the broadcast frame, represented by Jerry standing between the stage and audience. Jerry does not just speak from the studio frame; he must also intervene in the frame of the stage to maintain the sense of controversy. This is difficult when they complain to him, as Christina does here. He has to train the participants to keep addressing their remarks to each other, and in the course of doing so, to draw attention to their lapses. Notice how Christina's and Tina's pronouns shift in the discussion that follows, from directly addressing Diane ("your father") to talking about her in the third person ("younger than she is"):

Extract 6

C he's almost old enough to be your father
T his kids . his oldest child is twelve years old . five years younger than she is
Aud xxxxx

C they lived with her mother for a month . then lived with his ex sister-in-law . for a month . then his other ex sister-in-law and / now she lives with me
JS /talk to her. I'm out of it you guys argue
Aud xxxxxx

Jerry interrupts Christina's turn to redirect her attention to Diane. In doing so, he confirms that her conflict is to be enacted on the stage, not addressed to him or the audience. In terms of participation roles (Goffman, 1981), we must remain eavesdroppers for the controversy to be enacted. However, even with this juxtaposition of differing views, emphasized by spatial arrangement and audience alignment, there is still no drama, no narrative of how the views conflict, no pattern of tension rising and being released. Something else has to *happen* in the show.

MAKING IT DRAMATIC

The Jerry Springer Show is famous for its fights. As with the development of controversy, the show's performance of conflict depends on a shifting among several frames, bracketing off the actions of guests while also interpreting them. As with any entertainment program involving violence, however, the thrill is in the potential for violence, in emotional conflict pushed that far and released that quickly, rather than in the clumsy amateur fisticuffs themselves. The tension has to be so strong that it threatens to overwhelm the studio setting of the show. Whereas the essential tension in the development of controversy was between stage with guests and studio with audience, here it is between frontstage and backstage, with the sense of barely suppressed anger being kept just off the set.

The frontstage–backstage division can be seen in one surprising cut, that passes unnoticed at first between two of Jerry's sentences: "There's another member of the family now that has an opinion on this / first Jim you are the uncle of Diane." Jim is now introduced at a moment of tension, but unlike the other guests, he is not seen coming on stage. A section has been cut out, and we are soon given a reason for this cut. Jim, like Diane, is introduced in courtroom examination style:

Extract 7

LS of JS in studio audience	JS	um there's another member of the family now that has an opinion on this
MS of Jim on stage		first Jim you are
LS of JS		the uncle of Diane
	J	yes I am
	JS	you also
CU of Jim		knew know um Kenny
MS of JS	J	very well
	JS	how do you know Kenny
CU of Jim	J	I met him . about six seven years ago through . <u>my</u> wife
MS of JS		and her brother
	JS	and Kenny lived with you for a while
CU of Jim	J	no: yes . yes he did
	JS	ok . so you and Kenny were friends
inset box showing Kenny	J	yes
captioned BACKSTAGE	JS	you in fact introduced . uh Kenny to your niece Diane

	J	right
MS of JS	JS	and yet when you come out here now . you attack him like
	Aud	hh . hh [two short laughs]
	J	Diane
	JS	what was <u>that</u> about

Each of Jerry's statements, because they convey information known to Jim and flout the maxim of quantity, carry the implicature for the audience that this information is relevant to Jim's stance: he knows Kenny, Kenny lived with him, he introduced Kenny to Diane. Then the unseen violence is presented as relevant to this line of questioning and to his interactions on stage. The audience is laughing here after a reference to an event they have seen and we have not; the tension is built without us having to see the violence. In a similar way, bringing Kenny back on stage, accompanied by two beefy security guards ostentatiously holding his arms, suggests the possibility of physical violence.

Jim responds to the question about his outburst by telling a story, still short of breath, and by making a promise. When Kenny is brought out, Jerry does the kind of summary for Jim that he has offered to the other participants, summarizing the case from one stance:

Extract 8

MS of Jim	J	Diane was ten years old . and she used to come down and spend the the summers with me when school was out .
MS of JS		cause me and Diane are real close .
MS of Jim. He looks to the right. Kenny is brought out, arms held by two security guards		she's my favourite niece . and . I'll protect her to my dying day . ok
	Aud	hh [scattered laughter]
JS	JS	ok . ok what if you're but these two <u>love</u> each other .
CU of Kenny		
JS		you introd<u>u</u>ced him to her she is now seventeen just about eighteen years of age .
MS of Jim and Christina		<u>you</u> may not have chosen him .
JS		for her but <u>she</u> is making a decision now that she loves him <u>he</u> loves her apparently . what are you doing fighting him?
LS of whole stage	J	he loves her?
MCU of Jim		loves her my ass .
CU of Kenny		(he don't know what love is)
LS of whole stage	Aud	xxx hhh (7.0)

MS of JS then JS walking back across the audience, head down	JS	ok (1.0) without fighting you guys talk you talk

Jim's first conclusion gets no applause, even though the explicit promise would usually signal audience response. He is looking to the right, at Kenny's entrance, but he is lacking an opponent here and must turn to Jerry for a receipt. Once Kenny is brought out, Jim's overt hostility is greeted with applause.

Again Jerry disaffiliates himself both from Jim and from the applause of the audience; he reasserts the stage frame of "you guys talk." His movement back across the studio enacts his own withdrawal. He is not so much the ringmaster to the circus (as his autobiography would have it) as the Governor in *Romeo and Juliet*, or the Duke of Vienna in *Measure for Measure*, looking on and trying to persuade the participants to be wiser. This is a pattern repeated throughout the show: Different stances lead to conflict and to outbreaks of violence or overt hostility, but then Jerry aligns the program with lawyerly questioning, reasons, discussion. It is the rhythm of rising tension and sudden release that enacts the emotional drama of the controversy. Even if the fight is cut out, the spectacle of Kenny flanked with guards conveys its own sense of imminent conflict. The tension must be maintained, and built, until the planned climax, when the mother comes in.

MAKING IT MEANINGFUL

The difficulty for the *Jerry Springer Show* is not provoking conflict, but concluding it. This is not a therapeutic show, like *Donahue*, *Oprah Winfrey*, or even the early *Ricki Lake*, where conflicts may be resolved, people brought together, judgment or advice given, lives changed. The conflict that has been dramatized has to be reinterpreted to have general meanings apart from this case. This is not just to provide a gloss of respectability on voyeuristic entertainment; the emergence of more general meanings is part of the process of making the enactment available to a broadcast audience. After the enactment of particular conflicts and the unpacking of particular grudges (did Kenny ask Jim for drugs? does Diane have to live with Christina?), the case is restated as a single issue, and as an issue on which one can refer to general norms, on which the broadcast viewer can, and indeed must, have an opinion.

The usual resolution comes with Jerry's "Final Thoughts." This is a slot that he began when he was a newscaster, a brief homily to camera, off the usual stage of the show, without audience response. As he has noted

(Springer, 1999), he has to write this speech out before the program, so it is about the abstract issue to be presented, not the interaction we just saw:

Extract 9

title: "Springer's Final Thoughts"

JS you know older men younger women . in
other societies it's hardly an issue . but
here age differences tend to raise
eyebrows and looks and comments of
disapproval . I admit I'm often amazed at
how judgmental so many of us become about
other people's romances . inevitably we
hear criticism where wherever there's a
difference in age race religion or income
. how could those two be together we
wonder . and yet shouldn't the real
question be . if two people like each
other or love each other so long as
they're both adults why should anybody
else care . after all with all the hate
that still exists in the world why get
bent out of shape when two people choose
to love one another . that's not to say
that the relationship we observed today
doesn't have problems . it does . but the
problem is not age . it's character . it's
whether Kenny really loves Diane . whether
he's willing to work at the relationship .
provide and sacrifice for her . whether
he's the best choice for her regardless of
their age . maybe this relationship is
wrong . but if we're focusing on the age .
we're missing the point . till next time .
take care of yourself . a:nd each other

Jerry's closing speech, the longest turn in the program, does not just provide a moralistic commentary; for our purposes, what is important is that it makes the particular case general. Rapley and Antaki (1998), drawing on Billig (1987), showed how such a move is characteristic of research interviews. In their data, the interviewer formulates the interviewee's responses to make them useful in the frame of the research, and thus trains the interviewee to recognize what kind of response is needed. Here the issue is what sort of generalization can be made from the story of Diane, Kenny, and the family, a generalization that can make it useful in the frame of the broadcast. Jerry generalizes their particulars in a series of stages:

- our setting is invoked as one society among many: "here"
- viewers are included in a collective "we"
- they are made plural: "older men younger women"
- rejected opinions are attributed to hypothetical reported thought: "How could those two be together?"
- the problem is rephrased in general, hypothetical terms: "If two people like each other"
- evaluations are made by reference to commonplaces: "with all the hate that exists in the world"
- the problem is rephrased, "not age. it's character"
- the conclusion is a moral evaluation of our own position, not that of the guests, in a conditional form that makes it relevant to future action.

This is not a resolution for the guests themselves, then, but a sermon on the text of the program. In this respect it is similar to the homilies delivered in other talk shows where guests' problems are the focus for consensual moral lessons (Brunvatne & Tolson, chapter 6, this volume). However, Jerry's "Final Thoughts" are distinctive in that (a) they are spoken by the host himself and not an invited expert and (b) they are separate from the studio frame, with no pretense that they are "live." At the same time however, although Jerry always gets the final word, the guests and audience members have been trying throughout the show to support their own generalizations while rejecting others: love cannot be thwarted, marriage requires both partners to contribute, children must be protected from child abuse, children must show respect to older members of the family. The sensational titles, the defensive responses to Jerry's questions, the accusations between guests, and the "ooo"s of the audience are premised on the assumption that there are shared and invariable standards for judgment of what is acceptable.

This formal conclusion is brought off by a complicated diegetic reshuffle of events that we must assume happened in this order:

1. audience greets Jerry
2. Jerry greets guests
3. audience responds to guests
4. Jerry says good-bye to guests and audience
5. audience departs
6. Jerry records final thoughts
7. Jerry and guests reassemble in green room after the show.

However, in this particular show these events are shown in this order: 1, 2, 3, 4, 5, 7, 6. In this broadcast, after all the participants have been introduced, and after the comments from the studio audience, we see Jerry in the empty studio, after the guests have gone:

Extract 10

wipe to empty studio, JS sitting in one of the seats	JS	hi normally at this point we would end the show . but things got so heated after the show that we decided to show you what happened . so . what you're about to see now is what happened in the green room once the guests left the stage . take a look at this

The move backstage is typical of the program, as we have seen, but this sort of disruption of temporal sequence is not. This suggests the real drama is always being acted out backstage: "Take a look at this." The suggestion is that we see these people off camera (though of course there is a single hand-held camera there, whipping back and forth between them as they speak, in the style of fly-on-the-wall documentaries). The surprise is that there are no surprises; what they are like backstage is what they are like on stage, except that now we are told to see this as "so heated." It works, not by what people say or do in the green room, but by how it is framed, as the climax to the process of setting up stances and dramatizing controversy.

CONCLUSION

I maintain that the interaction on *The Jerry Springer Show* can be seen as a process of making an issue out of a particular situation that was not necessarily an issue before this work. The process involves the turn-taking of host, guest, and audience; articulation of the frames of stage, studio, and broadcast; and stages of representing stances, juxtaposing them in controversy, enacting a conflict, and bringing resolution by generalizing the meanings.

This analysis draws on other recent analyses of conflict talk (Anderson, 1999; Hutchby, 1997) and other analyses of the talk show format (Haarman, 1999, & chapter 2, this volume; Tolson, 1991). However, the focus on issue making leads to a new perspective on common criticisms of talk shows. These criticisms might be summarized under the headings of *sincerity* (how guests' performances relate to their real feelings), and *spectacle* (how watching these performances affects the audiences's judgment).

Worries about sincerity and authenticity of the performances run through press reports, audience comments, and Jerry's own responses. Some aspects of staging are taken as part of the format: the flowers provided by the show, ready for Kenny to offer clumsily to Diane, the bouncers in their front row seats ready for fights, the carefully controlled structure of introduction of participants, and the participants' own sometimes wooden delivery. However, the audience cannot simply take it all as a simulation; these have to be particular people with real problems to have the desired effect. Kenny's outrage at the accusation, or Diane's worry about how her relationship looks, must be real; otherwise the response to them would be like the response to soap opera characters, which it is not. A way of understanding this tension might be found in Goffman's (1974) comments on frames and sincerity: "To be 'natural,' then, is not merely to seem at ease, but to be acting in such a way as to convince others that the apparent frame is in fact the actual one. That is what is meant, functionally speaking, by sincerity and spontaneity" (p. 487). In *The Jerry Springer Show*, the effect of insincerity arises when a participant performs in one frame what would be appropriate only to another. I argued that the show depends on keeping the frames of stage, studio, and broadcast distinct. It will seem insincere if Kenny offers Diane flowers as an intimate gesture (stage) but conveys in any way that the gesture is for the camera (broadcast). It will seem insincere if Diane's gesture of dismissal of Christina with her hand is seen as saving face with the audience, rather than as a spontaneous response to Christina's question. It will seem insincere if an audience member gives advice to the guests on stage, but seems to be holding on to his or her turn of talk, stepping outside his or her role as representative of the audience.

On the other hand, host, guests, and audience can convey naturalness when they stay within the frame, even if the frame itself is highly artificial. Thus Christina's opening outburst, or later, Kenny's angry entry on stage, are seen as natural in the progress of the conflict set up on stage. The "ooo"s and applause and laughs of the audience are seen as natural to their position of watchers who share a normal code of behavior. "Naturalness" means not just doing the appropriate thing, but doing it with detail of gesture, and the right timing, and in the right setting. Diane's delay in responding to Tina and Christina in Extract 3 plays as appropriate to the frame of the family argument on stage; her response to the audience's "ooo"s conveys her awareness of how her words are taken up. Kenny's sincerity of anger is conveyed not just by his violent outbursts, but by his controlled nodding, back in the studio frame, listening to Jim. The issue, as Goffman (1974) reminded us, is not whether a given set of actions is real or unreal, but how it is performed and interpreted.

The other criticism often made of such talk show programs concerns their effect on the television viewer, who comes to treat such intimate, private encounters as spectacle. Some earlier discussion of talk shows (e.g., Livingstone & Lunt 1994) focused on the engagement of the audience in a mediated public sphere. Here the audience seems only to watch. Accordingly, *The Jerry Springer Show* seems to fit Barthes' (1972) description of wrestling as spectacle (a connection also made by Haarman in chapter 2):

> We are therefore dealing with a real Human Comedy, where the most socially-inspired nuances of passion (conceit, rightfulness, refined cruelty, a sense of 'paying one's debts') always felicitously find the clearest sign which can receive them, express them, and triumphantly carry them to the confines of the hall. (p. 18).

Gestures on *The Jerry Springer Show* are also calculated to carry clear signals of good and evil to a baying audience, an audience that can be relied on to share a clear moral code.

Barthes was talking about wrestling seen live in some smoky, noisy, spot-lit hall, however, not about the mediated passions of talk shows with their double audience. Thompson (1995) focused on this doubleness, and on the double role of the studio audience as spectators to talk shows: providing feedback to the guests on stage, and modeling responses for the broadcast audience, members of which may be watching alone. However, neither Barthes' "intelligible spectacle" nor Thompson's "mediated interaction" quite fits the process we saw here, in which the different frames of stage, studio, and broadcast are carefully articulated. The studio audience for *The Jerry Springer Show* is not an assembly of witnesses to an event, they are part of the event. They have a range of functions at different stages of the development of the issue: taking sides, evaluating performances, keeping score. They are not models for the response of the broadcast audience, they are another part of the cast, a chorus commenting on and reaching out to join in the action. The broadcast audience is given a range of ways of responding, in a development that allows for conflict, closure, and the usability of the particulars.

The real topic of *The Jerry Springer Show*, week in and week out, is what can be discussed, and how, and by implication, what can't be discussed. It makes public interactions that would usually remain private, and dramatizes conflicts that, without the cameras, might not break out at all. It works the other way as well, developing these materials so that they can be related to other lives. Long before Jerry Springer, Goffman (1974) asked us to see television watching as an extension, not a denial, of our individual projects of identity:

> For there is one thing that is similar to the warm hours we now spend wrapped in television. It is the time we are prepared to spend recounting our own experience or waiting an imminent turn to do so. True, we seem to have foregone some of this personal activity in favor of the work of professionals. But what we have given up thereby is not the world but a more traditional way of incorporating its incorporation of us. (p. 550)

Goffman compared the experience of television watching, not to other experiences of performance, but to the ordinary round of talk at dinner or in a pub. His last phrase pointed to the reflexivity that seems to be involved in the experience of television. The television watcher is not simply drawn into this world of freaks and weirdoes and misfits, but considers how this world includes him or her. Television is not separating us from the world, but providing another form of the endless provisional tries we make at performing ourselves and observing the performances of others.

REFERENCES

Abt, V., & Seesholtz, M. (1994). The shameless world of Phil, Sally and Oprah: Television talk shows and the deconstructing of society. *Journal of Popular Culture, 28*(1), 171–191.

Acland, C. R. (1995). *Youth, murder, spectacle: The cultural politics of "youth in crisis."* Boulder: Westview Press.

Anderson, L. (1999). Audience participation and the representation of political process in two British talk shows. In L. Haarman (Ed.), *Talk about shows: La Parola e lo Spettacolo* (pp. 53–100). Bologna: CLUEB.

Antaki, C. (1998). A conversation analytic approach to arguments. In M. Bondi (Ed.), *Forms of argumentative discourse* (pp. 71–84). Bologna: CLUEB.

Atkinson, J. M. (1984). *Our masters' voices.* London: Methuen.

Avery, R., & Ellis, D. (1979). Talk radio as an interpersonal phenomenon. In G. Gumpert & C. Cathcart (Eds.), *Inter/Media* (pp. 108–115). New York: Oxford University Press.

Bamberg, M. (1997). Positioning between structure and performance. *Journal of Narrative and Life History, 7,* 335–342.

Bakhtin, M. (1968). *Rabelais and his world.* Cambridge, MA: MIT Press.

Bakhtin, M. (1986). The problem of speech genres. In *Speech genres and other late essays* (V. W. McGhee, Trans., pp. 60–102). Austin: University of Texas Press.

Barker, M., & Petley, J. (Eds.). (1997). *Ill effects: The media/violence debate.* London: Routledge.

Barthes, R. (1972). The world of wrestling (pp. 15–26). In *Mythologies* (A. Lavers, Trans.). New York: Hill and Wang. (Original work published 1957)

Bauman, R. (1992). Disclaimers of performance. In J. Hill & J. Irvine (Eds.), *Responsibility and evidence in oral discourse* (pp. 182–196). Cambridge, UK: Cambridge University Press.

Bell, P., & van Leeuwen, T. (1994). *The media interview: Confession, contest, conversation.* Kensington, NSW: University of New South Wales Press.

Billig, M. (1987). *Arguing and thinking.* Cambridge, UK: Cambridge University Press.

Blum-Kulka, S. (1997). *Dinner talk: Cultural patterns of sociability and socialization in family discourse.* Mahwah, NJ: Lawrence Erlbaum Associates.

Blum-Kulka, S. (2000). Gossipy events at family dinners: Negotiating sociability, presence and the moral order. In J. Coupland (Ed.), *Small talk* (pp. 214–240). London: Longman.

Blumler, J., & Gurevitch, M. (1995). *The crisis of public communication*. London: Routledge.

Brown, P., & Levinson, S. (1987). *Politeness: Some universals in language usage*. Cambridge, UK: Cambridge University Press.

Bruner, J. (1986). *Actual minds, possible worlds*. Cambridge, MA: Harvard University Press.

Carbaugh, D. (1988). *Talking American: Cultural discourses on Donahue*. Norwood, NJ: Ablex.

Carpignano, P., Andersen, R., Aronowitz, S., & Difazio, W. (1990). Chatter in the age of electronic reproduction: Talk television and the "public mind." *Social Text, 25*(6), 33–55.

Clayman, S. (1988). Displaying neutrality in television news interviews. *Social Problems, 35*, 474–492.

Clayman, S. (1992). Footing in the achievement of neutrality. In P. Drew & J. Heritage (Eds.), *Talk at work: Interaction in institutional settings* (pp. 163–198). Cambridge, UK: Cambridge University Press.

Coates, J. (1996). *Women talk: Conversation between women friends*. Oxford: Blackwell.

Coates, J. (2000). *Men's stories: The role of narrative in men's talk*. Oxford: Blackwell.

Cohen, S. (1972). *Folk devils and moral panics*. London: MacGibbon & Kee.

Crittenden, J. (1971). Democratic functions of the open mike forum. *Public Opinion Quarterly, 35*, 200–210.

Dahlgren, P. (1995). *Television and the public sphere*. London: Sage.

Davis, S., & Mares, M. (1998). Effects of talk show viewing on adolescents. *Journal of Communication, 48*(3), 69–86.

Drew, P., & Heritage, J. (Eds.). (1992). *Talk at work: Interaction in institutional settings*. Cambridge, UK: Cambridge University Press.

Fairclough, N. (1989). *Language and power*. London: Longman.

Fairclough, N. (1994). Conversationalization of public discourse and the authority of the consumer. In R. Keat, N. Whiteley, & N. Abercrombie (Eds.), *The authority of the consumer* (pp. 253–268). London: Routledge.

Fairclough, N. (1995). *Media discourse*. London: Arnold.

Ferrara, W. K. (1994). *Therapeutic ways with words*. Oxford & New York: Oxford University Press.

Firth, J. R. (1950). Personality and language in society. *Sociological Review*, 42, 37–52.

Fiske, J. (1987). *Television culture*. London: Routledge.

Foucault, M. (1977). *Discipline and punish*. Harmondsworth, UK: Penguin.

Foucault, M. (1978). *The history of sexuality: Vol. 1*. New York: Random House.

Foucault, M. (1982). The subject and power. In H. L. Dreyfus & P. Rabinow (Eds.), *Michel Foucault: Beyond structuralism and hermeneutics* (pp. 208–226). London & New York: Harvester Wheatsheaf.

Garcia, A. (1991). Dispute resolution without disputing: How the interactional organization of mediation hearings minimizes argument. *American Sociological Review, 56*, 818–835.

Garnham N. (1995). The media and narratives of the intellectual. *Media, Culture & Society, 17*, 359–384.

Giddens, A. (1984). *The constitution of society*. Cambridge, UK: Polity Press.

Gledhill, C. (1987). The melodramatic field: An investigation. In C. Gledhill (Ed.), *Home is where the heart is: Studies in melodrama and the woman's film* (pp. 5–39). London: BFI Publishing.

Goffman, E. (1959). *The presentation of self in everyday life*. New York: Doubleday.

Goffman, E. (1971). *Relations in public: Microstudies of the public order*. New York: Basic Books.

Goffman E. (1974). *Frame analysis: An essay on the organization of experience*. (Reprinted in 1986). Boston: Northeastern University Press.

Goffman, E. (1981). *Forms of talk*. Philadelphia: University of Pennsylvania Press.

Goldberg, J. A. (1990). Interrupting the discourse on interruptions: An analysis in terms of relationally neutral, power and rapport-oriented acts. *Journal of Pragmatics, 14*, 883–903.

Goodwin, M. H. (1990). *He-said–she-said: Talk as social organisation among Black children*. Bloomington: Indiana University Press.

Gray, E. D. (1989). The daytime talk show as a women's network. In R. R. Rush & D. Allen (Eds.), *Communications at the crossroads: The gender gap connection* (pp. 83–91). Norwood, NJ: Ablex.

Greatbatch, D. (1986). Aspects of topical organisation in news interviews: The use of agenda shifting procedures by interviewees. *Media, Culture & Society, 8*, 441–455.

Greatbatch, D. (1988). A turn-taking system for British news interviews. *Language in Society, 17*, 401–430.

Greatbatch, D. (1992). On the management of disagreement between news interviewees. In P. Drew & J. Heritage (Eds.), *Talk at work* (pp. 268–301). Cambridge, UK: Cambridge University Press.

Grice, H. P. (1975). Logic and conversation. In P. Cole & J. Morgan (Eds.), *Syntax and semantics* (Vol. 3, pp. 41–58). New York: Academic Press.

Guardian (1998). Jerry Springer show to ban all violence. *May 2*, p. 17.

Guardian (1999a). BBC admits talk shows were faked. *February 12*, p. 5.

Guardian (1999b). Talk show accused of driving man to murder. April 3, p. 19.

Haag, L. (1993). Oprah Winfrey: The construction of intimacy in talk show settings. *Journal of Popular Culture, 26*(4), 115–121.

Haarman, L. (1997). Argument style and performance in the audience discussion show. In G. Bussi, M. Bondi, & M. Gatta (Eds.), *Understanding argument: La logica informale del discorso* (pp. 71–90). Bologna: CLUEB.

Haarman, L. (1999). Performing talk. In L. Haarman (Ed.), *Talk about shows: La Parola e lo Spettacolo* (pp. 1–53). Bologna: CLUEB.

Habermas, J. (1984). The public sphere: An encyclopedia article (1964). *New German Critique 3*, 49–55.

Halliday, M. A. K., & Hasan, R. (1985). *Language, context, and text: Aspects of language in a social-semiotic perspective*. Oxford: Oxford University Press.

Heaton, J., & Wilson, N. (1995). *Tuning in trouble: Talk TV's destructive impact on mental health*. San Francisco: Jossey-Bass.

Heritage, J. (1985). Analyzing news interviews: Aspects of the production of talk for an overhearing audience. In T. van Dijk (Ed.), *Handbook of discourse analysis* (Vol. 3, pp. 95–117). New York: Academic Press.

Heritage, J., Clayman, S., & Zimmerman, D. (1988). Discourse and message analysis: The micro-structure of mass media messages. In R. P. Hawkins, J. M. Wiemann, & S. Pingree (Eds.), *Advancing communication science: Merging mass and interpersonal processes* (pp. 77–109). London: Sage.

Heritage, J., & Greatbatch, D. (1991). On the institutional character of institutional talk: The case of news interviews. In D. Boden & D. Zimmerman (Eds.), *Talk and social structure: Studies in ethno-methodology and conversation analysis* (pp. 93–137). Cambridge, UK: Polity Press.

Heritage, J., & Watson, D. (1979). Formulations as conversational objects. In G. Psathas (Ed.), *Everyday language* (pp. 123–162). New York: Irvington.

Hester, S., & Fitzgerald, R. (1999). Category, predicate and task: Some organizational features in a radio talk show. In P. Jalbert (Ed.), *Media studies: Ethnomethodological approaches.* Washington, DC: University Press of America.

Holmes, J. (1995). *Women, men and politeness.* London: Longman.

Horton, D., & Wohl, R. (1956). Mass communication and para-social interaction: Observations on intimacy at a distance. *Psychiatry, 19,* 215–229.

Hutchby, I. (1991). The organization of talk on talk radio. In P. Scannell (Ed.), *Broadcast talk* (pp. 119–137). London: Sage.

Hutchby, I. (1995). Aspects of recipient design in expert advice-giving on call-in radio. *Discourse Processes, 19,* 219–238.

Hutchby, I. (1996a). *Confrontation talk: Arguments, asymmetry, and power on talk radio.* Mahwah, NJ: Lawrence Erlbaum Associates.

Hutchby, I. (1996b). Power in discourse: The case of arguments on a British talk radio show. *Discourse and Society, 7,* 481–498.

Hutchby, I. (1997). Building alignments in public debate: A case study from British TV. *Text, 17*(2), 161–179.

Hutchby, I. (1999a). Frame attunement and footing in the organization of talk radio openings. *Journal of Sociolinguistics, 3,* 41–64.

Hutchby, I. (1999b). Rhetorical strategies in audience participation debates on radio and TV. *Research on Language and Social Interaction, 32*(3), 243–268.

Hutchby, I., & Wooffitt, R. (1998). *Conversation analysis.* Cambridge, UK: Polity Press.

Hymes, D. (1967). Models of the interaction of language and social setting. *Journal of Social Issues, 23.*

Hymes, D. (1974). *Foundations in sociolinguistics: An ethnographic approach.* Philadelphia: University of Pennsylvania Press.

Hymes, D. (1981). *"In vain I tried to tell you": Essays in Native American ethnopoetics.* Philadelphia: University of Pennsylvania Press.

Jefferson, G. (1978). Sequential aspects of storytelling in conversation. In J. Schenkein (Ed.), *Studies in the organisation of conversational interaction* (pp. 219–248). New York: The Free Press.

Joyner Priest, P. (1995). *Public intimacies: Talk show participants and tell-all TV.* Cresskill, NJ: Hampton Press.

Krause, A., & Goering, E. (1995). Local talk in the global village: An intercultural comparison of American and German talk shows. *Journal of Popular Culture, 29*(2), 189–206.

Labov, W., & Fanshel, D. (1977). *Therapeutic discourse: Psychotherapy as conversation.* New York: Academic Press.

Labov, W., & Waletsky, J. (1967). Nararative analysis: Oral versions of personal experience. In J. Helm (Ed.), *Essays on the verbal and visual arts* (pp. 12–44). Seattle: University of Washington Press.

Landeman, J. (1995). The discursive space of identity: *The Oprah Winfrey Show. Metro, 103,* 37–44.

Langer, J. (1981). Television's "personality system." *Media, Culture and Society, 3*(4), 351–365.

Leith, D. (1995). Tense variation as a performance feature in a Scottish folktale. *Language in Society, 24*(1), 53–75.

Levinson, S. (1988). Putting linguistics on a proper footing: Explorations in Goffman's concepts of participation. In P. Drew & A. J. Wootton (Eds.), *Erving Goffman: Exploring the interaction order* (pp. 161–227). Cambridge, UK: Polity Press.

Liebes, T. (1998). Television's disaster marathons: A danger for democratic processes? In T. Liebes & C. Curran (Eds.), *Media, ritual, and identity* (pp. 71–85). London: Routledge.

Liebes, T. (1999). Displaying the news: The Israeli talkshow as public space. *Gazette, 61*(2), 113–125.

Livingstone, S., & Lunt, P. (1992). Expert and lay participation in television debates: An analysis of audience discussion programmes. *European Journal of Communication, 7*(1), 9–35.

Livingstone, S., & Lunt, P. (1994). *Talk on television: Audience participation and public debate.* London: Routledge.

Lupton, D. (1994). Talking about sex: Sexology, sexual difference, and confessional talk shows. *Genders, 20*, 45–65.

Marriott, S. (1996). Time and time again: "Live" television commentary and the construction of replay talk. *Media, Culture & Society, 18*, 69–86.

Masciarotte G.-J. (1991). C'mon girl: Oprah Winfrey and the discourse of feminine talk. *Genders, 11*, 81–110.

McGuigan, J. (1992). *Cultural populism.* London: Routledge.

McLaughlin, L. (1993). Chastity criminals in the age of electronic reproduction: Re-viewing talk television and the public sphere. *Journal of Communication Inquiry, 17*(1), 41–55.

McQuail, D. (1987). *Mass communication theory: An introduction.* London: Sage.

Meyrowitz, J. (1985). *No sense of place.* Oxford: Oxford University Press.

Montgomery, M. (1986). DJ talk. *Media, Culture & Society, 8*, 421–440.

Montgomery, M. (1991). "Our Tune": A study of a discourse genre. In P. Scannell (Ed.), *Broadcast talk* (pp. 138–177). London: Sage.

Montgomery, M. (1999). Talk as entertainment: The case of *The Mrs. Merton Show.* In L. Haarman (Ed.), *Talk about shows: La Parola e lo Spettacolo* (pp. 101–150). Bologna: CLUEB.

Munson, W. (1993). *All talk: The talk show in media culture.* Philadelphia: Temple University Press.

Myers, G. (1994). *Words in ads.* London: Arnold.

Myers, G. (1998). Displaying opinions: Topics and disagreement in focus groups. *Language in Society, 27*, 85–111.

Myers, G. (2000a). Sincerity and entitlement in broadcast interviews about the death of Princess Diana. *Media, Culture & Society, 22*, 167–185.

Myers, G. (2000b). Unspoken speeches: Hypothetical uses of reported speech. *Text, 19*, 571–590.

Negt, O., & Kluge, A. (1990). Selections from "Public opinion and practical knowledge: Toward an organizational analysis of proletariat and middle class public opinion." *Social Text, 25/26*, 24–32.

Nelson, E., & Robinson, E. (1994). Reality talk or telling tales? The social construction of sexual and gender deviance on a television talk show. *Journal of Contemporary Ethnography, 23*(1), 51–78.

Norrick, N. (1998). Retelling stories in spontaneous conversation. *Discourse Processes, 22*, 75–97.

Ochs, E., & Taylor, C. (1992). Family narrative as political activity. *Discourse & Society, 3*, 301–340.

Peck, J. (1995). TV talk shows as therapeutic discourse: The ideological labor of the televised talking cure. *Communication Theory, 5*(1), 58–81.

Probyn, E. (1993). Television's *Unheimlich* home. In B. Massumi (Ed.), *The politics of everyday fear* (pp. 269–283). Minneapolis: University of Minnesota Press.

Rapley, M., & Antaki, C. (1998). "What do you think about . . . ?": Generating views in an interview. *Text, 18*, 587–608.

Rimmon-Keenan, S. (1983). *Narrative fiction: Contemporary poetics.* London & New York: Methuen.

Sacks, H. (1978). Some technical considerations of a dirty joke. In J. Schenkein (Ed.), *Studies in the organisation of conversational interaction* (pp. 249–269). New York: Academic Press.

Sacks, H. (1992). Lectures on conversation (Vols. 1 & 2). Cambridge, MA, & Oxford: Blackwell.

Scannell, P. (Ed.). (1991a). *Broadcast talk*. London: Sage.

Scannell P. (1991b). Introduction: The relevance of talk. In P. Scannell (Ed.), *Broadcast talk* (pp. 1–13). London: Sage.

Scannell, P. (1996). *Radio, television, and modern life*. Oxford: Blackwell.

Scannell, P., & Cardiff, D. (1991). *A social history of British broadcasting, Vol. 1*. Oxford: Blackwell.

Schegloff, E. A. (1981). Discourse as an interactional achievement: Some uses of "uh-huh" and other things that come between sentences. In D. Tannen (Ed.), *Analyzing discourse: Text and talk* (pp. 71–93). Washington, DC: Georgetown University Press.

Schegloff, E. A. (1988/9). From interview to confrontation: Observations on the Bush–Rather encounter. *Research on Language and Social Interaction, 22*, 215–240.

Schegloff, E. A. (1991). Reflections on talk and social structure. In D. Boden & D. Zimmerman (Eds.), *Talk and social structure* (pp. 44–70). Cambridge, UK: Polity Press.

Schiffrin, D. (1984a). How a story says what it means and does. *Text, 4*(4), 313–346.

Schiffrin, D. (1984b). Jewish argument as sociability. *Language in Society, 13*, 311–335.

Searle, J. (1969). *Speech acts*. Cambridge, UK: Cambridge University Press.

Shattuc, J. (1997). *The talking cure: TV talk shows and women*. London: Routledge.

Snow, C. E. (1991). Building memories: The ontogeny of autobiography. In D. Cicchetti & M. Beeghly (Eds.), *The self in transition: Infancy to childhood* (pp. 213–242). Chicago: University of Chicago Press.

Springer, J. (1999). *Ringmaster*. London: Boxtree.

Squire, C. (1994). Empowering women: *The Oprah Winfrey Show*. *Feminism & Psychology, 4*(1), 63–79.

Thompson, J. (1995). *The media and modernity*. Cambridge, UK: Polity Press.

Thompson, K. (1998). *Moral panics*. London: Routledge.

Thornborrow, J. (1997). Having their say: The function of stories in talk show discourse. *Text, 17*(2), 241–262.

Tolson, A. (1985). Anecdotal television. *Screen, 26*(2), 18–27.

Tolson, A. (1991). Televised chat and the synthetic personality. In P. Scannell (Ed.), *Broadcast talk* (pp. 178–200). London: Sage.

Toolan, M. J. (1988). *Narrative: A critical linguistic introduction*. London: Routledge.

Turner, V. (1974). *Dramas, fields, and metaphors*. Ithaca, NY: Cornell University Press.

van Zoonen, L. (1998). A day at the zoo: Political communication, pigs and popular culture. *Media, Culture & Society, 20*, 183–200.

Verwey, N. (1990). *Radio call-ins and covert politics*. Avebury, UK: Gower.

White M. (1992). *Tele-advising: Therapeutic discourse in American television*. Chapel Hill: University of North Carolina Press.

Yatziv, G. (2000). *Introduction to normative sociology*. Claremont, CA: Foundation for California.

Index

D

E

F

G

H

N

O

P

R

S

T

U–V

W

Y